D1617163

SUNY series in Global Politics

James N. Rosenau, editor

Water Resources and Inter-Riparian Relations in the Nile Basin

The Search for an Integrative Discourse

Okbazghi Yohannes

STATE UNIVERSITY OF NEW YORK PRESS

Nile River photo, courtesy of Karen Miller / iStockphoto

Published by
State University of New York Press, Albany

For information, address State University of New York Press, Albany, NY
www.sunypress.edu

Production by Kelli W. LeRoux
Marketing by Michael Campochiaro

Library of Congress Cataloging-in-Publication Data

Yohannes, Okbazghi.
    Water resources and inter-riparian relations in the Nile basin : the search for
an integrative discourse / Okbazghi Yohannes.
        p. cm. — (SUNY series in global politics)
    Includes bibliographical references and index.
    ISBN 978-0-7914-7431-0 (hardcover : alk. paper)   1. Water-supply—
Nile River Watershed—Management.   2. Water supply—Political aspects—
Nile River Watershed.   3. Nile River Watershed—Environmental conditions.
4. Regional planning—Nile River Watershed Region.   5. Riparian areas—
Political aspects—Africa.   6. Food supply—Africa.   I. Title.

HD1699.A3512N559   2008
333.9100962—dc22
                                                                        2007035472

10 9 8 7 6 5 4 3 2 1

In memory of

Carolyn Garner,
who devoted her entire life here on earth in service to others,

and

my mother, Wozr Tesfaghiorghis,
who taught me the art of patience

Contents

Acknowledgments

This book was conceived almost thirty years ago, when I floated in a walking steamer on the White Nile for sixteen days from the river port of Koasti in middle Sudan to Juba in the southern part of the country. My encounter with the river and its environs, as well as the indigenous communities who depended—and who still depend—on this life-giving river left a memory so indelible that I have always wanted to write about my experience and more. However, my desire to write about the river and the riverine people had in the meantime been eclipsed by other social priorities until the growing ecological degradation, economic stagnation and political turmoils taking place throughout the Nile basin grabbed my attention and finally made postponement of my research project impossible.

In writing this book, I have stood on the shoulders of countless researchers and writers, who explored, studied, analyzed and documented the manifold features of the Nile system, ranging from its watershed ecology to its hydrology, ethnography, politics and economy. For all that, I remain in their debt. My special thanks go to Dean James Hudson, who generously helped me to secure the seed grant to begin the research project. Dewey Clayton also played an important role in securing this grant, and for that, I am grateful to him.

I have also immensely depended upon the steadfast support, insight and inspiration of many colleagues and friends both within and outside my home university. Charles Ziegler, Chair of my home department, has always been prodigious in his guidance, encouragement and support. I am grateful to Ron Vogel for his always sharp and critical insight, friendship and counsel. I have handsomely benefited from the hydrological expertise of Yohannes Woldemariam of Fort Lewis College in Durango, Colorado, for which I remain in his debt. My special thanks also go to Mary Ann and Robert Ziegenfuse, Kibrom Yohannes and Kinfu Addisu for their support and insights.

I am equally grateful to the anonymous reviewers of the manuscript; their detached evaluations and insights have indeed been highly constructive and helpful in shaping the final product of my effort. This book also reflects the insights I gained from students in my political economy of natural resources course. The contribution to the project from my diligent graduate assistants has also been immense. In this respect, Kristine O. Toole, Abi Smith and Isabella Christiansen deserve special mention. Isabella in particular worked untiringly on various phases of the project, ranging from tracking sources, double checking facts, organizing the bibliography, and proofreading and editing the original manuscript; for all that, I am grateful to her.

I can by no means forget the superb editorial support I received from the SUNY Press. I am grateful to both Kelli LeRoux and Rosemary Wellner Mills for the thorough and meticulous way in which they handled the editorial phase of the book.

I reserve the final commendations for my family. Just as in my previous work, this book has been a family affair. My wife, Tamara, has remained my guide, partner and personal editor; she kept me throughout the undertaking on the right track, often rebelling against my unwarranted digressions. Without her deep involvement with the project, this book might not have been possible. My daughter, Keren, has played a tremendous role in arranging and/or rearranging the materials, and often offering unsolicited opinions, for all of which I am thankful. More important, whenever my energy level got low, Keren's demonstration of her commitment to social justice always refueled my tank and kept me going. However, whatever mistakes and gaps are left in the book, the burden is exclusively mine.

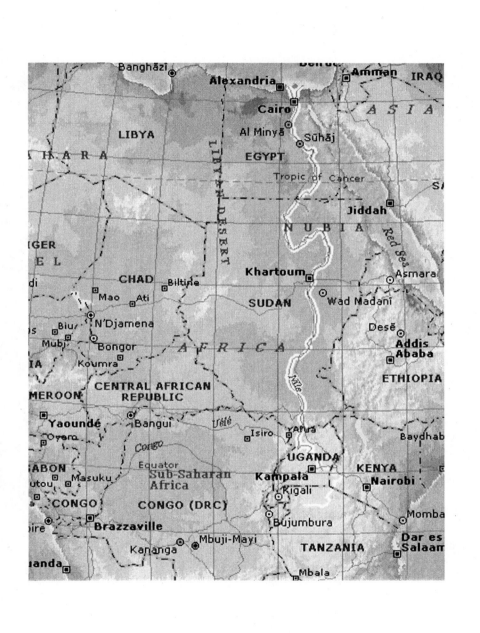

Chapter One

Toward a Provisional Understanding

Framing the Challenges

Over the centuries, the Nile basin has attracted the attention of explorers, geographers, ethnographers, and naturalists, each hoping to unlock its elusive mysteries by pinpointing the precise location of its source and by understanding the flora and fauna of its basin. Empire builders seeking to harness the river's resources to meet the burgeoning needs of modern capitalism soon followed. Indeed, Winston Churchill, anticipating the hydrographic future of the Nile, presciently observed over a century ago that the Nile, if forced into multiple canals of various claimants, "shall perish gloriously and never reach the sea."[1]

Today, environmental analysts, hydrologists, demographers, development economists, theory builders, and policy makers display competing interests in the Nile basin. Their competitive interests follow primarily from concerns that the basin might become one of the weakest links in the regional and international order. Early warning indices support these perceptions: the U.S. intelligence community categorizes the Nile basin as one of the ten flash points in contemporary international relations.[2]

The Nile basin is both geopolitically and ecologically sensitive. It extends from what U.S. policy makers call the "Greater Horn of Africa" to the great lakes region in the heart of the continent. The Nile basin is frequently portrayed as the most vulnerable to recurrent drought and famine, as well as to internal and interstate conflicts. Like many observers, I am deeply interested in the present and potential future sensitivities of the basin in the context of a collapsing hydrology and ecology. It is clear that the Nile basin's regional order, mediated not only by climatic and hydrographic, but also by socioeconomic and political factors, bears close watching.

My research vision entails the explication of the fundamental contradiction between the environmental/hydrological capacity of the basin and

1

the competing national development priorities and objectives of the riparian states. My point of departure differs from existing relevant literature, both in emphasis and orientation. Many analysts have viewed water scarcity as the determinant factor in the presentation of the hydrographic problem. By contrast, I take water scarcity in the Nile basin as an effect, the external expression of the potential collision between the social and natural worlds.

I argue that the source of this potential collision comes from the presentation of the hydrographic problem as rooted in the scarcity problematique, which is further reinforced by the unfettered perspective of nature as an object that humanity may exploit in pursuit of competing social goals. In this conventional view, it is assumed that water, as the essence of nature, is a given, constrained only by supply or quantity. Under this perspective, the uneven distribution of resources and the division of societies into territorially bounded entities go hand in hand, making interstate cooperation difficult, if not impossible, without a central enforcing agency or external imposition of power to condition and control state behavior. By contrast, I argue that, when social goals and needs exceed the supply of water resources or when internal elites seek to cover their incompetence, states begin to externalize the problem; water scarcity becomes both an economic and a political issue. The source of the problem therefore is that the Nile states, as elsewhere, are socialized into the fiction of a sacrosanct state sovereignty that claims exclusive internal autonomy and nonnegotiable external equality with other like actors. In the context of this socialization, it is natural for each riparian state to protect and promote its own hydrographic interest. In advancing state self-interest, decisions are made not only without regard to the interests of other states, but also without regard for the natural integrity of the biotic diversity of the entire basin.

For purposes of preliminary presentation, I thus argue that the problem is not scarcity, but rather the externalization and politicization of the scarcity notion within the context of the prevailing mode of capitalist production in the Nile basin. After all, research in the field of hydrology reports that, while the amount of water on earth today is almost exactly the same as when human civilization began, water resource quality has been substantially altered by anthropogenic-induced pollution and contamination. Caroline Sullivan of the Center for Ecology and Hydrology perceptively notes that "it is not the amounts of water resources available that determine poverty levels in a country, but the effectiveness of how you use those resources."[3]

I hasten to add that distorted priorities and the misuse of resources by human communities are at the root of the problem. Knowledgeable people tell us that with less than $100 billion a year, humanity can:

- Provide safe drinking water and sanitation services to those lacking them
- Reduce poverty

- Halve the number of hungry people worldwide by 2015
- Provide reproductive health care to all needy women
- Prevent soil erosion
- Promote environmental sustainability

Considering that the global military expenditure is $1 trillion annually, and the global crime syndicate grossed $2 trillion in 2003 alone, a $100 billion investment in human necessity is relatively small.[4]

This provisional position suggests that, on the basis of discursive rationality and dialogical communication, the supposed problem of water scarcity can be solved by establishing an equitable and democratic water regime in the Nile basin that takes grassroots democracy, ecological equity, and social justice as the central pillars of a just and sustainable order. Achievement of this task will require the socialization of states and societies away from the belief that the supply and demand of water are quantitatively determined and toward a dialogical understanding of the qualitative dimensions of water resources.

This work makes a normative case for establishing a democratic water resources regime in the Nile basin. This chapter develops the textual foundations of my normative commitment to a dialogical politics of governance in which the focus is more pedagogical than theoretical. Although my normative commitment to a particular outcome will be explicit in this and other chapters, my purpose is not to superimpose a particular vision of the future, but rather to contribute to the ongoing discourse in a positively sustainable direction. The pedagogical narrative developed here advocates for a progressive discourse that contests the prevailing social order and negotiates the outcome based on the following three interrelated theoretical propositions.

First, the discussion of water resources should serve as an entry point for analyzing other facets of development. It is futile to focus on how to divide the available water resources among riparian states without giving proper attention to their contexts. Second, the term "state" in this work is used as a generic agent for change. However, when referring to the state as the negotiating agent, I am not considering the state in its present constitution. Rather, the present use of the term "state" references a politically transformed state, either from within via adaptation or exhaustion, or from without through grassroots contestation, mobilization, and eventual liberation of power from urban kleptocrats and their rural hangers-on. Third, any water resources regime is unsustainable in the long run under the prevailing neoliberal economic order. It is clear by now that a belief in democratic capitalism's potential for self-replication in the Nile basin is self-delusional; the necessary internal conditions and external factors are not present on a pattern analogous to that which prevails in the global north. These three propositions hold throughout this work. In general, I will outline the contextual facets of hydrology in this chapter while deferring the details to subsequent chapters.

Almost a decade ago, I heard an interesting exchange on National Public Radio. Responding to a media person's questions, a biologist observed that economists generally think in terms of six months and their predictions are often in error. By contrast, biologists think in terms of millennia, since present actions may not manifest their effects until much later. A useful lesson, deduced from the biologist's wisdom, is that understanding the physical and biological structure of our environment is crucial to comprehending the values and limitations of water resources. The broad conceptualization of water resources to include innumerable internal and external influences, along with ecological and climatic determinants, is necessary for any effort to frame viable strategies to cope with the potential conflicts within and among Nile riparian states over the availability and allocation of water resources.

The American economist Lester Thurow borrowed and amalgamated two concepts to make sense of the nature and evolution of the contemporary global economy: plate tectonics from geology and punctuated equilibrium from biology.[5] In Thurow's illustration, the constant motion of earth's plates is unnoticeable to humans until manifested in the form of volcanic eruptions, earthquakes, and tsunamis. Likewise, biotic entities are undergoing incremental changes, continually adapting to new circumstances to ensure survival. However, the cumulative effects of gradual changes sometimes preclude adaptation to sudden and unexpected circumstances in many biotic species; thus, many perish and some survive. Let us consider the evolution of lakes (which is germane to this research project) in order to appreciate the heuristic and pedagogical significance of the preceding insight.

Limnologists tell us that lakes, like all natural and social entities, have beginnings and endings. Lakes begin as oligotrophs with clear and deep waters, little organic matter, and limited biological activity. As organic matter, sediments, and nutrient-rich substances enter the lakes, they begin to age through a natural process known as eutrophication, a condition in which nutrient concentrations in lakes stimulate algae blooms. Left alone, the eutrophication of lakes over millennia precedes their transformation into marshes, wetlands, and finally woodlands.[6] However, the natural aging of lakes is accelerated through anthropogenic eutrophication from the increases of nutrient-rich substances (the result of agricultural and urban runoff, sewage discharge, and other elements from point and nonpoint sources). The nitrogen, phosphorus, and carbon in these substances cause aquatic ecosystems to become swamped by the growth of algae, resulting in the death of plant and animal species from the lack of dissolved oxygen.

Thus, human-induced eutrophication of lakes has serious implications not only for aquatic species, but also for the availability of lake water for human consumption. When speaking of water, we must consider the interaction of water with multiple sources or "plates" (including anthropogenic sources) that will determine the future quantity and quality of water resources available to all species. Only through the comprehension of the nature (characteristics and dynamics) of the "plates" can we fully appreciate the hydrographic complexity, social significance, economic utility, and ecological vulnerability of the Nile river system. In the next sections, the major sources of "plates" are examined.

The Political Challenge

The Nile River is 6,800 km from source to mouth. It crisscrosses 35° latitude and encompasses ten sovereign nations. The Nile drains 2.9 million sq km (one-tenth) of the entire continent of Africa. The swamps of the Nile basin cover 69,720 sq km. Its lake areas cover another 81,500 sq km.[7] Burundi, Egypt, Eritrea, Ethiopia, Kenya, Rwanda, the Sudan, Tanzania, and Uganda all make entitlement claims to this vast ecological system, even though the contributions of the co-basin states vary considerably.

Historically, the nations of the region generally treated water as a low policy priority. Whenever concerns over the water supply arose, they were (usually) understood in hydraulic terms in the sense that supply could be increased through engineering. Today, however, the nexus between the shrinking supply of and rising demand for freshwater has placed water resources at the front and center of national policy priorities, regional competitions, and international concerns. The demographic boom, development imperatives, climatic fluctuations, and poor water management are among the factors responsible for supply-induced concerns over water shortages. For example, two important U.S. allies, Egypt and Ethiopia (pivotal states in the regional subsystem), are each adding one million people every eight months. Such a demographic boom requires not only an increased supply of potable water, but also an acceleration of urban, agricultural, and industrial developments. Necessities of life must be increased in proportion to the rising demands of the expanding population. Well-reasoned estimates suggest that, between 1990 and 2025, the rise in population alone in the Nile countries would reduce the per capita water availability from 1,070 to 620 cu m (cm) for Egypt; from 2,360 to 900 cm for Ethiopia; from 2,780 to 900 cm for Tanzania; from 590 to 190 cm for Kenya; and from 660 to 280 cm for Burundi.[8]

It is in this context that the elevation of water resources to a high policy priority has impelled some states in the region to define water resources in geopolitical terms. Among the early geopoliticians who saw the rising currency of water resources in regional politics was Anwar Sadat of Egypt, who predicted unavoidable conflict in the Nile basin. Following the Camp David Accords that ushered in reconciliation between Egypt and Israel,

Sadat cautioned upstream riparian states: "The only matter that could take Egypt to war again is water." Since then, other Egyptian leaders have echoed Sadat's warning. For example, former UN Secretary General Buotros Buotros-Ghali warned: "The next war in our region will be over the waters of the Nile."[9] The warnings are particularly directed at Ethiopia, where 86 percent of Nile water resources originate. Egyptian leaders are not alone in thinking that they can rely on their superior relative military capability to influence the allocation of water resources. Realist scholars subscribe to the somewhat antiquated notion of relative capability as an important factor in influencing outcomes. John Waterbury, for example, notes that "Egypt is capable of imposing a preferred solution."[10] It is against the backdrop of this prevailing conceptual linkage between hydropolitics and geopolitics that the U.S. intelligence community regards the Nile basin as one of the ten flash points in contemporary international relations.

Although Egypt's repeated warnings may indicate the seriousness of the hydrographic problem, the posturing in favor of the utility of force is dangerous and hollow as well. In the nineteenth century, Egypt's leaders made several military attempts to control the source of the Nile, but to no avail. I don't believe that Egypt is any better prepared today to influence the status of the Nile by military means; claims of modern Egypt's superior relative capability are grounded in illusion. The country is dependent on unsustainable American economic largesse and military protection to the tune of $2.1 billion a year. With such foreign dependency, Egypt hardly enjoys relative capability vis-à-vis its immediate rival, Ethiopia. Aside from nightmarish logistical problems (troop deployment and prepositioning of war material over an extended geographic space), Egypt's position is complicated by Ethiopian nationalism and pan-African sentiment.

Furthermore, even assuming relative capability in the short run, Egypt lacks the means to establish long-term colonial occupation of Ethiopia and the east African states in order to ensure a permanent flow of Nile waters. More important, defining water resources in merely geopolitical terms is self-defeating because the definition rests on the faulty presumption that water resources are only a matter of interstate relations. The factors that influence the supply of water are manifold. Indeed, innumerable internal factors (such as complicated interethnic relationships and the vulnerability of local ecosystems to degradation) are complicated further by other factors having the dimensions of law, institution, and policy that could compete with each other in the absence of a regional consensus. The maintenance and proper management of water resources are contingent on the integrity of the Nile ecology as a whole. Recognition of this reality in part requires the establishment of broader legal, political, and institutional frameworks that might prevent interstate conflict over the ownership of water resources or the nature of the jurisprudence governing the Nile water regime. In fact, in implicit recognition of these limits of power, Egypt has lately tempered its geopolitical posturing by invoking customary international law to justify its priority claims on Nile waters.

Egypt is put in a quandary by the hardening of upper riparian states' positions on the principle of equitable utilization of Nile waters. Ethiopia and the east African states appear committed to dam construction to meet the urgent necessities of their peoples, regardless of Egyptian consent. Pressure from international institutions and donor countries is also affecting Egypt. Since the end of the cold war, various UN agencies have been actively seeking to facilitate a water sharing arrangement from which the ten Nile states could benefit. The negotiations, with the World Bank, UNDP, and FAO playing active roles, have intensified since 1999 under an interim water regime dubbed the Nile Basin Initiative (NBI).

As confidence-building measures, twenty-two feasibility studies and projects were launched in 2001 with $140 million in grants from donors. In the hope of enticing both sides into a permanent and viable water regime, donor countries have attached $3 billion in promissory notes for projects in the Nile basin to this preferred outcome.[11] Noting the significance of the NBI, James Wolfeson, president of the World Bank, characterized the initiative as "a remarkable and fragile first step. It may be the first time in history that we are able to have the scientific and technical resources, the capacity, the knowledge, and the expertise to come together."[12]

The co-basin states' formal acceptance of the NBI by no means signals the resolution of the legal, political, and economic aspects of the Nile question. Yet, despite the potential for the protagonists' legal presentations to crystallize into dogmatic positions, the fact that riparian actors have adopted the language of law offers some rhetorical promise. Overcoming the juridical obstacle to the sustainable use of the Nile water resources will obviously be the first major step forward, but it is not an end in itself. Actors will ultimately have to face the challenges of regional poverty, underdevelopment, and other aspects of ecology, social justice, and political freedom. Although I do not minimize the tentative steps taken by the riparian states to deal with the quantitative determinants of water sharing under the Nile Basin Initiative, I question whether the NBI's objectives can be achieved within the prevailing structures; these limiting structures will be identified and evaluated in later chapters in the context of the scramble for security and poverty alleviation in each riparian state.

The Demographic Challenge

Ever since Thomas Robert Malthus wrote his controversial essay on the principles of population in 1798, the relationship between people and the carrying capacity of their environment has preoccupied population biologists. Current estimations of the earth's carrying capacity still range wildly, from two to several hundred billion people. Although the UN guesses that the global population will eventually stabilize at 11 billion, the emerging consensus among ecologists is that the earth can only support between 1.5 and 2 billion people at a reasonably acceptable living standard.[13] Neo-Malthusian analysts suggest that the production and supply of food and water are unlikely to keep pace with population growth in developing countries, including those states in the Nile basin, and with prevailing consumption patterns in the global north. Paul and Anne Ehrlich find that overpopulation in the global south and overconsumption in the global north, leading to finite resource depletion, are mutually reinforcing causes of human poverty, ecological degradation, and atmospheric deterioration.[14] In their view, until and unless these two fundamental problems are resolved, the very survival of humanity is at stake. Brown and Kane echo this concern, warning that the earth's carrying capacity is fast approaching its limits, owing to unsustainable exploitation of fish, rapid urbanization, dirty industrialization, and expansion of global water demand despite hydrological limits.[15]

The empirical evidence is overwhelming. Over the past thirty years alone, the general health of ecosystems has declined by 33 percent, while the general human demand for ecological resources has increased by 50 percent.[16] The average number of hectares (ha) of cultivable land per human fell from .23 ha in 1950 to .13 ha (moderately or highly degraded) in the mid-1990s. The human being had 0.23 ha of farmland to grow food, which fell to 0.13 ha by the mid-1990s, mostly moderately or highly degraded.[17] The steady diminution of cultivable acreage is complicated by the shrinkage of water resources, resulting from simultaneous rises in human population and consumption levels that, taken together, act to accentuate demand for water resources. For instance, in the year 1900, the world as a whole used 400 bcm of water. Forty years later, this figure had jumped to 800 bcm, and the world population had increased by 40 percent.[18] By the mid-1970s, countries of the world were annually withdrawing 2,838 bcm of water for industrial, agricultural, and municipal usages.[19] The U.S. Council on Environmental Quality, in its 1980 report to the president, assessed that demands for water withdrawals would rise between 200 and 300 percent by the year 2000. By the mid-1990s, the United States alone was withdrawing 584 bcm of water annually to maintain its prosperity.[20]

The prediction is credible, since world water consumption has doubled every twenty years during the twentieth century.[21] In fact, 180 million tonnes of world grain are said to be produced with nonreplenishable waters. Such rapid depletion of freshwater is occurring despite predictions that 2,000 additional cu km of water will be needed by 2025 to feed the world population.[22] Moreover, in the second half of the twentieth century, the gap between the supply of and the demand for water resources widened alarmingly; this gap continues to grow. In 1982, the WHO reported that only 29 percent of rural populations in underdeveloped countries were provided safe drinking water.[23]

It does not seem that chronic water resource shortages will be ameliorated any time soon. If the present projection holds, fifty-two countries, housing 3.5 billion people, will experience acute water shortages by 2025. Presently, 450 million Africans cannot access potable water, and 3 million die each year from waterborne and sanitation-related diseases. The average African uses just 10 to 20 liters of water a day, while the average American consumes 600 liters per day; the United Nations estimates the absolute minimum of daily water need for cooking, drinking, bathing, and sanitation at 50 liters.[24] These figures do not include water used by agriculture and industry; in terms of total usage, the average American consumes 5,200 liters daily, the global daily average is 1,750 liters.[25]

A number of irreversible ecological changes can also be observed. Over the last half-century, Africa has lost 75 percent of its water resources and is projected to lose another 13 percent by 2025.[26] To give tangible expression to this data, it is useful to note that, since the 1960s, Lake Chad (once the sixth largest lake in the world) has shrunk from its original size of over 350,000 sq km to 2,000 sq km.[27] The predictable implication of this scenario is not only a shortage of potable water but also of consumable food supplies, given the FAO's projection that the 2025 world food requirement will represent a 50 percent increase over the currently available supply.[28]

We should bear in mind that, today, 2 billion people worldwide suffer from various levels of nutritional deficiencies. We should also keep in mind that Africa's malnourished population is expected to rise from 315 million in 1995 to 404 million in 2015, representing a full 32 percent of the continent's people.[29] The data released in August 2005 by the International Food Policy Research Institute also do not inspire optimism. According to this study, the proportion of Africans suffering from malnutrition has remained constant at 35 percent since 1970, meaning that there were 200 million malnourished Africans in 2001, including 38.6 million children. The authors took pains to point out that at least $303 billion in new investments in agriculture, water management, and other facets of development would be required just to halve the number of hungry Africans by 2015.[30]

The consequences of this scenario inevitably include the recurrence of acute food and water shortages, degradation of ecosystem services, massive internal and interregional migrations, social convulsions, and political instabilities. The UN seemed to endorse this line of argument when it gave to its 1994 Cairo conference the title: "Population and Development"; this emphasized the presumed existence of crucial linkages between population size and the imperatives of economic development as determinants of the expected pace of progress. Thus, increased rates of population growth and economic development presuppose relative abundance and regular provision of water resources; the present 360 million people in the ten Nile riparian states are projected to reach 812 million by 2040.

However, cornucopian commentators, who belong to a class of optimists, openly challenge the glum neo-Malthusian assessment that overpopulation causes underdevelopment, poverty, or critical resource shortages. They find that overpopulation, if it exists, inevitably results from a lack of development. In 2003, for example, the ten Nile riparian states, with a total population of 358 million, and a total land area of 8.9 million sq km, had a combined gross domestic product (GDP) of $146 billion. By comparison, the three small Benelux countries, with a total population of 27.6 million, and a total land area of 74,632 sq km, had a combined GDP of $889.9 billion.[31] Therefore, the optimists contend that there is more to development than the quantitative determinants of growth seem to suggest: temporal and spatial factors and the interplay of natural and anthropogenic processes are crucial. But, while optimists may be right in that overpopulation, like poverty, is much less a factor than a consequence of underdevelopment,[32] their argument cannot erase the fact that the Nile states must cope first with their immediate problem: their inability to provide potable water and adequate food to their present peoples, on the one hand, and the imperatives of building internal capital accumulation to spur development, on the other.

At the moment, it doesn't seem feasible to pursue both social goals simultaneously within the prevailing socioeconomic and political structures. After all, according to the water poverty index that ranked 147 countries in 2002 in terms of their water resources and capacity to access and use those resources, the bottom ten countries included Ethiopia, Eritrea, Rwanda, and Burundi.[33] Moreover, Ethiopia's 1981 food production declined by 30 percent from the 1961 level, even as its population doubled.[34] In light of this, the demographic factor is likely to greatly influence water policies and interstate behavior in the basin. In the early 1990s, six of the co-basin states (Egypt, Sudan, Ethiopia, Kenya, Uganda, and Tanzania) planned to irrigate a combined area of 3,152,000 ha of agricultural land.[35] It does not appear that the search for more irrigable land will stop here. With the rising demand for food, the co-basin states will increasingly come under pressure to bring more land, including marginal land, under irrigation.

Such moves by co-basin states to boost food production in tandem are likely to put much stress on the hydrological and ecological determinants of the Nile system. Noting the enormity of the hydrological problem, Abu Zeid, Egypt's minister of water resources, projected that the Nile countries would face serious demands from growing populations in the coming decades, since worldwide demands on water resources were rising at three times the rate of the global population.[36] Moreover, on average, 48 percent of the population in the ten Nile states is under the age of fourteen; feeding, housing, and educating such young populations is enormously expensive. Over the long range, overpopulation may not become problematic when, and if, the Nile countries achieve the sort of development presently enjoyed by the Benelux countries. In the short to medium term, though, overpopulation is bound to contribute to the dire state of underdevelopment, mass poverty, social disintegration, ecological deterioration, and political instability throughout the basin—the kinds of stagnant turmoil we are witnessing today.

In light of the arguments made in the previous paragraphs, the debate between the neo-Malthusians and the cornucopians is abstract, unhelpful, and reductionist. A meaningful and useful population discourse cannot be understood apart from spatial, temporal, and contextual dimensions. I tend to agree with Athanasiou that "Overpopulation is a real threat, a multiplier of stress and tension, a variable in the equation of a crisis. But it is, as well, a heavily warped political category. Malthusians see overpopulation as a cause of a biological crisis, not as one of its key biosocial factors."[37]

To present overpopulation as one of the many factors retarding progress in the Nile basin is not to suggest that it is a cause of underdevelopment in the region. That said, a radically new population policy is urgently needed in the Nile basin. If the ten Nile states are presently helpless to provide safe drinking water and adequate food to their combined peoples of 360 million, it is difficult to imagine how they will be able to supply those necessities of life to 812 million people some forty years hence. At the moment, I believe that achieving demographic stability, along with a substantial reduction in human numbers throughout the region, ought to be among the immediate goals of all riparian states. This requires synchronized population policies: a regional bureau of population control must be established for purposes of coordinating efforts to promote the education of women, family planning, and reproductive health, and to combat pathogenic sources of diseases. The Nile states have valuable lessons to learn from the experiences of the Indian states of Kerela and Tamil Nadu. Led by progressive and enlightened groups of political cadres, these two states challenged the all-embracing capitalist order in favor of a progressive socioeconomic system that made the people in general, and women in particular, central to their policies. The leaderships introduced a series of policies that included agrarian land reform, universal health care, literacy, training, nutritional support, and distribution of free condoms. As a result, these Indian states managed to regulate their population sizes, as both fertility and mortality rates sharply declined.[38] In the same way, the Nile states can, and should, manage their population sizes primarily by encouraging delayed marriages and pursuing active policies to promote universal female education, female social emancipation, and economic empowerment.

The Economic Challenge

The ten sovereign states that share the Nile basin are all developing nations. Indeed, Eritrea, Ethiopia, Rwanda, and Burundi, with per capita income of between $100 and $200, are among the ten poorest countries in the world, where degradation of ecosystem services, rapid population growth, instability, and stark poverty are all defining features of their existence.[39] It thus goes without saying that the ten co-riparian states have to initiate comprehensive development programs in the form of both rapid industrialization and accelerated agricultural modernization if they are to meet the basic necessities of their growing populations and, by extension, buttress their own legitimacy.

The first priority for all states is to achieve food security, a phrase featured in virtually every public utterance today. Of course, if the experiences of advanced countries are a useful guide, the idea of food security presupposes industrialization of agriculture, ranging from cultivation to production, from processing to marketing, under technologically advanced conditions. That is how the advanced countries have not only achieved food security, but also squeezed substantial transferable surpluses from agriculture to fuel the industrialization of the manufacturing sector. Supported by modern means of production, the average American farmer, who barely fed himself two centuries ago, today feeds seventy-eight other persons and himself. Even though the proportion of land devoted to food production remained relatively stable between 1920 and 1978, food production in the US doubled during this period, due to agricultural industrialization.[40]

Modern activities revolving around agriculture perform a number of functions, in addition to producing food. Indeed, the whole range of tasks associated with cultivating, harvesting, processing, and selling food products are major sources of national employment. It is rarely emphasized that, for example, the biggest employer in the United States is not the manufacturing sector, but rather the agricultural sector. In 1986, U.S. agriculture employed 27 million Americans, representing one out of every five jobs, who were engaged in various phases of growing, producing, and marketing agricultural products; actual farmwork involved only 3.4 million workers.[41]

Attaining food security thus entails the agricultural industrialization. But here is the rub: industrializing agriculture requires a number of important aspects, including deployment of sizable capital, modern farm machinery, heavy uses of fertilizers and pesticides, substantial amounts of energy, and construction of dams to continuously supply irrigation water. For example, a full 27 percent of American crops are grown on just 12 percent of the country's total cropland of 169 million ha, supported by 2.5 million dams.[42] Moreover, of the 1,600 billion liters of water the US withdrew daily in the 1980s for various purposes, excluding hydroelectric use, 600 billion liters per day (or 38 percent of the total daily withdrawals) was for agriculture, with 99 percent used for irrigation.[43]

Central to American agricultural prosperity has thus been the heavy use of water from its 2.5 million dams and bountiful groundwater endowment, as exemplified by the great Ogallala aquifers. In the 1980s, the US withdrew 29.1 trillion liters per year from its groundwater reserves.[44] The Ogallala aquifers, central to America's hydrological wealth, cover half a million sq km, hold four trillion tonnes of water, and support over 200,000 modern wells that supply water to 3.3 million ha of farmlands.[45] There is an interesting parallel between irrigation-based American agricultural prosperity and its water endowment and water use. For example, in 1950, total U.S. withdrawals from its surface and groundwater reserves, excluding hydroelectric uses, were 250 bcm a year; this rose to 500 bcm a year in 1980.[46]

Irrigation-based agriculture is key for the United States, as for humanity as a whole. Today, 40 percent of global food crops are grown on irrigated fields.[47] Although Nile states may separately find independent sources of capital, they cannot find an independent source of water or a separate ecology. By compulsion of nature, they have to share the waters of the Nile and the various streams and lakes that make up the Nile system.

It is here where a dialogical discourse becomes useful to negotiate the nature of a democratic water regime. Dialogical discourse is also critical to avoid or overcome the downsides of industrialized agriculture. As is the case with most negotiations over natural resources under the prevailing mode of production, national and transnational actors are more often preoccupied with sharing than with resource conservation, protection, and management. As Poincelot perceptively notes, "Resources are threatened in two ways: by depletion and by contamination such that the resources become unusable. Both problems have an impact far beyond agriculture in that the resulting loss of food production and environmental damage threaten and diminish our quality of life."[48]

Depletion of Nile water resources can result from the riparian states' race to construct dams in order to modernize their agriculture, whereby they create permissive conditions for evaporation from a widespread network of reservoirs. It is instructive to bear in mind that 170 cu km of water annually evaporate from the world's dams.[49] Degradation of Nile water resources can also result from the growing use of the Nile system for navigation, as has been the trend worldwide. For instance, there were fewer than 9,000 waterways in the world in 1900; today there are more than 500,000.[50] Contamination of Nile waters can also result from problems associated with agricultural modernization: heavy pesticide and fertilizer usage, saltwater intrusion, salinization, sedimentation, and soil erosion. Water quality degradation and contamination associated with agriculture, for example, annually costs the United States between $6 and $9 billion.[51]

Other consequences are associated with the industrialization of agriculture. The first involves the risk of centralizing agrarian production in few hands. The agricultural sector in the Nile countries, from which 80 percent of the populations earn their living, is highly fragmented. In order to achieve scale efficiency in terms of both inputs and outputs, aggregation of farmlands would seem natural. The experience of advanced countries supplies evidence for the necessity of the concentration of agricultural capital and centralization of farmlands. In the United States, for example, the number of farms fell from 6.1 million in 1940 to 2 million in 2000.[52] The concomitant social consequence of the concentration of agriculture in fewer hands is urbanization, as more and more persons displaced by mechanized agriculture flock to the city in search of livelihoods. Urban growth, of course, requires simultaneous provision of jobs and water. When one talks about the city, it is important to keep in mind Odum's words: "The city is the parasite of the rural environment. It produces little or no food or other organic materials, purifies no air, and recycles little or no water or inorganic materials."[53]

Industrialization of agriculture signifies a distinct stage of development in a country. The gap between countryside and city narrows, and income levels between the regions tend to grow closer. Labor composition also changes as more and more workers are employed in manufacturing and service sectors. In this situation, industrial and municipal water usage intensifies. In addition to intensification of water consumption, industrialization and congregation of people in ever larger cities have important effects on resource utilization and environmental quality. The veritable lesson that should not be lost on Nile actors is the fact that modernization of agriculture and industry, on the one hand, and growing urbanization, on the other, readily lend themselves to simultaneous intensification of resource use and resource quality degradation. Contaminant inputs to the ecology are proportional to the level of industrialization. In the underdeveloped world, where environmental regulations are weak to nonexistent, industries and cities are major sources of pollution and water contamination. By some estimates, 90 percent of wastewater generated in the underdeveloped world is dumped untreated into rivers and lakes. Millions of tonnes of raw sewage from east African cities are annually discharged untreated into Lake Victoria, the source of the White Nile.[54]

One side effect of industrialization, equally worrisome to developing and advanced countries, is the growing acidification of rivers, lakes, and streams. Not only does acidification affect water quality, but it also undermines the food source. For example, studies found 200,000 lakes in Norway to be sensitive to acidification; 78 percent of the lakes in southern Norway have become completely barren of fish. It is alarming that the number of barren lakes in Norway has doubled since the early 1970s.[55] In the early 1990s, Sweden also saw 95,000 km of streams becoming acidified; by then half of its 90,000 acid-sensitive lakes were showing considerable levels of acidification.[56] In the early 1990s, 350,000 lakes in eastern Canada were found to be acid-sensitive, of which 14,000 had become acidified and another 150,000 were demonstrating considerable effects. In the Canadian province of Ontario, 48,000 lakes were showing serious ecological effects from acid deposition.[57] Acidification of lakes, by undermining the physiology and reproduction of aquatic species, undermines human food security. Acid precipitation also has a serious impact on watershed vegetation. In 1990, it was estimated that Europe as a whole lost $30 billion from timber production because of acid rain.[58]

The cautionary value of the advanced countries' experiences for the riparian states in the Nile basin is apparent. The lesson is twofold. First, industrialization under the prevailing mode of production inevitably entails negative externalities such as air pollution, contamination of water resources, acidification of rivers and lakes, and soil deterioration. Second, despite multiple layers of regulatory agencies and environmental groups, coupled with relatively ample resources earmarked for environmental protection, even the advanced countries have not been able to effectively mitigate or manage the effects of industrialization. Destitute both in resources and regulatory machinery, the Nile states are ill-equipped to deal with the harmful effects of industrialization. Therefore, the challenge for the Nile states is to fashion an economic order that is ecology-friendly and efficient in terms of resource use.

One of the major difficulties in the Nile basin is the fact that the actors are multiple, distinct, and sovereign. Most of the demographic increases are likely to occur in urban areas, not necessarily due to only natural urban birth rate, but largely because of rural to urban migration following the classic trajectory of modernization. Impounding water in gigantic dams or artificial lakes will become unavoidable; diversion of a sizable quantity of water to irrigate ever-expanding agricultural areas will be required to ensure national food security. These competitive programs will certainly accentuate the demand for water throughout the basin. The conventional wisdom is that instrumentalist national policy priorities will be competitive, setting the stage for inter-riparian conflicts. The impact of the divergent programs on regional hydrology will be severe, bringing land reclamation imperatives and sustainability principles into collision. Short of policy coordination at the regional, national, and subnational levels, the development imperatives of the riparian states can generate severe stress on the environment, undermining the hydrological sustainability of the Nile basin, and weakening the integrity and buffering capacity of local ecosystems.

According to the World Bank, the UNDP, and other international agencies, the solution is the creation of a regional water regime modeled after the Mekong River. As the story goes, Vietnam, Laos, Cambodia, and Thailand have hammered out their differences by creating a regional water regime to promote economic development in the Mekong river basin. The reported positive outcome is the Nam Ngum hydroelectricity plant in Laos, which supplies 80 percent of Thailand's and 100 percent of Laos's energy needs. Thus, the Mekong River has become an engine of regional integration rather than one of inter-riparian conflict.[59]

The lessons of the Mekong River were not lost on the 400 Nile state delegates to the eighth NBI session, held in July 2000. At the conference, proponents of inter-riparian cooperation proposed that the Nile states could benefit from a comprehensive, transboundary integrated management system, as well as from the promotion of economic development in the Nile basin by allocating internationally supported development projects throughout the basin under an equitable water utilization regime. To showcase this orientation, as noted earlier, the World Bank, UNDP, and FAO began funding twenty-two projects with $140 million. The World Bank also pledged to raise $3 billion to accelerate economic development in the basin as the necessary precondition toward regional integration.

Despite the NBI's positive superficial appearance, it is nonetheless flawed. A base focus on sharing Nile waters and initiating projects throughout the basin evades fundamental issues of democratic governance, social justice, and ecological equity. Dividing Nile water resources among the ten riparian states and impounding their respective shares for purposes of irrigation and hydropower generation does not guarantee them food security. On the contrary, impounding water resources throughout the basin can have huge ecological and economic costs, unless accompanied by a radical transformation of existing political structures and an open contestation of the prevailing mode of production. For example, FAO studies show that 30 million ha of the world's 240 million ha under irrigation are severely salinated, and another 80 million ha suffer from waterlogging and salinization.[60]

The Hydrological and Ecological Challenge

Various studies indicate that water availability is a function of both natural supply and human demand. There is an inexorable relationship between human actions and the laws of hydrology.[61] The availability of water resources to humans is thus determined as much by the hydrologic cycle as by human effects on the ecological determinants of civilization. Understanding this complex interaction between human needs and nature's capacity to meet them becomes crucial. In this sense, the hydrologic cycle is as much a function of geomorphology as of anthropogenic participation. It is repeatedly stated that over 97 percent of all water on earth is found in the form of seawater and therefore unusable by humans. Theoretically, only 2.7 percent of the earth's water is freshwater and thus accessible to humans; in reality, though, only a small proportion of this freshwater is readily available to humans: 77 percent of the freshwater is trapped in ice caps and glaciers; another 22 percent is detained in the ground.[62] Equally important to acknowledge is the fact that the hydrologic cycle is greatly influenced by the exchange between the earth's energy cycle and solar energy fluxes. It is estimated that some 500,000 cu km of water annually is evaporated from surface water bodies, surface land, and vegetation into the atmosphere by solar radiation; this returns to the earth in the form of rain and snow. Of the gross returning water, the share of the land surface is 110,300 cu km, even though the contribution of the land surface to the evapotranspiration regime is only 72,900 cu km.[63]

The vexing paradox posed by the hydrologic cycle is that the seasonal and annual distribution of rain and snow is geographically uneven. For example, the annual per capita runoff in Egypt is less than 1,000 cu m compared to 100,000 cu m yearly per capita runoff in Canada. The annual runoff in two-thirds of the African continent is one-third less than the global annual average.[64] This suggests that the thermodynamic relationship between solar energy fluxes, geographic configurations, types of vegetation, evapotranspiration, and precipitation regimes is unmistakable. Conversely, the human role in the thermodynamic relationship is seldom recognized as critical to the hydrologic cycle.

A continual rebalancing process, heating up and cooling off the earth, results from the interaction between incoming solar radiation and outgoing energy from earth. As Berner and Berner coherently note, ocean currents transport warm water from the equator to the cold polar regions of the earth; winds circulate warm air through the atmosphere; and the water vapors in the atmosphere carry latent heat.[65] These three modes of energy transmission are sensitive to human actions. Burning more fossils can easily influence the circulation of heat, in the process warming the earth's atmosphere. In the absence of the right counteraction between the outgoing and incoming energy fluxes, the relationship between the evaporation and precipitation regimes can be significantly altered. A small rise in the earth's surface temperature due to greenhouse gases can substantially change the hydrologic cycle, resulting in uneven distribution of precipitation. Some regions become wetter, while others become drier.

As paleoclimatologic data suggest, the African continent has seen dramatic shifts in the hydrologic cycle over the past 14,000 years. Prior to the dramatic hydrological shifts pounding the continent, for example, the Sahara Desert was once endowed with lush landscapes, expansive shallow lakes, and vast groundwater resources. Today, the Sahara Desert is moving southward, placing the Sahel region extending from Niger to Ethiopia under its powerful influence. It is worth noting that the hydrological circulation on the African continent is a function of the interaction between solar radiation and the highly seasonal African and Indian monsoon. The alternating wet and dry seasons and the interannual rainfall fluctuations in the Nile basin are determined by the monsoonal circulation in interaction with the solar energy in the atmosphere, in the oceans, and on land.[66] Perhaps a useful way to look at the hydrological determinants germane to the Nile system is to conceive of the regional water budget as a function of the global water budget. The conditions that generally affect the composition of the atmosphere will have a direct bearing on the region's climate, temperature, and precipitation. For example, climatologists warn that carbon dioxide buildup in the atmosphere and consequent warming can radically alter the global cycling of water; some places are likely to become wetter and other areas drier. The resulting unusual events (severe storms, floods, heat waves, droughts, the spread of pathogens and diseases, sea level rise, and acidification of water) will gravely affect human health, water supply, agricultural productivity, and ecosystem services, as well as internal and regional microclimates.[67]

Interannual fluctuations of the Nile during the last century are suggestive of the radical shifts in precipitations that can arise with variegated implications. For example, the years 1913, 1984, and 1987 were periods of extremely low Nile flows. By contrast, the years 1946, 1954, 1961–1964, and 1998 were the wettest of the twentieth century. The 1961–1964 flood years were particularly costly in economic, social, and human terms.

The hydrologic cycle is not solely determined by geomorphologic processes, but is also significantly influenced by human actions. Even if the riparian states are able to reach agreements on the basic questions of law and policy, they still must face the science of the environment. National hydrological security cannot be separated from the environmental security of the region as a whole. The environmental security of the Nile basin can be threatened by factors from within and from without. Ecological degradation, deforestation, desertification, atmospheric degradation, migrations of the intertropical convergence zone, changes in oceanic temperature, and a radical shift in global climatic conditions can easily weaken the requisite conditions of sustainability of the water regime. Human-induced or naturally occurring processes can affect the hydroclimatology of the basin, the precipitation regime, and the discharges of the Nile in unpredictable ways. The recognition of negative environmental implications should be a sufficient basis for proposing changes to state behavior and policy priorities.

Of course, formidable impediments exist to realizing such a vision. Significantly, an insufficient understanding of the intrinsic relationship between hydrology and ecology may be compounded by the dominant view of policy makers and their economic advisers. The call for a sustainable water regime must be embedded in regional unitary decisions undertaken to fashion, develop, and promote integrated ecological policy. This involves the total negation of positivist dichotomies between high and low politics, sovereignty and anarchy, economy and ecology, order and justice, equity and efficiency, equality and liberty, and between society and nature as terms in opposition to one another.

For example, politicians seeking legitimacy and economists seeking efficiency often speak of a necessary trade-off between such oppositional terms as equity and efficiency on the faulty presupposition that the values of the terms in presumed opposition cannot be realized without the subordination of one to the other. In truth, they are not. On the contrary, they function as harmonious and holistic complements, in organically complex and interdependent relationships. An economy that does not nurture the ethics of conservation, preservation, and protection of ecological resources will in the long run undermine the foundations of its operations. The logic of efficiency, which does not celebrate equity as the ethical foundation of human civilization or promote the ethics of doing with less in order to share ecological resources in the present and the future, will in the long range erode the basis of orderliness, human solidarity, and the co-evolution of human societies with the living ecology.

A society that objectifies nature will hasten its own demise. The ethics of nature thus demand the complete repudiation of the hitherto dominant anthropocentric practices, which put human interests and needs above those of other living things that share the ecology with humans. The point to be emphasized here is that the living ecology can continue its evolutionary course without the presence of man, but man cannot survive unless the integrity of the living ecology is preserved. To appreciate this point, a brief discussion on ecological imperatives is in order.

Ecology is not only a living entity where "organisms, animals, plants, and microbes interact with the natural world," but also a science by which we study these complex interactions among living entities in the context of their environment.[68] Biological transformations in ecosystems cannot be understood apart from the physical compositions of the ecology and the chemical reactions that take place within it. The ecology is a synergistic system in which energy fluxes and nutrient cycling continually occur as a result of the mutual dependence and interdependence of all living things on and with their nonliving environment, in the process modifying the conditions of their evolution and co-evolution. The positive or negative effects of co-dependence, of living things on one another and on the physical environment, arise from the very unity of the ecology itself. This ecological reality is strengthened or weakened by the magnitude of such physical phenomena as water movements, wind currents, and solar radiation. To capture the full range of the complex interdependencies of biological entities and physical forces, the British scientist Charles Elton once used the notion of thermodynamics as key to understanding ecology. In fact, he aptly defined the earth as a "giant thermodynamic machine driven by the solar radiation."[69]

This is exemplified by the ecology of the Nile watershed where all living organisms are affected in various ways by such natural events as drought or the spread of disease vectors, and by such human actions as deforestation or dam construction at various points in the catchment. Extensive deforestation, for example, can expose denuded landscapes to rapid evaporation rates, decrease the amount of rainfall, or alter the patterns of heating and cooling and the character of microclimatic zones. Likewise, removal of topsoil from exposed landscapes can encourage the transportation and deposition of sediments in waterways.

The cumulative effects of ecological deterioration can thus erode the basis of human survival. The report of the Millennium Ecosystem Assessment, prepared by 2,000 world scientists and other experts representing a variety of fields, presents an alarming scenario. According to the report, 60 percent of ecosystem services that support life on earth in fundamental ways have been degraded or exploited unsustainably. "Any progress achieved in addressing the goals of poverty and hunger eradication, improved health, and environmental protection is unlikely to be sustained if most of the ecosystem services on which humanity relies continue to be degraded."[70] The report adds that the hyperacceleration of human exploitation of ecosystem services in response to ever-expanding demands for fresh water, food, fiber, timber, and fuel could irreversibly impact supplies.

Biologists warn that the principle of punctuated equilibrium could be at work here. Small and incremental changes may go on unnoticed for a while, but these cumulative changes can produce abrupt, sudden, and enormous effects such as sudden shifts in local, regional, and global climates, the emergence and spreading of new human pathogens and diseases, sudden changes in the properties of water, the collapse of fisheries, and an unprecedented loss of biodiversity. The spread of malaria in the Nile basin and beyond exemplifies the effects of ecosystem service degradation. For instance, had only malaria been eradicated some thirty years ago, Africa's GDP would have grown to $100 billion today.[71]

On the microlevel, Rwanda typifies the dangers of climate change and the associated spread of malaria. Since the 1960s, average temperatures in Rwanda have increased by almost 1° Celsius; incidents of malaria doubled as the malaria-carrying anopheline mosquito continually climbed to high altitudes.[72]

One major cause of degradation in ecosystem services is the alarming rate of vegetation removal. When vegetation cover is removed, fragmented, or destroyed, valuable soil nutrients and chemicals are exposed to erosion by wind and water. In consequence, soil erosion starves farmlands of important minerals, nutrients, and chemicals. According to some studies, Africa loses up to 40 tonnes of soil per ha annually, compared with 7 tonnes for Europe and the United States.[73] Globally, approximately 2 billion ha of cropland and grazing range are suffering from various forms of soil degradation, compounded by enormous soil erosion as some 25 metric tonnes of topsoil are annually washed away from agricultural land. As a result, humanity loses 7 million ha of farmland (of the total global stock of 700 million ha) to soil degradation annually, depriving one billion people of their basic livelihoods. The loss of the agricultural value of another 140 million ha of farmland is expected by 2010.[74]

Moreover, the alarming rate of desertification, which presently affects 60 percent (or 2.6 billion ha) of range land and threatens the livelihoods of one billion people worldwide, is largely associated with radical alterations of the ecology. The annual economic cost of desertification is over $40 billion.[75]

Building on the previous discussion, I believe that it is in the collective interest of all Nile co-riparian states to promote the ecological integrity of the basin for three crucial reasons. First, since forests have a direct bearing on humidity, pressure, temperature, and precipitation regimes, their deforestation can affect the various microclimatic zones and, by extension, the whole regional climate regime. The buffering capacity of the Nile river system watershed can be highly compromised. By the complex processes of water retention, transpiration, and slowing of the evaporation rate, living plants and their litter make incalculable contributions to the modification and regulation of the climate regime. In the absence of plants to cycle and recycle water, an area becomes hotter and drier. In its lifetime, a large rainforest tree is said to pump 2.5 million gallons of water into the atmosphere.[76] By the role they play in the biotic sequestration of carbon dioxide, plants are similarly critical to climate regulation.

Second, living plants and their litter, by occupying vast areas and creating drag effects, protect the soil against erosion by wind and water movements. Removal of vegetation cover exposes the soil to powerful natural forces, like wind and water, that transport the soil nutrients; this accelerates the disintegration and weathering of rocks, creating the condition known as laterization. Stripped of its spongy top portion, the landscape cannot absorb water, and runoff is magnified. The result is that the land loses its productivity, and streams and reservoirs become choked from sediments; these impacts presently haunt both upstream and downstream Nile states. To replace lost nutrients, farmers increasingly use artificial fertilizers, which are equally subject to the erosion process. Transported chemical fertilizer residues contaminate streams, lakes, and reservoirs.

Third, forest cover is an important source of organic matter, which is key to soil formation, structure, fertility, water holding and buffering capacity, and maintenance. The degradation of organic matter resulting from the decomposition of leaves, dead plants, and grass by microorganisms is essential for recycling and recovering nutrients and for producing nutrient-rich soil. The earth's photosynthetic plants, which produce approximately 100 billion tonnes of organic matter annually by transforming solar energy into organic matter, supply the necessary ingredients to soil. Good agricultural soil, containing 5 percent of organic matter by weight, owes its health to the complex interaction between organic matter and biologically active living organisms of all sorts. For example, the estimated 71 billion bacteria per ounce of soil play a critical role in nutrient cycling throughout the decomposition process.[77] The nutrients and trace elements that are necessary for crop production are obtained from plant litter that is created through decomposition by microorganisms. Decomposition of organic matter involves both biological and physical processes, as microorganisms labor to adapt themselves to their physical environment while at the same time adapting the geobiochemical environment to their biological needs.[78] The dark organic matter that results from decomposition, known as humus, is essential to the nutrient retention of soil. Soil structure, aeration, water infiltration, and the buffering capacity of soil—the basic elements in humus, which help to prevent changes in pH—are very much affected by the level of organic matter in the soil. The nature of soil structure, high concentration of microorganisms, water retention, and iron exchange capacity of soil are directly connected with organic matter. When organic matter is eroded, the soil loses its water absorption and drainage capacity and becomes dry; this in turn makes it more vulnerable to erosion. Given these considerations, a Nile water regime that does not take seriously the ecological dimensions of hydrology is nothing but a facade.

Urbanization, Pollution, and the Challenge of Clean Water

The quality dimension of water resources is crucial, not only to the supply of water but also to the maintenance of sound public health systems. The Nile is not only a natural channel for the distribution of water resources across the entire region, but also a drainage system for the whole basin. As a result, the Nile River is vulnerable throughout the basin to municipal wastes and raw sewage, industrial pollutants, acid rain, agricultural runoff, and human and animal feces. These anthropogenic sources of pollution and contamination will certainly make the water of the river a major source of waterborne diseases.

According to the World Health Organization (WHO), around 500 million people worldwide are infected by waterborne diseases each year, and 10 million die annually from waterborne bacteria, viruses, protozoa, and other microbiological organisms.[79] Indeed, 80 to 90 percent of all infectious diseases worldwide are waterborne, mainly due to dumping of untreated urban sewage into rivers and lakes, the lack of access to safe and clean potable water, and proper sanitary services. Globally, over 2.2 billion people cannot access clean drinking water, and 50,000 children die each day for lack of clean drinking water.[80]

Medical experts put water-related health hazards into two categories.[81] The first involves a host of biological agents, which humans contract when either they ingest unsafe drinking water or are bitten by insects. The contamination of drinking water with pathogenic viruses, parasites, bacteria, and other biological agents in most developing countries is primarily caused by human and animal excretions and secretions, as well as by municipal effluents. Most people in developing countries, as in the Nile basin, use rivers, ponds, and canals to wash their clothes, dispose of their excretions, and obtain drinking water, creating permissive conditions for the development, propagation, and transmission of infectious diseases. It's a small wonder that 25 million people die each year from waterborne diseases, primarily because 90 percent of raw sewage in the underdeveloped world is dumped untreated into local ponds and streams.[82]

Schistosomasis is a paradigm example of the sort of danger associated with contaminated and infested water. According to the WHO, at any particular moment, up to 200 million people worldwide are infected by the parasite schistosoma.[83] When the schistosomasis reaches an endemic level, as in Egypt, over 50 percent of the population becomes host to the parasite. The damming of rivers and the construction of canals naturally favor the growth and propagation of the schistosoma-carrying snail population.

The increasing presence of artificial lakes and canals and of stagnant water in the environment also favors the growth and spread of water-associated insect vectors, such as mosquitos causing malaria and yellow fever, and the human African trypanosis tsetse fly. Worldwide, over 500 million malaria cases result in over one million deaths annually.[84] The human African trypanosis infects 30,000 Africans annually and threatens 55 million people in sub-Saharan Africa.[85] In addition, 18 million Africans suffer from river blindness, largely contracted from bathing in dirty rivers.[86] Floriasis is another water-associated parasitic infection affecting over 250 million people worldwide. The congregation of people in urban centers without proper sanitation and adequate supply of clean water worsens the situation. For example, 1.7 billion people worldwide are said to be carrying the bacterium that causes tuberculosis and 3.1 million people die annually from tuberculosis.[87]

The second category of public health hazards involves the dumping of harmful chemicals and radioactive pollutants and contaminants into rivers and reservoirs. The world as a whole produces $2 trillion worth of chemicals per year, most of which enter the global water system.[88] Undergoing further chemical and biochemical transformations once in water, these pollutants cause long-term harm to humans and aquatic species. Air pollution and seepage, or releases of carcinogenic substances into river systems, compound the public health problems. Worldwide, there are three million reported cases of pesticide-related poisoning, and five million children under the age of five die each year from respiratory complications.[89]

In the advanced capitalist countries, people have long suffered the adverse health effects of five primary air pollutants: sulfur dioxide, nitrogen oxide, carbon dioxide and carbon monoxide, solid or liquid particulates, and lead particulates. These pollutants, annually produced in millions of tonnes, are by-products of industrialization. Fossil-fuel combustion in the United States alone produces 25 million tonnes of sulfur dioxide, 20 million tonnes of nitrogen oxide, and 100 million tonnes of carbon monoxide each year. Once airborne, sulfur dioxide and nitrogen oxide chemically react with water vapor to produce sulfuric acid and nitric acid, respectively, which fall on terrestrial and aquatic ecosystems as acid rain or dry acid depositions.[90] Transboundary movements of humans, animals, and insects also facilitate the spread of all sorts of maladies. For example, before 1864, reindeer pest was known in Egypt, but not in east African societies. However, traveling either via the Sudan or Ethiopia, the reindeer pest was detectable in east Africa by the 1880s. The impact of the disease on east African cattle herders was devastating. In 1891, two-thirds of the Massai in Tanganika, known for being solely dependent on cattle for subsistence, died as a result of reindeer pest infestation. The impact of the same infestation on Kenyan and Ugandan cattle herders was similar as they lost 95 percent of their livestock.[91]

Another human illness detected in Uganda in 1901 was sleeping sickness, which killed 200,000 Ugandans by 1906. Similar outbreaks of sleeping sickness also occurred in the Congo, Tanganika, Rwanda, and Burundi.[92] Although there is no consensus among epidemiologists as to the origin of the illness, alteration of the ecology and intensified interactions between humans and other living members of the ecology are blamed for regional outbreaks.[93] Today, the public health threat comes from HIV-AIDS, Ebola, and similar contagious diseases. To be sure, given the complex hydrological and ecological interdependence of the Nile riparian states, the public health issue is no longer solely a national problem: vectors and waterborne pathogens easily cross national borders. In the first half of 2006, for example, cholera outbreaks swept the Nile basin and beyond. Between late January and early September 2006, there were 25,000 reported cases of cholera outbreak in the Sudan involving hundreds of deaths. Owing to heavy summer rains, nearly 200 persons also died in Ethiopia from waterborne diarrhea and another 19,000 fell ill.[94] Kenya, Uganda, and Tanzania also witnessed isolated cases of cholera outbreaks during the same period. The geographic fluidity of the public health problem suggests that a credible future Nile water regime must come to terms with the public health challenge at a regional level.

The Governance Challenge

The ability of the Nile states to meet the complex challenges discussed in this chapter ultimately depends on the domestic and regional institutions they design, the constitutive processes they foster, and the authoritative decisions they make; these institutional designs, processes, and decisions are captured by the notion of governance, a term that has been widely co-opted. Since the collapse of Soviet social imperialism and the subsequent triumph of the neoliberal discourse in international interactions, the terms of the debate in international economic relations have shifted from one based on social analysis to one based on the question of governance. In the new discourse on governance, the capitalist relations of production and the internationalization of capital are seen as functionally integrative and positively progressive. Accordingly, the lack of economic development and social progress in the global south is understood as primarily due to the internal shortcomings of the underdeveloped countries themselves. Insofar as the argument goes, at the root of the problem is the absence of accountable internal governance. This purportedly exonerates external agency from complicity in the perpetuation of the problem.

As a result, the term "governance" has become one of those overused concepts in both official documents and academic literature. For example, the authors of *Shared Vision* for the NBI have appropriated seemingly progressive normative concepts, such as good governance, rule of law, transparency, accountability, sustainability, environmental conservation and protection, local participation, indigenous rights, and so on. The authors of the document are certainly officials representing governments that are internationally known for their repression of their peoples, gross violation of human rights and civil liberties, wanton corruption, and their limitless contempt for political dialogue and political pluralism. In fact, the cooptation of norms is so sweeping that it makes one lose faith in the seriousness of the NBI document.

In a crucial respect, though, the sweeping cooptation or invocation of seemingly progressive norms simply confirms Gramsci's reflection on the co-dependence and mutual reinforcement of coercion and consent, obtained primarily through manipulation and deception. From the ruling elites' standpoint, exclusive reliance on power to maintain power is costly and perhaps unsustainable in the long run. For its maintenance, power requires the consent of the significant majority of the masses. This, in turn, requires the manipulation of language, symbols, myths, and other external markers of identity. This is what Gramsci called class hegemony, embedded in institutions, cultures, and political values, and intended to mask the social relations of production and, by extension, to thwart the emergence of counterhegemonic civic movements intent on overthrowing the prevailing order.[95]

The political practices in the Nile basin confirm Gramsci's reflection. Yoweri Museveni, before seizing power in Uganda, for example, plausibly argued that the key problem in Africa was that leaders stay in power for too long. As a demonstration of apparent sincerity, he made sure that the Ugandan president was constitutionally term-limited; after two electoral cycles he would leave. Now, after nineteen years in power, Museveni and his allies have amended the constitution to remove the "term-limitation" clause from the constitution. After parliament, packed with his supporters, approved the new constitution, Museveni submitted the constitution to the Ugandan people in a referendum on July 29, 2005, after administering a massive dose of propaganda, manipulation, and arm twisting. Fewer than half of the voting adults participated in the referendum and thus rewarded Museveni with a run for a third term. In light of the previous observation on the meaning and significance of governance, clarification of the term is in order. By "governance" I mean here a system that takes human political freedom, ecological integrity, and social justice as the central pillars of full human emancipation. The textual foundation of governance celebrates both the vertical and horizontal dimensions of a political system, whether it is arranged internally or regionally.

As a necessary prelude to creating a credible water regime, the Nile states must first simultaneously face up to the regional and internal dimensions of governance. At the regional level, the urgency of the question calls for a thoroughgoing reconceptualization of sovereignty as a fundamental prerequisite for spatial reconfiguration of the Nile basin. As Veronica Ward notes, the Westphalian definition of a modern state is embedded in such notions as absolute authority, autonomy, control, and territorial exclusivity.[96] This means that the modern state can do whatever it deems is its right within its physical environment and to its own people.

The definition of the modern state as sovereign entity stands in sharp opposition to the holistic concept of ecological integrity. For example, it is understood that conservation and protection of tropical rainforests are critical to both the climate and precipitation regimes, which are in turn necessary for the generation of water resources. The uppermost Nile co-riparian states, namely the DRC, Rwanda, and Burundi, are endowed with moist tropical rainforests. Under the logic of sovereignty, these countries have the absolute right to the forests. But doesn't this undermine the integrity of the hydrological system?

Pollution and contamination of the Nile river system by upstream states pose another set of problems that the notion of sovereignty cannot handle. Thus, a resolution of the clashing differences between the logic of sovereignty and the imperatives of ecological integrity is a necessary precondition for a redefinition of sovereignty, and the spatial transformation of the Nile basin on the basis of new identities, new institutions, and new ground rules. This can lead to a credible Nile water regime, one that moves the co-basin states from a cooperative mode of relationship as an interim arrangement to an integrative management as a long-term goal. This requires the co-riparian states to move from territory-based identity to a basin-wide institutional framework.

A Nile water regime ought to be surrounded by and anchored in a constellation of critical institutions, as in a population control regime, regional environmental agency, disease control organization, and so on. Central to any success at a regional level is the internal entrenchment of democratic governance. To be credible, real governance should address comprehensively and justly the gender, ethnic, and social relationships within a polity. A nation is a composition of many subunits, each manifesting a variety of characteristics that are natural, social, economic, and cultural. The human and material satisfaction of all societal units is best met by complete inclusion of local units in actual decision-making processes at the center, on the one hand, and by allowing them to preserve, nurture, and enhance their autonomy and authenticity, on the other. In this sense, local communities are the real building blocks of a democratic nation, just as democratic nations are the building blocks for a sustainable regional system.

The hydrological integrity of a basin is first and foremost impacted by developments internal to each riparian state. Interethnic and religious differences over the allocation and use of water resources can possibly lead to civil wars, as in the Sudan where the canalization project in the south of the country has been abruptly halted. The Sudanese civil war has resulted in the deaths of two million southerners since 1983, and has produced not only millions more of internally displaced persons but also hundreds of thousands of refugees who have enormously burdened other co-riparian nations. The Sudanese tragedy has yet to subside as the Islamic regime continues the interethnic conflict in the Darfur region, and the government-supported "Arab militia" unleashed ruthless campaigns of eviction, rape, and outright murder on other Sudanese of "non-Arab" origin. At present, two million Darfurians are either internally displaced or have become refugees in neighboring countries under appalling conditions. Another paradigm case of bad governance has prevailed in the DRC. Since 1998, a bloody civil war has been raging in that country. What is particularly appalling about the DRC is not only the extent of the savagery, but also the scant international attention paid to this tragedy. Various reports from nongovernmental organizations suggest that at least four million Congolese have died since 1998 alone from a combination of internal war, disease, hunger, and starvation.

The situation in Uganda is no different. The Lord's Resistance Army has battled the central government for nineteen years and is imbued with a bizarre mixture of Christian theology and traditional religious practices. The Lord's Army has continually resorted to savage acts of mutilation, abduction of children, rape, and burning humans alive. It has succeeded in driving over two million Ugandans out of their homes into neighboring countries or internal camps.

The tragedy of internal war is not limited to the Sudan, Uganda, and the DRC. Eritrea and Ethiopia, in addition to their recent bloody war, are beset by internal low-intensity conflicts. Rwanda and Burundi are battling internal rebellions at different levels of intensity. Even Egypt has to deal with violent opposition from religious extremists.

The internal conflicts and civil strife in the Nile basin have also generated a context within which several regional actors have conducted, or are surreptitiously conducting, nefarious proxy wars against each other. Thus, the enduring lesson from the experiences of internal instabilities and interethnic strife ought to be the veritable realization that absence of real governance can potentially produce propitious conditions for degradation of critical ecosystem services, social disintegration, internal instability, and massive migration and refugee formation, putting the security and stability of the entire region in jeopardy. This in turn will have serious ramifications for international security.

The way to thwart such tendencies is to take the governance challenge very seriously. The point I am trying to convey here is that, so long as the prevailing internal orders persist, no credible water regime can be created or sustained. Given the extent to which water resource utilization, the integrity of the environment, and inter-riparian relations and security are inseparable quantities, the prior promotion and establishment of real democratic governance in each riparian state ought to be seen as the inescapable prerequisite to the realization of those concerns.

The Neoliberalist Challenge

The prevailing notion of progress in contemporary lexicon demands the uncritical acceptance of Western capitalism, which is presented as a naturalized system without alternative. To blunt the negative effects of the anarchy of production and overaccumulation in the core capitalist countries, on the one hand, and to supposedly pull the underdeveloped countries out of poverty, on the other, unfettered globalization of the capitalist mode of production is advanced as the only viable system. In consequence, underdeveloped countries have been pushed into unquestioning acceptance of the Western prescription for development. Markets and the price mechanism are presented as cure-alls for underdevelopment.

In keeping with this dominant orientation, the World Bank, the IMF, and the World Trade Organization (WTO) have lately succeeded in defining water as a material value and therefore an exchangeable commodity.[97] This is the latest in a series of efforts toward completing the commodification or commercial enclosure of the global commons. Global neoliberal institutions are exerting enormous pressure on underdeveloped countries to adopt the market approach to their water requirements. It is instructive to note that the pressure to establish the demonstration effect of the Western model of progress is best exemplified by what has been taking place in the last fifty years in the area of agriculture, where the trend has been toward impounding water in ever-larger reservoirs to drive electricity turbines and irrigate vast farmlands. The number of large dams, 150 m high, jumped from 5,000 in 1950 to 50,000 by the mid-1990s, of which 85 percent were built in the early 1960s. These large dams together with the 100 superdams, over 150 m high, hold 6,000 cu km of water, accounting for 15 percent of global freshwater.[98]

Powerful economic forces underpin the race to construct megadams, as many developing countries imported the multiple-use irrigation model as an answer to their growing food deficit and industrial underdevelopment. With the rapid decline of tillable land, and the intensification of food production on existing lands, reliance on a continuous supply of irrigation water and chemical fertilizers becomes appealing, since multiple cropping could be achieved. Thanks to the internationalization of the multiple-use irrigation model, the world put 6 million ha of land under irrigation annually in the 1960s and 5.2 million ha per year in the 1970s. To be sure, the majority of the 50,000 large dams and the 800,000 small dams worldwide have been built since the 1950s. Even in Africa, the total hectareage under irrigation rose by 80 percent over the 1950 level by 1982.[99]

The export and universalization of the multiuse irrigation model was actively facilitated by the World Bank and other international capitalist institutions. After devoting $1 billion a year to dam building in the 1950s, the World Bank increased the loan amounts for dam construction to over $2 billion a year in the 1970s. Between 1975 and 1984, the World Bank and its satellite regional banks funneled over $40 billion into dam construction, mostly in the global south. The World Bank alone approved and financed the building of twenty-six dams per year between 1970 and 1985. Moreover, since the 1980s, some 80 percent of World Bank loans to the agricultural sector in the global south have been for irrigation infrastructure, such as building dams and distribution canals, along with power transmission lines. The amounts of loans devoted to such purposes averaged $2 billion per annum since 1980; in total, the World Bank alone spent $58 billion on 527 dams in ninety-three countries between its creation and 2000.[100]

As the World Commission on Dams documents, there is a powerful logic behind the push for building a huge irrigation infrastructure, since market opportunity in this sector is immense. Western corporations can supply such capital goods as construction equipment, bulldozers, rubble and dirt movers, pumps, tractors, turbines, regulators, and power transmission equipment. Once built, irrigation works and dams require continual maintenance services for which multinational corporations provide engineering services, advanced technologies, and massive quantities of spare parts year after year. In this sense, the mammoth irrigation works and dams in the global south are integral to capitalist accumulation in the global north. When the World Bank shuffles billions of dollars to the global south to construct hydroelectric dams and irrigation canals in the name of promoting development, the rationale is all too clear. It is this "one size fits all" model that the Nile countries are currently scrambling to emulate; this contextualizes the hydrographic race for Nile waters.

In addition to grappling with the major challenges discussed earlier, the societies and states in the Nile basin will have to deal with the dark side of globalization, especially the deepening of the objectification of nature, which now includes the commodification of water resources. The World Bank and the IMF have, for quite some time, been pushing a market solution to the presumed water crisis that features the privatization of water services. In 2000, the standby agreements signed by the IMF and at least six countries were said to have involved some degree of privatization of municipally controlled water services.[101] The IMF used its program known as "Poverty Reduction and Growth Facility" as a mask to force Tanzania to privatize its water sanitation services in the capital in order to receive debt relief. Rwanda is also required to place its water services under private management as a condition for receiving IMF help. In fact, in 1999, the World Bank played hardball with Mozambique. In order to receive $117 million in loans and some debt relief, the World Bank put Mozambique under compulsion to privatize its water utilities and sanitation services. The French water company (FAUR) stands to collect $9 million annually from this long-term contract with Mozambique. Similarly, the World Bank has been using its financial flagship, the International Financial Corporation, to bring private water corporations to Nigeria and Ghana with $2 billion of its own money in loans.[102]

Historically, water has been regarded as inseparable from nature and therefore a common heritage. But the belief in nature as the owner of water resources is quickly changing. In 1996, a World Bank official predicted that "one way or another, water will be moved around the world as oil is now. Within the next five years, we will see a rising recognition that water is an international commodity."[103] In an effort to universalize the commodification and privatization of water, the global capitalist institutions have problematized water, not as a right, but as an economic need. This places the demand for water within the context of the laws of supply and demand, mediated by the price mechanism. Defining water as an objective thing can readily justify the call for privatizing water resources. This would allow owners of capital to overcome the difficulty involved in the definition of water as a common heritage, to which everyone is entitled as a matter of human right. Indeed, since the second World Water Forum formalized the definition of water as a commodity in March 2000, thereby making it tradable like other commodities governed within the purview of WTO rules, global water corporations, fully supported by the World Bank and the IMF, have offensively moved to complete the commodification process by acquiring management rights to public water services. The question of whether the Nile states can resist international pressure to accept the commodification and privatization of their water resources is something that they must address.

Conclusion

The discussion in this chapter amply demonstrates that water resources involve manifold aspects of governance. The quantitative and qualitative aspects of water cannot be understood apart from the economic, social, political, and ecological dimensions of human civilization. Indeed, a discourse on hydrology ought to be part of a larger social research program to guide policy makers in the effort to generate material prosperity, social security, political liberty, and ecological equity for their societies. A sustainable and equitable water resources regime requires not only the widening and deepening of water-related issues, but also the forging of a seamless web of relationships and commitments, involving the cultivation of horizontal trade, democracy promotion, information sharing on hydrology and meteorology, and regional coordination of population control, public health, and environmental protection policies and programs. Therefore, the study of international water resources management requires a methodology that is grounded in an integrative discourse that overcomes two key deficiencies currently evident in mainstream literature. The first deficiency involves the exclusion of ecological demand for water. Sustainable utilization of a river system must allow a water flow that sufficiently meets the requirements of aquatic species and their ecosystems, wetlands, and riparian vegetation. Second, an integrative discourse, one that is holistic and comprehensive, must go beyond the official co-optation of such lofty notions as "integrative water resource management" and "integrative river basin management" to investigate whether these approaches are feasible under the existing neoliberal mode of production and political structures. Once the fundamental question regarding the appropriate economic system for the Nile basin is determined and the right political structures are put in place, then co-basin states can talk about the proper action plan. The right mix of economic and political strategies should be able to provide satisfactory answers to the following six questions:

1. How can the various stakeholders and communities in the ten riparian states of the Nile basin inaugurate an integrative discourse of communication, rationality, and understanding conducive to the formation of a sustainable hydrological regime?

2. How can the riparian states establish regional coordination mechanisms to ensure that disparate national policies are not pursued in manners that run counter to sustainability principles?

3. How can the riparian states put legal and institutional arrangements in place to meet the challenges of sustainable development and promote ecological security in the region on the basis of a comprehensive water resources research agenda?

4. What can be done to promote and accelerate the democratization process in each riparian state to thwart the conditions of instability and its attendant consequences?

5. How can nonstate actors, social movements, indigenous communities, cultural groups, and civic institutions be meaningfully included in an integrated hydrological regime to ensure the effectiveness of water resources management and planning and to optimize the net flow of Nile waters?

6. To what extent can extraregional bodies facilitate the forging of regional hydrological order in the Nile basin?

Chapter Two

Egypt
Gift of the Nile

Ever since Herodotus called Egypt the "gift of the Nile," the names of the country and the river have almost become synonymous. For millennia, Egyptians relied on the Nile for agriculture, drinking water, transportation, and energy. The country has long been totally dependent on the Nile and Egyptians have developed a deep sense of entitlement to the river. Egypt's dependence on the Nile is almost exclusively defined by the country's physiographical configuration and hydrological determinants. The entire population is congregated in the 15,000 sq km along the narrow green belt of the river (known as the Nile Valley), and in the exceptionally fertile delta. Together the Nile Valley and delta represent just 4 percent of Egypt's total land area, yet they hold the whole population; a full 96 percent of the country is unpopulated desert.

Just 200 km before reaching the Mediterranean Sea, its final destination, the Nile splits into two branches: the Damietta to the east and the Rosetta to the west. Between the branches is a triangular alluvial delta that is some 18 m thick and 200 km wide. Before the construction of the Aswan High Dam, soupy alluvium from Ethiopia annually replenished the topsoil of the flat delta plain, making it enviously fertile and productive. In effect, soil formation in Egypt has been tied to the continual deposition of Ethiopian silt along the river banks and on the delta. In the 1920s, some 110 million tonnes of silt passed through the Aswan dam annually; of this total, some 78 million tonnes were abandoned by the river along its banks, and some 22 million tonnes reached the Mediterranean Sea (Collins 2002).

Because Egypt and the Nile are inseparable and because Egypt without the Nile is unthinkable, the hydrographic conundrum has placed the contemporary Egyptian government between two blades of a pair of scissors.

Upstream co-basin states insistently charge Egypt with taking more than its share from the Nile waters; in consequence, the legitimacy of Egypt's presumed entitlement to the Nile has recently come under a ubiquitous challenge. The Egyptian regime must meet this external challenge as it seeks to establish a sort of modus vivendi with co-riparian states to ensure sufficient flow of the Nile. Yet it is also challenged internally by its own socially restive population. Not only the dispossessed peasant population and the unemployed urban youth, but also the rising living standards of the privileged classes are placing huge demands on the regime, compelling it to look to the river for an answer. This chapter examines the evolution of Egypt's water regime and the competing internal and external demands made on this regime, and evaluates the government's water resources development strategies in light of the evolving regional water discourse.

The Elusive Quest for Food Security and the Modernization Imperatives

The Napoleonic invasion of Egypt around the turn of the eighteenth century transformed Egyptian agriculture from one based on sustainable self-sufficiency into one based on modern market-oriented production. Mohammed Ali, whom the Ottoman sultan sent to Egypt to expel the French from the area, adopted the European method of primitive capital accumulation to begin the modernization process; this was the first overt commoditization of the Nile River. The adoption involved the concentration of agrarian property in the hands of the state (the royal house and client agents, in particular), heavy taxation of the peasantry, and the introduction of new cash crops. These arrangements stimulated the canalization of the river system.

With help from French engineers, the Egyptian ruler began the first canalization program. The effort, heavily dependent on forced labor, resulted in the construction of a complex network of canals, diversion dams, and barrages. The introduction of cotton, both long staple and short staple varieties, followed. Together, canalization and monocrop cotton cultivation achieved the perennialization of Egyptian agriculture.

During the last quarter of the nineteenth century, against the backdrop of intra-European rivalry over new colonies, the British provided the Egyptian canalization project with a fresh impetus. No other imperial power recognized (as did the British Empire) the centrality of Nile waters to the actualization of the colonial project. The British were elated by their control of the Nile flow and startled by the absence of irrigation works in Egypt. Colonel Moncrieff reflected this British mood when he opined: "When one sees the great monuments of Egyptian skill in classical times, it seems strange that a nation capable of designing and erecting such buildings apparently never thought of controlling the river on which they depended."[1]

The British quickly acted on their excitement, creating a new reality that would have profound implications for inter-riparian relations long after their departure. In fact, McFarlane made an early and insightful projection of the radical alteration to Egyptian agriculture that would result from the conversion to perennial irrigation and the future preponderance of the cotton crop. At the center of the revolutionary transformation was British ingenuity and power. McFarlane stated that, by virtue of the widespread cultivation of cotton, "[The] whole agricultural regime would have been altered. We believe that the results will justify the change. But we admit that it is an experiment, an experiment which will require for its success the continuance of British power in the basin of the Nile and British control of the irrigation works in Egypt for many years to come."[2] The British thought that it was an historic opportunity to take control of the river and make the colonial project a reality. They wasted no time in committing engineering skill and financial power.

In 1902, British engineers created a 200-mile-long artificial lake in Upper Egypt that they called the Aswan Dam. This gigantic breakthrough in dam building would soon transform Egypt into a primary cotton producer and supplier. It was a perfect union between the politics of British empire building and Egyptian canalization drive. British engineers had calculated that perennial irrigation demanded a continuous supply of 32,000 cu ft of water per second. The constant flow of the Nile in Egypt, at only 8,000 cu ft per second, was far below the necessary average. The engineers realized that the flood season might supply the missing 32,000 cu ft per second; seasonal flooding increased the flow to between 300,000 and 500,000 cu ft per second. The challenge was to harness the surplus water. Backing up the waters of the Nile over the 200-mile-long Aswan Dam solved the puzzle. Water from the dam continued to flow to existing cotton fields and, via a network of 8,500 large and 45,000 smaller canals, was also made to feed one million acres of new fields.[3] Encouraged by this success, British and Egyptian engineers built three more dams between 1903 and 1925 along the Egyptian Nile that, together, irrigated six million acres of farmlands. Two-thirds of the farms in the delta were placed under perennial irrigation, as were another 400,000 acres 60 miles southwest of Cairo.[4]

The speed with which perennial irrigation expanded in Egypt had important long-term economic, social, and environmental ramifications. First, the process of perennialization of agriculture shifted the agrarian equilibrium in favor of cotton production for export. In the early 1920s, as cotton exports topped $250 million annually, or ten times more than the combined value of Egypt's cereal and vegetable exports, Egypt happily devoted one-third of its land to cotton cultivation. British demand accounted for 50 percent of Egypt's cotton export.[5]

Perennialization of agriculture also profoundly affected agrarian relations of production. With water now available year-round, land value skyrocketed. In the Nile Valley, per acre land prices increased from $25 in 1900 to between $150 and $250; in the delta, the average price increased to between $700 and $800 per acre.[6] Landlessness and shrinking holding sizes increasingly defined the agrarian mode of production. The conversion of flood-based basin irrigation, which was compatible with the Nile's natural flow, to barrage-based perennial irrigation would eventually transform the river: British canalization presaged a hydrological revolution. In addition to the benefits accruing from the control of seasonal, historically deadly flooding, the dam allowed Egypt to store 9 bcm of water year-round for hydroelectricity generation and multiple cropping.[7]

Initial successes in dam construction and perennial cultivation prompted British hydrologists to strive to complete the hydrocolonization of Nile water resources. To guarantee Egypt's political stability, water security, and ability to supply global capitalism with long staple cotton, the entire watershed of the Nile had to be seen as a single patchwork of nature. All of its streams had to be integrated into a single hydrologic system to ensure the continuous supply of water to Egypt. This hydrologic necessity captured the imagination of Harold Hurst of the Egyptian department of public works. Hurst imagined that British imperial interests and Egyptian water needs could only be met by domesticating the Nile's flow.

Hurst's idea was captured in the notion of "century storage," and several committees were formed to make recommendations on the viability of this concept. Among these was the Jonglei Committee, assigned to undertake a comprehensive hydrological study of the Nile system. Prominent among its recommendations, contained in the Report on the Nile Valley Plan, was to dig a canal that would be sited from Bor farther south in the Sudan, before the water of the Bahr al-Jabal flashes into the Sudd swamp, all the way to Malakal, about 360 km north of Bor. Accentuating the strategic importance of this canal, the report noted: "The Nile basin must be treated, hydrologically speaking, as a single unit that the newly independent states must see beyond their narrow interests and work together."[8] However, despite British interest and Egyptian urgency, work on the Bor-Malakal Canal was postponed until the 1970s, for reasons discussed in the next chapter.

In the 1950s, the progressive utilization of Nile water resources received renewed attention, fueled by Nasser's personal ambitions, Egyptian nationalism, and popular expectations. Egypt's ruling elites believed that, by embarking on a new hydrological strategy of development, the country could eliminate its hydrological dependence on upstream co-riparian states, thwart its vulnerability to the potential instability in the upper reaches of the basin, and overcome its state of underdevelopment. Rearticulation of Egypt's long-term interest in the Nile system thus led Nasser to resurrect the British notion of century storage. The idea, as originally conceived by Hurst, presupposed the perennial flow of Nile water to Egypt by constructing permanent water storage dams along the entire length of the Nile, where resources could be conveniently stored during periods of high precipitation and flow and released during periods of low flow for use in Egypt.

Century storage would, by regulating the periodicity of flows, complete the domestication of the Nile. The plateau lakes of the great African rift valley, where rainfall amounts were thought to counterbalance the evaporation rate, were particularly considered ideal sites for the hydrological venture. Belief in the presumed limitless providence of the Nile supported the conception of the Aswan High Dam, which was essentially Nasser's equivalent of century storage. Hurst would have taken satisfaction from the implementation of his concept, despite differences in siting and, possibly, in environmental and social consequences.

When the Free Officers under Nasser came to power in 1952, Sudanese nationalism was bubbling, jeopardizing the terms of the 1929 Nile waters agreement. Sudanese nationalists complained that Egypt was overexploiting Nile waters at their expense, and threatened to ignore the terms of agreement by unilaterally placing 6.5 million feddans of arable land under irrigation. The Sudanese insisted on renegotiating a new water framework that would take full account of present and potential needs to expand irrigation. This meant that the Sudan was entitled to 35 bcm of Nile waters. Egypt rejected both the Sudanese demand and its basis. The Egyptians advanced historical rights and population size as critical determinants for any renegotiation, and indicated their willingness to increase Sudan's share from 4 bcm, under the 1929 agreement, to only 9 bcm.

The stalemate continued until General Ibrahim Abboud successfully staged the 1958 coup, altering the dynamics of the negotiation process. Bargaining and resolution were hastened by Abboud's need for Egyptian support for his military regime, Egypt's desire to quicken the construction of the Aswan High Dam, and Egypto-Sudanese fear of British meddling in the hydrographic dispute. Under the 1959 agreement, annual allotments were set at 55.5 bcm for Egypt and 18.5 bcm for the Sudan. Subsequently, both countries proceeded with building dams.[9] Having thus ensured the supply of water, Nasser began implementing his version of "century storage" with full Soviet financial and technical support. The principal aims of the Aswan High Dam were: continuous provision of irrigation waters; reliable hydropower generation; permanent flood control; irrigation of 1.2 million feddans of reclaimed land; and conversion of 800,000 feddans in the Nile Valley from basin to perennial irrigation farms.[10] At the start of Aswan High Dam construction, Egypt believed that the realization of these objectives would free its water security from the potential stranglehold of upstream states. In the words of Gamal Abdel Nasser: "Once the Aswan High Dam is built, Egypt will no longer be a historical hostage of the upstream riparians of the Nile basin."[11]

The dam, completed in 1971, is 980 m wide at its base, stands almost 111 m high, and averages over 10 km across. Lake Nasser's storage capacity, at 164 bcm, is roughly equivalent to two years of Nile flow. The dam has enabled modern-day Egypt to receive 30 percent of its hydroelectric power supply from Lake Nasser and to increase its cultivable area from 2.4 million ha to 3.4 million ha. With the completion of the Southern Valley and the North Sinai Development projects, Egypt plans to raise the latter figure to 4.6 million ha by 2017.[12]

Today, Egypt's irrigation system is among the world's most sophisticated and complex networks. The hydrological system's operation involves eight gigantic barrages, 30,000 km of public canals, 670 complex public irrigation pumping stations, 22,000 public water control systems, and 17,000 km long public drainage networks, augmented by 80,000 km of private canals and farm drainage systems and 450,000 private water pumping devices. Together, these systems distribute 59 bcm of water annually.[13]

Although the dam's contribution to Egypt's economy is undeniable, the ecological and social consequences of hypercanalization are less positive. Since 160 of the dam's 450 km length are located inside the Sudan, dam construction displaced not only 40,000 Egyptians but also 50,000 Sudanese Nubians.[14] Other troubling consequences include hypersedimentation of the upstream portion of Lake Nasser associated with silt accumulation, loss of fertility, erosion of the downstream delta, waterlogging and soil salinity, and the loss of fish species. Potential inundation of the delta with Mediterranean seawater and seismic activity resulting from the shifting weight of the lake are even more worrisome.

Egypt has become precariously and wholly dependent on Nile waters to meet its population's needs. Rather than developing alternate solutions, such as population size management and promotion of distributive justice, Egypt has sought solace in the overexploitation of Nile water, treating the Nile's availability to Egypt as a divinely sanctioned gift. It continues to view its 55.5 bcm share, per the 1959 agreement with the Sudan, as sacrosanct. Yet common sense dictates that a bilateral agreement on a sensitive and crucially important international river system is likely unacceptable to the other eight riparian states. In combination with the growing degradation of ecosystem services in the Nile basin, Egypt's insensitivity to the water needs of co-basin states could be a critical source of friction in the basin.

To make matters worse, Egypt launched two unilateral projects in the mid-1990s that, in the context of an intensifying race for water resources, may be both a basis for interstate conflict and the cause of basin-wide ecological disaster. The South Valley Development project, comprising the Toshka, East Oweinat, and Western Desert Oasis, is due for completion by 2017 at an estimated cost of between $90 and $145 billion. The second project, the North Sinai Development scheme, is also due for completion by

2017 at a cost of $20 billion.[15] The South Valley Development scheme will, over a twenty-year period, irrigate more than 400,000 ha of reclaimed desert land in southwestern Egypt, just 50 km from the Sudanese borders. Egypt hopes to relieve some of the crowding and congestion in Cairo by resettling six million people in the Toshka depression and its environs. The Toshka scheme, launched in 1997, represents the first phase of the South Valley Development.

The project will be extended by 30 km in its second phase and by 350 km in the final phase. The government has promised the area's potential settlers quick prosperity from the production and exportation of citrus fruits and cash crops. Egyptian peasants are offered 4 ha of free land per person and loans on easy terms. Large private concessionaires are also welcomed. In 1998, the Saudi billionaire Prince al-Waleed bin Talal purchased 50,000 ha of land in the Toshka scheme at a bargain price of 25 Egyptian pounds per ha, sweetened by a twenty-year tax holiday and other incentives. The Holding Company for Agricultural Development, representing eight privatized Egyptian corporations, bought 50,000 ha, and another consortium of Egyptian entrepreneurs bought 80,000 ha.[16] These concessionaires intend to grow and export crops and fruits, primarily to the European Union.

By the end of 2002, the government had already spent over $4 billion on various infrastructure projects meant to entice private investors. The Mubarak pumping station, composed of twenty-four separate pumps that together lift 25 million cu m of water daily, is the heart of the Toshka scheme. The second largest of its kind in the world, the Mubarak pumping station and its branches will require 375 MW of energy to transport water through the 360 km long canal from Lake Nasser to the Toshka depression, with a view to eventually irrigating 2,268 sq km of desert land.[17] The Toshka project is expected to support the development and expansion of eighteen cities.

The North Sinai Development, launched in 1994, consists of two subprojects. The Sheikh Gaber Canal is expected to irrigate a 600 sq mi. strip of Sinai desert land paralleling the Mediterranean Sea that will eventually house 3.2 million resettled Egyptians. The second component, Al Salam Canal, will irrigate over 100,000 ha of desert land west of the Suez Canal with water from Damietta at the eastern mouth of the Nile. The North Sinai Development project also has ambitious manufacturing, mining, and tourism components. Egypt's political technicians believe that, when these various projects are completed, the country's habitable area will have been increased from just 4 percent of total land area today to 25 percent twenty years hence.

Egypt's efforts to reclaim more desert land must be understood in context of the fact that, presently, 76 million Egyptians share a mere 4 percent of the country's total land. The average holding of Egypt's 3.5 million farmers is 2 feddans, which must be cultivated intensively.[18] To feed its population, the country depends on 3.4 million ha of irrigated land, or 0.004 ha per head. In contrast, when Napoleon invaded Egypt over two centuries ago, its 2.5 million people shared one million ha of cultivable land, or 0.4 hectare per head.

The choice facing Egypt is to either continue on the present course, expanding irrigation works farther into the desert, or to find alternative means to not only slow the growth but also reduce the size of its population. The Mubarak government chose the former. In the words of Dr. El-Quosy, the man heading the Toshka project:

> We have no other alternative. Our Nile valley and delta are becoming more and more overpopulated. We've reached a situation in the major urban centers like Cairo where there are 1,600 people per square kilometer, and that's intolerable. . . . This is the story: we are under pressure from a growing population but have a fixed area of agricultural land. In order to maintain that very tiny sliver of agricultural land, we have to recover and cultivate another 3.4 million ha by 2017.[19]

Dr. El-Quosy may correctly identify the source of the pressure for more cultivable land, but the policy choice rests on nebulous assumptions and expectations. After all, if Egypt's population keeps growing, the addition of 3.4 million ha is unlikely to solve the long-running demographic and social injustice problems. If the present projection holds, Egypt's population will reach 150 million by 2050.[20] Abu Zeid, Egypt's minister of irrigation and water resources, is trenchantly right when he observes: "Thirty years from now we'll have another thirty million people, so the effect on the population living in the Nile valley and delta is not going to be eased very much."[21]

The southwestern and Sinai land reclamation programs are also predicated on the false hope that Egypt is going to retain its share of 55.5 bcm of Nile waters. But even allowing for this assumption, Egypt will need more water. The total water available to Egypt in 1999 was 63.5 bcm, already 4.5 bcm short of national demand.[22] Even by the government's own estimation, the country will need 86.74 bcm of water a year by 2017; the Toshka project alone will require 5.5 bcm of water annually.[23]

Even if the current flow of the Nile is maintained, I don't believe that other riparian states will continue to tolerate the status quo. For example, when Mubarak approved the Toshka scheme in 1997 just as NBI negotiations for a broadly acceptable multilateral water regime were under way, upstream riparian states demanded a radical revision of the 1959 Egypto-Sudanese accord. In fact, Ethiopia and Uganda asked for some 18 bcm from the Egyptian and Sudanese apportionments.[24] Attempting to satisfy the demands of upstream states under the existing arrangement creates a hydrological paradox, since base maintenance of Egypt's growing population necessitates an additional 20 bcm of water annually.[25]

If clinging to its present share of Nile waters is Egypt's attempt at managing its population and buttressing its own legitimacy, it may be disappointed. The reclamation schemes could end up being mere "white elephant" projects. For example, the government suggests that farmers will be able to grow crops four or five times per year. To question the sustainability of this optimism, one only needs to consider that Egyptian farmers in the fertile delta or Nile Valley grow only two crops annually.[26] Thus, the government's plan may prove illusory and might even be a major source of internal instability and regional discord as the government resists the regional effort to create a new framework for equitable reallocations of Nile water resources.

This point must be understood in the context of Egypt's rapidly shrinking water budget. Both its surface and groundwater resources are fully exploited. In 1960, when Egypt's population stood at the 30 million mark, the per capita water availability was 2,100 cu m annually; when the population reached 72 million in 2003, availability decreased to 792 cu m per person per year. Projections place the population at 90 million in 2025, so that the per capita water consumption will be 337 cu m per year.[27] To give tangible reference to this point, the UNDP defines a water stress condition as 1,700 cu m per person per year and water scarcity as 1,000 cu m per person per year (Whibb 2001). Experts warn that the present mode of water utilization will ultimately prevent Egypt from irrigating 60 percent of its agricultural land, placing national food security in jeopardy.[28]

Moreover, critics, familiar with the physiography of the land reclamation sites, believe that Egypt could benefit more from redirecting the resources currently devoted to the reclamation schemes toward education, public health, and other projects. Egyptian soil experts at the University of Alexandria believe that no more than 33,600 ha of land in the Toshka area are considered moderately suitable for cultivation, and 77 percent of the land surveyed is considered utterly barren.[29] If one supplements these criticisms with a consideration of the projects' impact on ecological equity and social justice, the resettlement schemes become even more unsavory.

Even though the future environmental impact remains to be determined, knowledgeable people are not sanguine about the ecological unknowns. Professor Aaron Wolf, for example, believes that Egypt will suffer more environmentally than it is likely to gain from the execution of desert land reclamation programs. He foresees two fundamental problems. First, the withdrawal of the envisaged amount of water from the Aswan High Dam would substantially reduce the amount of water required to sufficiently dilute pollutants downstream, thereby increasing salinity. Second, the withdrawal of freshwater in the magnitude needed to irrigate vast desert land would undermine the delta's ability to withstand saltwater intrusion from the Mediterranean Sea. If this assessment holds, Egypt will lose more agricultural land than it will gain under the reclamation schemes.[30]

The gross social injustice embedded in the new schemes is equally apparent. By enticing private concessionaires with cheap labor, giveaway land, tax holidays, and other incentives, the Egyptian government has clearly determined in favor of capitalist accumulation. Echoes of the many false promises used to justify the Aswan High Dam are heard today, as the Egyptian people are assured that their prosperity lies with the completion of these projects. Egypt is currently one of eight countries whose rapidly diminishing water supply has inspired the concern of the international security community. The others are China, India, Iraq, Uzbekistan, Iran, Pakistan, and Bangladesh.[31]

The Egyptian hydrographic orientation is troubling because, despite the looming water crisis, policy makers and hydrologists continue to think within the box. They pin their hopes on four factors: supposed relative power to indefinitely keep the 55.5 bcm allotment; transformation of Lakes Victoria and Albert into storage facilities and completion of the Jonglei Canal in southern Sudan; application of technological prowess to improve efficiency and recycle more of existing water resources; and excavation of fossil water in the great Nubian sandstone formation. Each of these hydrological hopes presents a serious challenge to Egypt.

Egypt's ability to keep its existing share of 55.5 bcm of Nile waters is dubious for two reasons. First, there is no natural guarantee that the present Nile flow will remain constant. The climatological history of precipitation in the Nile basin is instructive of the sorts of long-range changes we should expect. Until 12,000 years ago, Lake Victoria had no outlet to the western Nile system. Even after the two Nile branches joined into the main Nile at Khartoum, the uneven discharge of the Nile has continued. As Mike Hulme notes, the discharge of the Nile has fluctuated wildly over time in response to a confluence of natural and anthropogenic factors. The mean annual flow of the Nile was 110 bcm between 1870 and 1899; 84 bcm between 1900 and 1959; and 72 bcm between 1977 and 1978.[32] While the third average dropped 15 percent from the preceding years' average, it was on the basis of the second average that Egypt and the Sudan concluded the 1959 water agreement. Indeed, the ten-year flows of the Nile during the twentieth century fluctuated between 67.7 and 93.6 bcm a year with serious implications for water resources management, particularly in Egypt.[33] Thus, the volume of water at Lake Nasser precipitously dropped from 110 bcm in 1978 to 72.9 bcm in 1984, and then to 41.4 bcm in 1988, due to an unprecedented decrease in annual Nile discharge. In fact, in 1987, the level of water at Lake Nasser became so dangerously low that Egyptians were asked, for the first time, to conserve water and major regions experienced electricity rationing and blackouts.

In a crisis mode, the regime hoped to save 86 mcm of water annually from irrigation through rationalization and to recover another 196 mcm a year by recycling drainage water.[34] The experience of the 1980s clearly demonstrates that "century storage" no longer guaranteed water security. If the trend of the 1980s becomes the norm, not only Egypt but also other co-riparian states are likely to experience serious water shortages.

Second, even if the generous Nile flow persists, upstream states are unlikely to forgo demands on Nile waters. With populations rising throughout the basin and nations seeking food security through irrigation, states will place increasing demands on Nile waters and ecology. Today, the ten riparian states together have 8 million ha of land under irrigation (in addition to rain-fed farms), producing all the crops on which the 360 million people of the region precariously depend. An estimated 10 million ha are said to be available for irrigation, assuming the availability of the necessary water resources.[35] Yet, water stress in every upstream state has already become of grave concern, and local communities are likely to exploit the local water resources, further stressing the system even in the absence of large governmental projects.

Moreover, watershed degradation due to heavy deforestation is likely to undermine the climatic and precipitation regimes, substantially affecting the Nile. Even if the Nile flow remains unchanged in quantitative terms, its quality might be degraded so that the amount of water actually available to Egypt will diminish significantly. Under these circumstances, to think that military power might be applied to perpetuate the existing water arrangement is not only foolish but also self-defeating. Egypt contemplates military action at its own peril. The grim reality is that there is no shortcut to regional cooperation on the basis of domestic legitimacy and regional solidarity.

The hope of transforming the east African lakes into storage facilities by raising their water levels is equally illusory, without prior radical transformation of each co-riparian state. The Nile basin is populated by states with dubious reputations in matters of democracy, rule of law, accountability, and social justice. Construction of dams in the east African lake plateau or the canalization project in the Sudan cannot proceed unless the pertinent issues of grassroots democracy, domestic social equity, and ecological integrity are first addressed.

Reliance on technological prowess to improve efficiency and distribution of water resources seems a good prospect. After all, Egypt is known for marked inefficiency in water resource utilization. The ranges of efficiency in Egypt's agriculture are between 60 and 70 percent; the efficiency rate in municipal and industrial sectors is even lower, between 50 and 60 percent.[36] If efforts to improve demand side management, conservation, and efficient use of water are not supported, the consequences could be dire. Note that in the 1980s China was able to treat only 2 percent of the 28 bcm of wastewater it generated annually; the rest was dumped into rivers and lakes, causing China to lose most of its inland fisheries.

An effective application of technological resources to amplify water uses through recycling allowed Egypt, in 1995–1996, to compensate for its 8 bcm water deficit by reusing its waste and groundwaters.[37] Recycling municipal and industrial water and using newer technologies can reduce the volume of water required in industrial plants while also improving water quality. Recent experiences in water resources management suggest that equipping plants with recirculating water systems could help to substantially reduce pollution and the volume of water used. However, it is not apparent that Egypt has sufficiently developed the necessary technology, and it is not known to what extent Egypt's water problem might be addressed through a technological approach. By some estimates, given the current state of technology and the quality of its administration, Egypt can squeeze only 4 or 5 bcm from intense use of drainage water.[38] In fact, Mohammed Abdel Hady, Egypt's minister of water resources, acknowledged in 1994 that his country had already reached the self-imposed efficiency target of 75 percent; this was allegedly comparable to the efficiency level achieved by Israel.[39] Although Abu Zeid's recent complaints about Egyptian wastefulness cast doubt on the minister's claim, his comment nonetheless highlights the limits to gains that can be expected just from efficiency. Technological prowess alone cannot solve Egypt's water problem.

Present Egyptian water policy and efficiency levels do not inspire confidence in elites' official pronouncements and national priorities. By some estimates, only 2 percent of Egypt's 3.4 million ha of cropland are irrigated by efficient modern methods.[40] The diversion of 5.5 bcm of Nile water to the western desert also casts a shadow on the elites' commitment to efficiency. The marginal soil of the western desert suggests that the investment return will not justify the use of Nile water. Indeed, Egypt might best improve its water security by committing to efficiency gains in the agricultural sector that, for the following reasons, consumes 84 percent of the national water budget.

Egypt's farmland is highly fragmented. In 1982, 2,470,000 landholders shared 2,770,000 ha of cropland, or slightly more than one ha per farmer.[41] Because the holding sizes are very small, unit efficiency is lost through water and other input use. Consequently, aggregation of the small holdings into manageable units under cooperative arrangements, not privatization for unbridled capitalist accumulation, must be seriously considered. Second, 2 bcm of water is lost annually from its crop fields through evaporation alone. Modernization of irrigation canals through the installation of subsurface canals would improve efficiency. Third, changing the nation's mix of crops would save a good amount of water annually. Some analysts suggest that Egypt can substantially reduce the water demand by growing sugar beets on the 130,000 ha now dedicated to sugarcane, and by decreasing its rice fields from 540,000 ha to 300,000 ha.[42]

Unless the cost of energy becomes prohibitive, Egypt might enhance its water security through technological innovation by desalinating seawater. In the late 1990s, there were over 11,000 water desalination plants worldwide, producing over 4 billion gallons of water daily. Middle Eastern countries accounted for 60 percent of these desalination plants.[43] Saudi Arabia, the world's leading desalinated water producer, has installed thirty desalination plants and has six more under construction. The kingdom's desalination plants presently produce 12 mcm of freshwater a day, providing 70 percent of the country's drinking water. The Shuaiba desalination plant, the largest of its kind in the world, by itself produces 150 mcm of freshwater annually. In 2000, the plants also generated 28 million megawatt hours of electricity. When the six plants currently under construction come on stream, the thirty-six Saudi desalination plants will produce 800 million gallons of freshwater daily.[44]

The prospects for desalination are likely to improve as the costs of new technologies fall and the taste of desalinated water improves. The World Bank estimates that investment in desalination ventures will be between $45 and $60 billion over the next decade, and will be concentrated in the Middle East.[45] Israel's water controller once observed that a $2.5 billion investment in desalination plants would yield enough water for everyone and render harmless the fractious regional politics of water.[46] Certainly, it would be cheaper to invest in desalination technology, however expensive, than in war preparations.

It seems to me that Egypt can sufficiently improve its water security by radically reviewing its water budget. By increasing investment in desalination technology, modernizing its irrigation system by installing subterranean pipelines in its farm fields to reduce evaporation rates, and avoiding water-intensive crops and instead promoting more drought-resistant ones, Egypt can mitigate its water deficit.

For example, by shifting from the gravity flow method for crop field watering to a combination of sprinklers and drip systems, Egypt can achieve efficiency rates between 75 and 90 percent. Important lessons can be distilled from Israel's experience. By relying on computer-aided irrigation technology, Israeli farmers have scheduled the watering of their fields so as to optimize the water requirements of their crops and minimize evapotranspiration rates. Eighty percent of Israel's irrigated farms rely on sprinklers and another 20 percent use drip systems.[47] As a result, Israel has reduced the amount of water used per ha by 20 percent between 1967 and 1981 while simultaneously expanding farmlands under irrigation by 39 percent.[48] By using similar technologies and lining irrigation canals, Egypt can substantially improve its efficiency rate, reduce the volume of water applied to crop fields and thereby avoid the problem of waterlogging, and mitigate the effects of evapotranspiration and the associated problem of primary and secondary salination.

Finally, Egypt expects to excavate fossil water in the great Nubian sandstone formation. Fossil water volume in the Nubian sandstone formation is estimated at 200,000 bcm, and is shared by five countries.[49] Egypt, claiming a share of 40,000 bcm, began excavating fossil water in the late 1990s to irrigate 200,000 ha of farmland.[50] Since fossil water is commonly found at a depth of 4,000 m, the necessary amount of energy and the kind of technology required will certainly be expensive. Furthermore, some of the water may be unusable because of its relatively high salt content. Since this water is not renewable, excavation can only serve as a stopgap measure.

At any rate, this is Egypt's new hydrological frontier. Libya has already been excavating the fossil waters of the Nubian Desert. Qaddhafi allocated $32 billion to construct a 1,800-km-long subsurface canal to transport the fossil water from the Nubian sandstone formation to the north of the country. The 1,000 wells already in operation are gushing 1 bcm of water annually; when fully operational, Libya will be able to mine 40 bcm of fossil water annually until entirely exhausting its supply in forty or fifty years.[51] The Sudan is also planning to excavate fossil water from the Nubian Desert to supply drinking water to the western region of the country.

After Modernization

From a macro perspective, the modernization of Egypt's irrigation system and hydroelectricity generation facilities has certainly made a huge difference in the life of the country. Certainty of water supply, increased acreage of cultivable land, multiple cropping in a single year, the availability of relatively cheap hydropower energy, the doubling of the food supply, and flood control are the principal benefits that Egypt has been enjoying since the completion of the Aswan High Dam. The twelve installed turbines, each with the capacity of 175,000 kWh, have enormously enhanced Egypt's energy resources. By reclaiming one million acres of cultivable land, it had eased the lives of four million peasants. Today, the Egyptian farmer can feed eleven persons by harvesting five crops over every three years, compared with four persons in 1800.[52]

Despite these gains, however, Egypt's structural problems remain unresolved. The population increases by one million persons every nine months, and landlessness remains acute. Moreover, 60 percent of the reclaimed land is either characterized by low productivity or abandoned; the remaining 40 percent is classified by moderate productivity. The major reason for diminishing returns on agrarian modernization is soil salinity. Since the completion of modern irrigation networks, the high evaporation and transpiration rates, characteristic of arid regions and aggravated by the absence of good drainage systems, have left six million tonnes of salt on Egypt's cultivated land. One-third of the irrigated farms suffer from a severe soil salinity, and two-thirds experience poor drainage.[53]

The bitter irony is that the country that promised its people abundant food has become one of the largest food importers in the world. Food security has been proven illusory. In the 1960s, Egypt was a net exporter of food; it became a net food importer by the 1980s. In 1961, Egypt imported just 7 percent of national food requirements; this rose to 80 percent by the 1980s. The country's net food imports increased from $427 million in 1973 to $4.4 billion in 1981. Food imports were 21 percent of total imports in 1998 and 28 percent in 2002. By 1983, Egypt had become the largest importer of American wheat and wheat flour, as 75 percent of its wheat consumption was accounted for by imports. On average, Egypt imported over 7 million tonnes of wheat annually in the 1980s and the 1990s compared with 2 million tonnes in the 1960s.[54]

Egypt's growing food deficit lubricated the evolution of U.S.–Egyptian relations: Egypt bought American food on concessionary terms, and the United States enjoyed important proxy services from Egypt in the Middle East. American shipments of wheat to Egypt under PL.480 (concessional sale), for example, rose from $2.6 million in 1974 to $287 million in 1981.[55] This seemingly symbiotic relationship transformed Egypt into a client state and the United States into a "generous" patron, with the former receiving $2.1 billion annually from the latter.

Egypt's dependence on food imports reveals a fundamental contradiction in its modernization drive. The regime's obsessive preoccupation with internal legitimacy has made it hostage to the urban population whose acquiescence has had to be bought with cheap subsidized wheat bread. Indeed, 30 percent of the 1974 national budget was devoted to wheat subsidies. The demands of the urbanites in combination with population growth worsened Egypt's structural food deficit. For example, the per head wheat consumption rose from 112 kg in 1970 to 185 kg in 1983. To put this in perspective, between 1956 and 1986, domestic wheat production increased by 71 percent and the population increased by 102 percent, while wheat imports during the same period rose by 612 percent.[56]

An attempt to buy social peace through food subsidization is a poor substitute for genuine social justice. It is a self-defeating and unsustainable policy, yet Egypt's elites continued to juggle dangerously with agriculture. Although the agricultural sector accounted for 16.1 percent of GDP in 2003, the sector employed 28 percent of the workforce.[57] Furthermore, the country remains condemned to the specialization in primary commodities, particularly long and extralong staple cotton. Even though Egypt is the world's primary exporter of long staple cotton, the crop is heavily subsidized to shield the one million employees of the state-owned spinning and weaving industry against foreign price competition. Even so, Egypt had to reduce the area under cotton cultivation from 924,000 ha in 1962 to 302,000 ha in 1996. In terms of tonnage, its long staple cotton production dropped from 345,700 in the 1996–1997 season to 206,300 in the 2000–2001 season.[58] Moreover, urban growth and the sale of farmland are decreasing the country's available farmland. In 1984 alone, Egypt's poor farmers sold 250,000 acres of farmland to brickmakers.[59]

All things considered, the long-term environmental and social costs of Egypt's policies will likely outweigh the more immediate benefits. So far, Egypt's priorities have violated principles of social justice and ecological integrity. In the first instance, the plight of the Sudanese Nubians is most telling.

As Robert O. Collins described with great sensitivity, the tragedy that beset the Nubians was immeasurably cruel. Without a scintilla of concern for the history, culture, and welfare of the Nubians, Nasser's Egypt planned and executed the construction of one of the largest dams in the world, which backed up into Sudanese territory for 160 km, submerging the country of the Nubians in toto. In 1963, forty-five countries rushed to raise $29 million, including $10 million donated by the Kennedy administration, for purposes of rescuing and preserving the relics of Nubian civilization, but no resources were devoted to rescuing the people. Both Sudanese and Egyptian governments relegated the cause of the Nubians to mere post hoc compensatory negotiations; in fact, the negotiations were designed to cover up the crime that was perpetrated upon the Nubian people.

The compensatory price suggested by the Sudanese was 36 million Egyptian pounds. Egypt offered just 10 million pounds, prompting the Sudan to counter with a reduced price of 20 million pounds. With characteristic Arab paternalism, Nasser personally intervened and proposed to divide the difference, which gave the Sudanese 15 million pounds, or only 4 percent of the relocation cost. If one divided this pitiful sum among the 50,000 Nubians who were displaced by Lake Nasser, each would have received a mere 300 Egyptian pounds. Moreover, in characteristic Sudanese fashion, the army ruthlessly suppressed Nubian protesters. By forcefully relocating the Nubian farmers to a socially and environmentally inhospitable zone around the Atbara River in eastern Sudan, the government also created the permissive condition for interethnic friction between the Nubian cultivators and the nomadic pastoralists of the area. Apart from the fact that, even after thirty years, the Nubians received no compensation, they were resettled twice.[60] If one puts this account in a broader context, the story of the Nubians becomes a footnote in the history of capitalism. Since 1945, the world has built 50,000 large dams and 800,000 small and medium-size dams, uprooting approximately 80 million people from their cultures, serene ecology, productive land, and holistic economies. These dams today generate 20 percent of global electricity and supply water to 250 million ha of irrigated crop fields to produce 40 percent of the world's food.[61] One of the many consequences of this industrial modernization is the growing concentration of people in megacities. This is partly due to internal growth and partly to rural to urban migration, associated with the degradation of rural ecosystem services.

For example, Cairo's population has ballooned over the last fifty years from 2.8 million to 15 million.[62] In the mid-1990s, the population density in greater Cairo was 40,000 persons per square kilometer; in Cairo's old sections, 100,000 persons per square kilometer lived without clean drinking water and safe sanitation services. Because of acute housing shortage, one million people were living in the city's graveyards and another million people were squatting in scattered corners of Cairo.[63]

Concentrations of factories and people intensify water use and transform the ecology of water, resulting in water pollution and degradation. A World Bank study showed in 1990 that 3.2 bcm of untreated water was dumped annually into Lake Manzala in the Nile Delta.[64] Approximately 350 industrial plants discharge their wastewaters into the Nile River, laden with microbial, toxic, and corrosive matters, pesticides, fertilizer residues, detergents, and organic and heavy metals. Moreover, 60 percent of the 1,250 industrial plants located near surface water in the Alexandria region are said to discharge wastewaters into Lake Marriott, which drains to the Mediterranean Sea.[65] Helwan (the industrial suburb of Cairo), known for its cement dust, carbon monoxides, nitrogen, and sulfur oxides, annually discharges 45 million cu m of industrial wastewaters into the river.[66] In total, Egypt's industrial establishments are said to treat 80 percent of their water for reuse while they dump the remaining 20 percent back into the water system untreated with all the hazardous health consequences. It is estimated that Egypt's industrial plants dump 500 mcm of industrial waste in the Nile River annually.[67]

Nadia El-Awady, in her award-winning article, bemoans these environmental crimes. She documents how raw sewage effluents from industry, agriculture, and homes are dumped daily into the Nile, irrigation canals, and drainage systems. The immediate casualties of these hazardous contaminants and pollutants are children who swim less than 100 m downstream from the dumping sites. She laments: "The river Nile has been Egypt's vein of life since time immemorial. Now facing a variety of threats ranging from bilharziasis to the dumping of raw sewage, industrial, and agricultural effluents, the longest river in the world has been slowly turned into a death sentence for Egypt's millions."[68]

As noted in the introductory chapter, water is the principal medium for the transmission of all kinds of pathogenic microbiological organisms. Schistosomiasis, cholera, paratyphoid, and typhoid are some of the waterborne diseases that regularly inflict tens of thousands of Egyptians annually. It is clear that a strong relationship exists between the damming of rivers and the proliferation of disease vectors, as illustrated by the history of schistosomiasis in Egypt.

The presence of schistosomiasis in Egypt is historically documented. However, the propagation of vector snails and the spread of schistosomiasis are closely associated with perennial irrigation. The slow-moving canal waters and the shorelines of the various dams have created ideal conditions for the growth and proliferation of the snail population. In the 1970s, 200 million people worldwide were known to have been infected by the disease, resulting in an annual productivity loss of $640 million.[69] Studies in Egypt show that schistosomiasis infections increased tenfold among villagers after the installation of canals and pumps. Villagers using traditional methods of basin irrigation, which depend on the annual floods of the Nile, had fewer incidents of schistosomiasis than farmers using perennial irrigation. In the 1930s, over 50 percent of people in the delta had the disease, and in some places the prevalence rate was 90 percent. In 1967, 14 million of Egypt's 30 million people carried the disease.[70]

Sensing the urgency of the problem and hoping to contain the spread of waterborne diseases, the USAID contributed $2 billion before the end of the 1990s for the establishment of national water treatment facilities in Egypt.[71] However, health conditions in Egypt have hardly improved. A growing number of Egyptians are suffering from bladder cancer, urinary tract infections, liver disease, schistosomiasis, and other ailments. As indicated earlier, the main reason for the spread of disease is the detention of water in large reservoirs, which creates permissive conditions for the growth and spread of disease vectors. For example, after the first Aswan dam opened in 1902, the number of schistosomiasis incidents rose from just 6 percent of the population prior to construction to 89 percent of the population afterward. Similarly, at the completion of the Aswan High Dam, cases among the general population jumped from 5 percent in 1968 to 77 percent in 1993.[72] Since almost all Egyptians live within 21 km of the Nile, they are extremely vulnerable to waterborne diseases and contamination.

In order to appreciate the long-range impact of pollution, let me bring three points into sharper focus. First, pollution and dumping of hazardous chemicals and metals into the river and channels are substantially affecting Egypt's irrigation drainage networks. Second, pollution and contamination of the hydrological system are making the country's water allotment exceedingly difficult to reuse and prohibitively expensive to treat for reuse.[73] Third, the discussion in this section elucidates the point, made in the introductory chapter, that a focus on the quantitative determinants of water alone is a misdirected approach to hydrology. How water resources can be used to meet present and future demands is primarily a fundamental principle of demand-side management.

Abu Zeid, Egypt's minister of irrigation and water resources, appears to appreciate the enormity of the problem when he notes that the country's urban consumers waste over 40 percent of their water resources. He blames the problem on the poor habits and lack of awareness of water users, as well as the absence of a transparent and efficient water pricing regime in the country.[74] This is probably true, but Abu Zeid forgets to add that the source of these bad habits (lack of consumer education and the absence of an equitable pricing system) is the presence of a bad government and a bad economic order. Unless one addresses the source, one cannot solve the problems.

The physical alteration of the area as a result of damming and water diversion is even more dangerous for Egypt in the long term. To their credit, it didn't take long for British empire builders to notice significant changes in Egypt's ecology associated with the new dams, even though cotton production doubled within two decades of their occupation of the country. "There is another aspect of the irrigation question which requires attention," McFarlane wrote in 1909, drawing particular attention to the environmental consequence of perennial irrigation and intense cotton cultivation. "The conversion of the delta and considerable part of middle Egypt from basin to perennial irrigation has resulted in a deterioration of the land. . . . as cotton is an exhausting crop, the land is gradually rendered poorer without having the elements of fertility restored to it. Over cropping is also a problem, that is, cotton is grown much oftener on the land than ought to be. The land is deprived of the fertilizing silt brought down by the river."[75]

McFarlane's observation was prescient: today, approximately 109 million tonnes of the 130 million tonnes of sediments that the Nile carries are trapped annually behind Egypt's dams and barrages, affecting the fertility and the physical structure of the Nile Valley and the delta; the deposition of sediments, composed of clay, silt, and fine sand, has resulted in the increase of bed level and the decrease of reservoir capacity as well as the formation of new delta, which is likely to significantly hamper navigation.[76] Prior to the construction of the Aswan High Dam, at least 32 bcm of Nile waters flowed annually to the Mediterranean Sea. This flow dropped to 6 bcm in the late 1970s; to 3 bcm by the mid-1990s; and, by the late 1990s, to only 1.8 bcm, released only during flood months.[77]

The continual addition of soil has had two critical determinants. First, 90 percent of the 130 million tonnes of silt was previously carried to the Mediterranean seacoast, where it strengthened the structural stability of the delta over the centuries against salty seawater intrusion and erosion. In consequence, it is estimated that the depth of the soil along the Nile in Egypt ranges between 9 and 11 m.[78] The deposition of the silt behind the Aswan High Dam starves the delta of millions of tonnes of silt a year crucial to the maintenance of the stability of delta structure. One result may be the creation of permissive conditions for the Mediterranean Sea to make a foray into the delta. If projections of global warming and consequent sea level rise hold, a massive inundation of the delta could cause Egypt to lose up to 15 percent of its habitable land area and 15 percent of its economically active population over the next sixty years.[79] Climatic patterns support this concern: between 1993 and 1997, 131 million people were affected by flooding, while similar phenomena affected just 19 million people between 1973 and 1977.[80] Changes in traditional economies are also telling: Egypt's brickmakers, who traditionally produced bricks with silt dredged from the river, now must purchase expensive topsoil from Egyptian peasants.

Second, significant amounts of the soupy silt of the 130 million tonnes of silt from Ethiopia historically fertilized the riverbank lands, renewing the topsoil and obviating the need for artificial fertilizers. In 1960, Egypt's farmers used 192,000 tonnes of chemical fertilizers; this figure jumped to 791,000 tonnes by 1990. Phosphate applications rose from 48 to 190 tonnes over the same period.[81] Chemical fertilizers have negatively affected water quality and fish species. Egypt's forty-seven commercially viable fish species historically supported over one million Egyptians in the delta; thirty of these species are now extinct.[82] Reliance on these chemicals also undermines the chemistry, physical composition, and water retention capacity of the soil, causing productivity to diminish and salinization to increase.

Irrigating in arid lands presents a classic double jeopardy: overapplication of water, intended to mitigate the effects of salinity, heat, and aridity on crops, simply worsens the problem. Primary salinization occurs when water evaporates from fields, leaving salt on the land surface. Farmers attempt to rid the soil of the salt by applying a good amount of water. The soil's decreased water-retention capacity and insufficient drainage infrastructure result in waterlogging and a rising water table. When the table approaches the root zone, capillary action pushes the water and its residue load to the surface. Secondary salinization results as exposure to solar radiation causes the water to evaporate, leaving another layer of salt. Not surprisingly, half of Egypt's irrigated land suffers from primary and secondary salinization.[83] Installation of adequate drainage networks would alleviate the problem; yet, given Egypt's economic and technological challenges, this seems a distant prospect. Even the United States, with massive agricultural infrastructure investment, finds that salinization affects one-third of its irrigated acreage.

Finally, there is the question of the hydrological life of Lake Nasser. Originally, engineers assumed that the dam would function for some five hundred years before silt accumulation could overrun the live storage capacity of Lake Nasser. However, the lake's dead storage capacity is fast filling with silt, and the original time frame has likely been shortened by 190 years.[84] Anthropogenic causes are exacerbated by natural phenomena like the Saharan windstorms that regularly dump huge amounts of sands into Lake Nasser. As Robert Collins poignantly reminds us, the area is also vulnerable to earthquakes. In November 1981, an earthquake measuring 5.3 on the Richter scale struck some 72 km southwest of the Aswan High Dam.[85]

The Puzzle

Egypt is the critical player in the regional reconfiguration of the Nile basin because it is the chief beneficiary of Nile waters and it is most vulnerable to any significant changes in the Nile ecological system. In light of these two crucial factors, Egypt must play a constructive role, not out of altruism, but out of necessity. However, despite Egypt's need to improve its hydrological security and reduce its vulnerability to uncertainty, Egypt seems deficient in its learning capacity.

Egypt's regional posturing lacks the capital of sincerity. On the one hand, it appears to accept the notion of equitable utilization of Nile waters by promising to enhance its water resources through the promotion of efficiency, conservation, recycling, and desalination. On the other hand, it seeks to perpetuate the inherited water regime. In 1993, for example, Egypt joined Ethiopia in a pledge not to harm each other. The joint communiqué issued by the countries' leaders stated that: "Future water resource cooperation would be grounded in international law."[86] Yet, the Toshka and Peace Canal schemes model Egypt's insincerity and disregard for the interests of other riparian states; these projects were planned, without prior consultation with other riparian states, at the same time that the NBI was created. If Egypt's present hydrological orientation persists, regional fragmentation and ecological disintegration could well be the outcome. The history of Egypt's hydrological policy does not inspire confidence in its capacity to supply needed leadership.

Egypt pursues three strategies to perpetuate the hydrological status quo. First, it constantly reminds co-riparian states that it is willing to use its presumed preponderance of power to defend its water security. Second, Egypt advances a legal argument in defense of the status quo. Third, its diplomacy, geared toward denying upstream states access to international financial and technical resources, is coupled with nebulous attempts to cajole them into acquiescing to the status quo.

For the most part, Egypt has successfully denied upstream states access to donor agencies and countries. Egypt's pivotal role in Middle East politics, its dependence on American patronage, and the support it gets from oil-rich Arab states have proved effective weapons for quashing the demands from upstream states for international help to develop their water resources. However, Egypt also recognizes the importance of promoting a regional cooperation that would solidify Egypt's hydrographic preponderance in the Nile basin.

To this end, in 1967, Egypt made the first regional diplomatic move and spearheaded the formation of the Hydro-Meteorological Survey of the Equatorial Lakes (Hydromet). The organization, supported by the World Meteorological Organization and the UNDP, was entrusted with meteorological data collection, considered key to understanding the water balance in the west Nile watershed. Egypt, Sudan, Uganda, Kenya, Tanzania, Rwanda, and Burundi were its constituent members. Ethiopia and Zaire rejected membership in Hydromet, opting for observer status. Ethiopia openly criticized the exclusion of the water redistribution issue from the organization's mission.[87] When Hydromet thus failed to legitimize the hydrological status quo, Egypt again led the way in 1983, creating Undungu (brotherhood in Swahili) to ostensibly promote basin-wide solidarity and cooperation in matters of trade, culture, environmental protection, and infrastructure development.

Again, the question of "equitable utilization" of Nile waters was not included in Undungu's agenda. While Zaire joined the new organization as a full member, Ethiopia, Kenya, and Tanzania chose observer status in demonstration of their reluctance to legitimize the Egyptian-dominated regional water regime. Like its predecessor, Undungu was soon abandoned. In 1992, the Technical Cooperation Committee for the Promotion and Development of the Nile (TECCONILE) was formed to tackle issues of water quality control and environment. Ethiopia, Eritrea, Kenya, and Tanzania, finding the new organization still deficient, opted for observer status. In hopes of attracting Ethiopia, TECCONILE adopted the notion of "equitable sharing" of Nile waters in principle as one of its goals in 1995.

The World Bank, FAO, and UNDP worked to make TECCONILE a success. Their bait, intended to reconcile the regional actors, was the twenty-two projects funded by $140 million from donor countries. In 1999, TECCONILE became the NBI and expanded its mission (see chapter one). Like all internationally sponsored documents, the NBI white paper contains a laudable list of goals, including poverty eradication, promotion of regional economic integration, and development of Nile water resources in order to ensure equitable and sustainable regional prosperity, security, and peace.

These statements raise more questions than they answer: will donor countries and institutions really commit billions of dollars to realize the stated goals? Are these objectives really achievable within the existing political structures and the prevailing mode of production? Is Egypt really prepared to accept a diminution of its water resources to redress the growing water imbalance elsewhere?

The puzzle's internal dimension raises still more questions. Today, 24 million of Egypt's 76 million people remain attached to an ever-shrinking agrarian sector. Rural poverty and landlessness are increasing. In 1999–2000, there were 42 million (upper line) incidents of poverty.[88] The result has been increasing conflict and violence. In 2004, land disputes resulted in forty-nine deaths and 430 arrests. In late April 2005, forty peasants were arrested after two landlords in the delta were killed in a land dispute.[89] In this struggle for land, the landlords enjoy full backing from the state and its repressive institutions, including courts, police, and state-owned propaganda instruments.

The government's answer to the land hunger is privatization. The market-oriented land law, operative since 1997, enables big landowners to freely buy and sell land holdings, and landlords to reclaim old possessions that were taken by the state for purposes of addressing the land issue. The rationale is familiar: privatization of agriculture encourages land concentration, input rationalization, and higher agrarian returns on investment. On paper, the prescription looks logical. However, at least two difficulties inhere in the logic of agrarian capitalist accumulation under privatization. First, concentration and rationalization of agrarian assets substantially reduce the human numbers engaged in the sector. Although the policy does not specify how, it is clear that these numbers must be transferred to nonfarm sectors; failure to do so can only result in overcrowding of cities and the creation of slums, and thereby in instability and violence. In recent years, the Egyptian economy grew only 3 percent per annum on average, half the rate needed to resolve the growing problem of joblessness.[90]

Second, privatization and concentration of land in fewer hands do not guarantee national food security. Egypt's agricultural history belies the prospect of a beneficial agrarian capitalist accumulation. Before the 1952 revolution, one-third of Egyptian agriculture was concentrated in 12,000 large estates, dependent on tenant labor.[91] Beginning in 1902, rural poverty and landlessness grew in proportion to the agrarian accumulation that paralleled the canalization drive. By 1952, this volatile situation provided the necessary precondition for revolution and justified subsequent land reforms.

President Nasser and fellow officers blamed Egypt's rural poverty on the increasing concentration of land in the hands of the agrarian oligarchy under private property rights and found it therefore necessary to dismantle large estates for distribution to the landless. Even though land redistribution under the Nasserite program was modest, the new tenancy law did curb the landlords' powers of arbitrary eviction and hyperexploitation of tenants. The land reform program was, of course, undertaken to buttress the legitimacy of the Nasserite state. But the motivation for legitimacy itself stemmed from the recognition that increasing agrarian concentration and consequent, growing landlessness and rural poverty would threaten regime survival unless and until the land issue was carefully addressed.[92] Given this nutshell recounting of Egyptian agricultural history, it is reasonable to ask how the restoration of the agrarian order of yesteryear might achieve future agrarian prosperity.

Perhaps it is possible to speak of a consensus regarding the need for agrarian concentration. The issue is: "concentration" in whose hands? My opinion, informed by history and the experience of Egypt itself, is that the solution is to initiate an authentic process of agrarian accumulation under a farmers' cooperative regime on a national scale. This involves allowing Egypt's farmers to control the full spectrum, from field sowing to marketing, of agrarian production. Ruling elites would surely find this alternative threatening to class interests, as well as to existing political power and control of the state. Given this reality, the emergence of self-reliant farmers' cooperatives will not be permitted, and the containment of the agrarian crisis will continue to be the preferred strategy.

Karem Saber, director of the Land Center for Human Rights in Egypt, trenchantly observed that "What happens with the peasants and farmers will be the real litmus test of political change in Egypt. Right now, liberalization is just for big businessmen. Workers aren't free to unionize, and farmers can't form cooperatives or associations to protect themselves."[93] Both the trend toward agrarian concentration under the privatization regime and the growing incidents of land disputes must be understood as manifestations of a system in deep crisis. For over half a century, Egypt has been ruled by three military officers, each preoccupied with the preemption and containment of opposition. Since the 1970s, the political class has forged relationships with the new bourgeoisie (themselves products of economic liberalization) and with the officer corps of the armed forces, who skim revenues from special economic facilities that are under direct military control and beyond the scrutiny of any government entity.[94]

Egypt's national elites continue to play at multiparty politics in the hope of buttressing regime survival. Reacting to domestic and international pressure for accountable governance, Hosni Mubarak simulated a multiparty presidential election on September 7, 2005. The misnamed "independent electoral commission" barred domestic and internal poll-watchers from electoral monitoring. Guessing the likely outcome of the highly publicized simulation, most Egyptians stayed home; only 23 percent of the eligible voting population actually cast a ballot. Mubarak claimed a landslide victory, allegedly capturing 88.6 percent of the vote. Alas! This is the Egyptian style of democratic governance.

In sum, Egypt's general political life and its particular hydrographic strategies, as explored here, suggest that the country is far from meeting the challenges outlined in the introductory chapter. The pathological pursuit of power and the perpetuation of the unjust social order by a narrow circle of elites are major impediments to internal progress and to the needed rearticulation of Egypt's hydrographic orientation. To risk repetition, grassroots democracy, social justice, and a genuine appreciation for ecological equity are requisite foundations of integrative discourse. None of these preconditions appears to be in prospect in Egypt. The terrible conundrum is that Egypt plays a pivotal role in the hydrographic configuration of the Nile basin. No sustainable water regime can be established without a radical reorientation of Egypt's position and without constructive, regional leadership by Egyptian elites.

Chapter Three

The Sudan
A Hydrographic Bridge?

The Beginnings

In hydrologic terms, the Sudan enjoys twin geographic advantages. The first involves its receipt of 17 bcm of rainfall annually, which makes rain-fed cultivation possible. The second involves the inflows of some 120 bcm of water annually from outside its territory.[1] Inundation of vast areas along the banks of visiting rivers makes traditional irrigation possible. Because of the hydrographic configuration of the Nile system, analysts view the Sudan as uniquely positioned as a bridge between the major producers of water resources (to the south and east) and the chief Nile water user (to the north). By accommodating the flows of the Blue and White Niles over its vast territory, the country provides transitional storage for precious water resources.

In historical terms, the Sudan has been seen as a hydrographic bridge and Egypt's backyard, waiting (on the one hand) to be domesticated for purposes of protecting its bridge status, and exploiting (on the other hand) its human, material, and water resources. On its eastern borders, the Sudan receives the Blue Nile River and its tributaries from the Ethiopian highlands, carrying vast quantities of water loaded with nutrient-rich sediments. The Blue Nile system annually dumps almost 60 bcm of water into the Sudan, while the Atbara River makes an annual contribution of 10.6 bcm to the main Nile. On its southern borders, the Sudan welcomes the White Nile, carrying some 22 bcm of water annually from Lake Victoria and its satellite lakes. Once inside the Sudan, it is baptized as Bahr el Jabal and enriches itself with the addition of some 4 bcm of water from a half a dozen seasonal streams. However, some 14 bcm of water from the Bahr el Jabal disappears into the swamps of the Sudd, mostly by evaporation and seepage. Eventually, the Bahr el Jabal sluggishly zigzags northward to the shallow Lake No and formally assumes the title White Nile. After traveling for some 130 km northward from Lake No, the White Nile replenishes itself again with waters from the Sobat River, which originates with the Baro-Akobo tributaries in the Ethiopian highlands. It also receives some additional water from the Pibor River, which rises in southern Sudan itself. The Sobat and Pibor rivers together donate 13.6 bcm of water annually to the western Nile system, although the Sobat River's share of the donation represents 72 percent of the total.[2] Having welcomed the Sobat River as its last tributary, the White Nile travels without further obstruction for 860 km northward to join the mighty Blue Nile in Khartoum.

In its role as a hydrological bridge, the Sudan had historically been expected to use Nile waters without affecting the overall natural flow of the river; however, because the Sudan does receive a good amount of rain, especially in the south of the country, its water needs had been underestimated. With the colonization of the Sudan in the early twentieth century, substantial modification of its hydrographic character began out of British and Egyptian necessity. First, imperial overstretch made the British keen on discovering how the Sudan could generate the means for its colonial administration.

When the British conquered it, the Sudan was totally dependent on gum arabic as its leading exportable commodity, accounting for over 75 percent of external revenue.[3] Income from this export alone was not sufficient to sustain the colonial administration, and another cash crop was needed to augment revenues. Second, empire builders believed that the provision of internal security maintenance also required fungible resources. Rain-fed agriculture in the Sudan was not reliable. Depending on the frequency and length of rainfall events, grain production varied wildly. In 1904, for example, cultivation of 750,000 feddans yielded 240,000 tonnes of durra, while in 1912, 1,450,000 feddans produced a mere 200,000 tonnes of durra because of poor rain.[4] Thus, considerations of external revenue and internal security prompted a turn to the vast potential of agricultural land and Nile waters.

The conception of the Gezira irrigation scheme was the immediate answer to the revenue question. From the British point of view, growing cotton on such a huge scheme addressed two needs at once: supplying cheap cotton to British textile mills while enabling the Sudan to generate important revenue by exporting cotton. Small-scale experimental projects were carried out between 1906 and 1925. The Sennar Dam south of Kartoum, completed in 1925, was designed to store 500 mcm of Blue Nile waters, providing a steady water supply to the initial 300,000 feddans committed to the Gezira cotton scheme. To reassure Egypt that such an irrigation work would not disrupt the natural flow of Nile waters, the British built the Jebel Aulia Dam to store White Nile waters primarily for Egypt's use.[5]

Perhaps the most veritable British contribution to the emergence of modern Sudan is the agrarian mode of articulation, symbolized by the Gezira scheme. The colonial empire builders quickly identified some five million acres of potentially irrigable land between the two branches of the Nile. To meet the land and labor requirements of the new scheme and its planned expansions, the British ingeniously devised a system, which they euphemistically dubbed the profit-sharing tenancy system; 40 percent was given to the tenants, another 40 percent to the state, and 20 percent to private capitalists. In 1925, the Sennar Dam's 80 deep gates and 112 overflow spillways were let loose to water a vast area of crop fields. By 1931, over 300,000 acres had been irrigated, growing long staple cotton and its derivatives (sorghum, millet, and lubbia). The cotton crop lived up to its promise, both in terms of productivity and value. Sharecroppers were able to produce more then 400 pounds of cotton per acre; during the 1950–1951 agricultural season, production averaged 648 pounds an acre.[6]

The scheme provided the government with 25 percent of its annual revenue prior to World War II, 50 percent after the war, and 60 percent by 1990; cotton was now considered the pinnacle among exportable crops, taking over the traditional privilege assumed by gum arabic.[7] The Gezira scheme assumed a place at the epicenter of the Sudanese political economy, setting a lasting pattern for the agrarian model of production and development. Subsequent constellations of schemes revolved around the Gezira project, both before and after independence, yet none has rivaled the long-term economic, social, and ecological implications of the Gezira scheme.

An Arab "Breadbasket"?

Lured by the vast clay plains, lying between the two Niles and stretching to the Ethiopian borders, the colonial administration of the Sudan invited Sir Alexander Gibb in 1950 to carry out a comprehensive survey of the Sudan's potentially cultivable area. At the conclusion of the survey, Sir Alexander Gibb and his consulting firm identified some two million additional irrigable feddans and recommended construction of the Roseires Dam near the Ethiopian border with annual storage capacity of 3 bcm of water. This recommendation was made against the backdrop of two previous developments: the Gezira scheme and the spread of pump irrigation schemes, both public and private.

The British plan was to ultimately commit five million acres of cultivated land, two million in Egypt and three million in the Sudan, to cotton production.[8] The Gezira area was gradually expanded to cover one million feddans on the eve of independence (by the year 2000, the Gezira scheme covered two million feddans, divided into 114,000 tenancies, supporting 2.7 million people).[9] Following independence in 1956, a confluence of internal and external factors heightened interest in the Sudan's hydrographic position. The Sudanese elites, realizing that the country could overcome its relative backwardness via agricultural modernization, created a distinctly Sudanese orientation toward the Nile's hydrology.

At the same time, the oil-rich Arab states saw enormous agricultural potential in the Sudan. By relying on cheap grain from a sisterly Arab country, the rich Arab states could reduce their dependence on grain from outside the Arab world. These conditions allowed for a perfect union between Sudanese agriculture and the Arab petrodollar. The potential benefits of this arrangement prompted the Sudanese elites to look to the Nile for precious water resources. This new hydrological orientation, however, required a radical revision of the 1929 Anglo-Egyptian Nile water agreement, by which the annual flow of the Nile water had been divided between the Sudan and Egypt: 4 bcm and 48 bcm of water, respectively. This lopsided distribution in favor of Egypt would prevent the Sudanese elites from transforming their country into an Arab "breadbasket." The Sudanese request for renegotiation thus led to the 1959 agreement by which the two countries divided the 84 bcm waters of the Nile as measured at Aswan High Dam. The Sudan received 18.5 bcm of water and Egypt got 55.5 bcm; the remaining 10 bcm was expected to evaporate in Lake Nasser.

With the resolution of the Egyptian dispute, Sudanese elites focused their attention on harnessing Nile waters to accelerate agricultural modernization. In 1961, General Abboud's regime issued a seven-year economic and social development plan with a particular focus on agriculture. The plan was prepared with the assistance of the World Bank, demonstrating the national and international consensus on the importance of agriculture to Sudanese modernization. The initial cost was 240 million Sudanese pounds, supplemented by loans from the World Bank and West Germany. The plan devoted 75 percent of budgetary allocations to three projects: expanding the Gezira scheme, constructing the Roseires multipurpose dam on the Blue Nile near the Ethiopian border, and building the Khashm al-Girba multiple dam on the Atbara River near the Kassala province.[10] Completion of the three agricultural projects would have increased Sudanese farms under irrigation by 46 percent.[11]

Completed in 1966, the Roseires Dam provides hydroelectric power to Khartoum and its environs, as well as irrigation water for the Managil Extension, which is part of the gigantic Gezira scheme. The Khashm el-Girba Dam, completed in 1964, was designed to have a storage capacity of 1.3 bcm of water. The 500,000 ha put under irrigation and the minor hydropower station it supports were intended to provide the means of livelihood to the 50,000 Nubians displaced by the construction of the Aswan High Dam.[12] Cotton, groundnuts, and wheat were first introduced into the Khashm al-Girba scheme, followed by sugarcane plantations. A sugar factory, with an annual capacity of 60,000 tonnes, was established to mill and refine the sugarcane. However, by the late 1970s, the Khashm al-Girba Dam had already lost more than 40 percent of its storage capacity due to heavy siltation, thus undercutting its ability to meet power and water requirements of the projects. The irrigated fields in the Gezira and Khashm El-Girba were augmented by 300,000 feddans of the Rahad scheme on the right bank of the Blue Nile, which also draws water from the Roseires Dam.[13]

With the completion of the dams, the realization of the Sudan's agrarian hopes seemed possible. The Gezira scheme was (and still is) the major source of revenue for the government, accounting for 60 percent of the country's foreign exchange earnings.[14] Since the Gezira scheme, cotton has been the leading crop in Sudan's development. Rising domestic and regional demands for sugar prompted equal attention to growing and refining sugarcane. The "breadbasket" of the Arab world ideology stimulated this orientation toward sugarcane plantations. It is instructive to note that Arab countries together expected to import about 5 million tonnes of sugar annually (from Japan and Sri Lanka alone) beginning in 1980. Expecting to export sugar to Arab markets, the Sudanese government drew plans to export 775,000 tonnes of its projected annual production of 1.2 million tonnes of refined sugar.[15] By the mid-1970s, annual production had reached 120,000 tonnes, satisfying 43 percent of domestic requirements. By 1981, the Sudan had five sugar factories, each processing sugarcane grown on its own irrigated ha. Of these, the Kenana scheme was one of the largest of its kind in the world, producing 330,000 tonnes of fine sugar in 1985–1986. By 1989, sugar production from the five factories combined reached 400,000 tonnes.[16]

The new irrigation schemes ushered in an ideology supportive of capitalist agrarian accumulation. The country's arable potential was placed at 84 million ha, 60.5 million of which are in the Nile basin.[17] The provision of abundant Nile water and the supply of exploitable labor were assumed. Even after such figures proved highly inflated, official utterances and nonofficial estimates still put the Sudan's cultivable land at over 84 million ha. Even if the often-cited figure were true, the Sudan could not possibly find enough water to irrigate more ha. In fact, the 18.5 bcm of Nile water allotted to the country under the 1959 agreement with Egypt could irrigate only 1.7 million ha, or about 5 percent of the potentially irrigable land.[18] This explains why, by 2002, the Sudan had managed to put only 16 percent of its total arable land under cultivation (rain-fed farming included).[19] At present, the Sudan's annual water budget (excluding rainfalls) is 26.3 bcm. Of this total, 18.5 bcm comes from the Nile and its tributaries, 1.1 bcm comes from two seasonal non-Nile rivers (el Gash and the Khor Baraka, both rising in Eritrea), and some forty wadis or rivulets contribute 6.7 bcm annually. The country annually taps 1.3 bcm of its estimated 9 bcm underground water reserve. Some 450 mcm of this withdrawal is annually used for domestic purposes, while another 850 mcm is used to irrigate 67,200 ha of land.[20] By early 1990, in addition to the 4.4 million ha under rain-fed mechanized farms, the Sudan had 2 million ha of agricultural land under irrigation, which consumed approximately 25 bcm of water annually. If the Sudan desires to double the total acreage under irrigation, which will represent only a tiny fraction of the often-cited figure of 84 million ha, it will need 25 bcm of additional water, over and above its present water budget.

Where can the Sudan find such an amount of water? When placed in the context of increasing desertification, urbanization, and overpopulation of humans and livestock, the idea of irrigating 84 million arable ha is a pipe dream. In 2004, the Sudan's population (34 million) put per capita water availability under 1,000 cu m, categorizing it as a chronically water-scarce nation. Because the duration of rainfall is very short and its distribution during the growing season is highly erratic, the country increasingly relies on surface water originating in other countries.[21] The combination of huge livestock and human populations exerts enormous stress on the country's biotic environment and water budget.

It is useful to note here that, in 2000, the Sudan had 124 million heads of livestock, ranking second in this category in Africa.[22] Both the government and the pastoralists have great incentives to increase livestock production for pure existential reasons; in 1999, the livestock sector accounted for 22.4 percent of the GNP and $142.3 million in foreign exchange earnings.[23] As with food and sugar production, incentives to increase livestock production have had an Arab breadbasket component. In the 1970s, owners of petrodollars began to invest in the livestock sector. The Saudi financier and arms dealer Adnan Khashoggi led American and Sudanese investors to develop a one-million-acre commercial ranch with the aim of slaughtering 100,000 head of cattle annually to produce 17,000 tonnes of meat for export.[24]

The Arab League rushed to create an Arab Authority for Agriculture and Development, headquartered in Khartoum in 1976. Its specific mandate was to facilitate a union between Sudan's natural endowment, the Arab petrodollar, and Western agricultural technology. The Arab Authority announced the deployment of $6.6 billion to finance one hundred agricultural projects in the first decade, as part of its twenty-five-year plan to make the Sudan the breadbasket of the Arab world. The anticipation was that the Sudan would meet 40 percent of the Arab world's agricultural and livestock needs by 1985.[25]

In the long range, the Arab breadbasket ideology provided the motivation for accelerating agrarian accumulation. The Arab oil embargo on the United States (for its unconditional support of Israel in the wake of the 1973 war) gave tangible expression to the urgency of reducing Arab vulnerability to potential retaliation by promoting Arab food security. In this context, the elites in Khartoum became lavish in their promise to put at least one million additional ha under irrigation within ten to fifteen years.[26] The six-year plan of 1977, for example, promised to put 6 million feddans of land under cultivation to produce grain and livestock for the Arab market.[27]

The cruel irony was that the Sudan proved incapable of feeding itself, let alone the larger Arab world. By 1985, the breadbasket ideology was clearly a fatally flawed proposition. By then, the per capital grain production had fallen sharply, and massive food imports were needed to thwart widespread starvation. In 1984, the country managed to produce less than 1.5 million tonnes of grain, or 1.9 million fewer than projected.[28] In fact, during the 1984–1985 famine, two million people in western Sudan survived on a bush berry known as Mukheit, which can be poisonous if it is not soaked in water for at least three days before its consumption.[29] So, in times of food stress, the Sudanese look not to the government's make-believe granary, but to nature.

Although the envisioned transformation of the Sudan into an Arab granary proved a dubious proposition, the country has managed to put 2 million ha of land under irrigation (1 million ha added since independence), producing exportable cash crops and grain for domestic consumption. Ninety-three percent of the landed properties under irrigation are in government-owned schemes. The remaining 7 percent are controlled by a class of new petty bourgeoisie. Interestingly, despite the seriously flawed agrarian system, the ideology of an Arab breadbasket still holds sway among Sudanese elite, who continue to believe that the country can escape poverty and underdevelopment through agrarian capitalist accumulation. Until the late 1990s, when oil exports assumed importance in the Sudan's economy, the agricultural sector commanded 80 percent of export earnings, bringing in $600 million in 1999. The sector still accounts for 48 percent of GDP and 65 percent of national employment.[30]

Maladministration of irrigation schemes, soil degradation, sedimentation, and evaporation are today major threats to the elites' vision of agrarian modernization. Mechanized agriculture, mainly owned and operated by the urban petty bourgeoisie, is particularly taxing on the ecological health of the country's arable land. By 2005, there were around 10,000 big farmers, whose farm sizes range from 400 ha to 850 ha.[31] These owners of mechanized farms, eager to accumulate wealth quickly, rely on "soil mining," a practice of sowing the same area with the same crop (sorghum in this case) year after year. Without crop rotation, the soil nutrients are not replenished, and the soil becomes degraded. The country's irrigation works are also suffering from mismanagement, excessive siltation, and high evaporation rates. When the Roseires Dam was built, engineers expected that the annual sedimentation rate would not exceed 15 mcm a year; but in the first decade, the actual sedimentation rate proved to be 55 mcm per annum. As a result, by 1985, the dam had lost 75 percent of its capacity, as a massive annual flow of 1.4 tonnes of sediments arrived at the dam's dead storage from Ethiopia. The 7 bcm of water annually diverted from the Roseires to the Gezira scheme are loaded with five mcm of silt and clay, choking the irrigation canals. Likewise, both the Sennar and Khashm al-Girba dams lost half of their storage capacities to sedimentation. Indeed, the extent of reservoir degradation led the Sudan to spend $1 billion between the late 1970s and late 1980s to rehabilitate its dams, yet deterioration of irrigation and drainage infrastructure persisted. By 2000, over a million ha were actually taken out of agrarian production because of water supply degradation and heavy siltation. In the Gezira scheme, crop intensity dropped from 80 percent in the 1991–1992 growing cycle to 40 percent in the 1998–1999 season, compelling management to take 16,000 ha out of production.[32] Moreover, the detention of water in large surface areas in the country's arid regions (where the annual evapotranspiration rate is 3,000 mm) has accentuated the evaporation rate. For example, the old Jebel Aulia Dam loses 2.5 bcm of its 3.5 bcm of stored water annually to evaporation.[33] These problems are contextualized by gross technical deficiencies, maladministration, and unrealistic expectations. For example, the price tag for the Rahad-I irrigation project was assessed at $125 million in 1973. Upon completion in 1983, however, the project's cost overrun had reached $400 million, prompting the regime and donors to postpone work on Rahad-II indefinitely.[34]

The cumulative effects of these conditions are reflected in the country's cotton output. The average yield of cotton fell from 408 kg per ha in the first half of the 1990s to 397 kg in 1997; this decline occurred while the worldwide average yield stood at 560 kg per ha, and several countries were enjoying an average yield of 1,500 kg per ha under modern conditions of irrigation.[35] According to FAO studies, the current productivity rate of 42 percent for wheat, sorghum, and cotton in the Gezira scheme can be raised to 112 percent under proper planning and management.[36]

Sudan's answer to its internal inadequacies is to increase its dependence on supply augmentation strategy. Like all riparian states, the Sudan is increasingly looking to the Nile for economic and energy solutions, without learning much from past practices. The government seeks not only to expand existing facilities but also to build new schemes. In 1989, expansion work on the Roseires began with $400 million to increase its storage capacity to 7 bcm.[37] The Sudan emulates Egypt's Toshka project. The Merowe-Hamdab Dam project under way, some 350 km north of Khartoum, illustrates the Sudanese determination to become an active player in the regional hydrographic competition. Sudanese efforts are strongly supported by the presence of Chinese capital and technology;

75 percent of technicians and 90 percent of engineers involved in its construction are Chinese.[38]

If completed by 2009 at a cost of $1.8 billion, with a storage capacity for Nile waters of over 12 bcm, the Merowe-Hamdab Dam would add another 1,250 Mw annually to its current hydroelectricity generation capacity of 580 Mw.[39] The dam is 200 km long and more than 10 km across, detaining sufficient water to drive ten turbines. In addition to providing electricity and protecting 450 km from flooding, the Merowe-Hamdab Dam will irrigate 600,000 ha of agricultural land. The Merowe-Hamdab multipurpose scheme is supplemented by the Kajbar project on the third cataract to the north. When completed, the Kajbar project would add another 300 Mw to the Sudan's stock of electricity. Such a rush by downstream states for Nile waters can only encourage upstream states to do the same.

The Politics of Internal Governance

Contrary to the much touted expectation, irrigation-based agriculture has not resolved the structural contradictions of the Sudan. Instead, it has widened the gap between the wealthy few and the poor majority. Exploitation of agricultural labor in the context of poor planning and gross maladministration of irrigation schemes has simply served to expose the inequitable agrarian formation. The dismal performance of three schemes illustrates the point. When the Khashm El-Girba project was originally envisaged, the 50,000 resettled Nubians and local nomads were supposed to earn their livelihoods by growing crops on 400,000 to 600,000 feddans. However, unable to sustain their existence under wretched conditions, the Nubians left the scheme and the resettled local nomads followed suit. As a result, by the late 1980s, the project was limited to irrigating a mere 150,000 feddans, or a third to a quarter of the expected acreage.[40]

Modeled after the Gezira scheme, the Guneid sugarcane scheme is another interesting case. Drawing water from the Blue Nile, the Guneid scheme began growing sugarcane in the 1960s on 37,500 feddans. Before the state appropriated the land, locals ran rain-fed traditional farming, growing durra. When water shortage became problematic in the 1980s, management ordered the tenants to stop growing durra, the staple food of the tenant population, as well as lubbia, the major source of fodder for their livestock. The plan was to conserve water for the sugarcane plantations, but the heavy siltation of the canals cut the supply of irrigation water to the plantations by as much as half of the water required for profitability. Tenant families not only lost milk and other livestock products but also income as a result of the declining sugarcane production.[41]

The El Ela scheme, located in the Blue Nile province, is another illustrative case. Modeled after Gezira, the intent was to grow cotton and groundnuts on 85,000 feddans by transforming the nomads into settled tenants. Under the terms of the arrangement, the tenants, government, and management would each receive a third of production. However, insufficient supply of energy and water combined with pest infestation severely cut into productivity. Even the supply of fertilizers was cut from eight bags per tenant to four or five partial bags. As cotton prices on the world market declined, it became common for tenants not to be paid for three or four consecutive years. Having already given up their pastoral lifestyle, they had no option but to migrate elsewhere.[42]

Since the 1970s, the steady state expropriation of land for irrigation schemes and the rise of a private commercial class engaged in mechanized agriculture have combined to drive small farmers and pastoralists from their biosocial environments. The prelude to the perpetual domination and control of the agrarian formation was manipulation and subversion of customs and traditions in the name of modernization. The 1921 Gezira Land Ordnance provided the legal framework for appropriating both communal land and labor. This ordnance empowered the state to rent land from its original owners on demand. In return, the original owners would enjoy the presumed privilege of tenancy. That the tenants were to claim 40 percent of the production on the scheme created the illusion of tenant participation and, by extension, acquiescence in the arrangement.[43] In this way, the crude separation of land from its actual owners passed as partnership and the permanent alienation of labor from the pastoralists and farmers was justified in the name of modernization. In essence, tenancy ensured the continuous supply of labor, while also allowing the managers of the scheme to determine the regular cultivation of cotton. Frank testimony from Arthur Gaitskell (British manager of the Gezira scheme from 1945 to 1952) reveals the manipulative nature of the arrangement: "The ordnance provided an ingenious way of establishing control over land, without outraging the traditional right of proprietors."[44]

The veritable legacy of the Gezira paradigm is the enduring framework that it provided for the universalization of the tenancy system. After independence, the Sudanese elites found the inherited Gezira framework to be perfectly in keeping with their class interests. Without creating a landless class of peasants and pastoralists, they could not continue to appropriate land and labor. Because the tenants could theoretically claim 40 percent of the production, the state bourgeoisie was freed from worry about wages or benefits, even when the value of cotton on the world market bottomed out. Since the variable costs of inputs, processing, transporting, and marketing cotton are normally reduced from the gross revenue of the scheme, the tenants are often left empty-handed after sale; since the profit-sharing arrangement (by definition) exonerates the state from responsibility to look after the tenants in times of bad harvest or price slump, the tenants are bound to bear a disproportionate risk.[45]

In the end, the introduction of modern irrigation systems in the Sudan, represented by the Gezira paradigm, placed the Sudan's rural population under double jeopardy: first through property loss, and, second, through extraction of surplus value by selling their labor to the various schemes under tenancy arrangement. There have been incalculable social costs as well; these are hard to quantify since they involve quality of life. The detention of water over wide-open space has created ideal conditions for aquatic weed infestations and the propagation of water-related diseases.[46] The shift from traditional methods of farming to perennial irrigation has compounded the problem since most of the combined length of major, minor, and field canals (estimated at over 90,500 km) is covered with water year-round. Even though the government established the Blue Nile Health Project in 1979 to fight schistosomiasis by controlling the snail population in the canals, the vector snails have proved resilient and recolonization of treated sites by these intermediate hosts is common.[47] Historically, because the Blue Nile is a rough river with swift waters, its ecology had not been hospitable to the growth and proliferation of snails. In fact, before the construction of the Gezira scheme, the presence of schistosomiasis was hardly known in the Sudan. The prevalence of malaria was historically seasonal, subsiding during dry seasons and reappearing with the rains. The constant presence of stagnant water in open canals now provides a conducive environment for the vector mosquito. According to one study, there were 100,000 cases of malaria every year between 1959 and 1967 in the Blue Nile province where the Gezira and Rahad irrigation schemes are found; the malaria prevalence rate in and around these schemes was 15.6 in 1990.[48]

Contamination and pollution of water and food sources are another legacy of the Gezira paradigm. The increasing resort to pesticide applications to protect the quality of the cotton harvest has contributed significantly to water-quality degradation. In 1976, a study revealed that up to 2,500 tonnes of insecticides, two-thirds of which was DDT, were deposited annually in the Gezira scheme fields and adjacent grassland. The deposition of insecticides and pesticides increased over time in proportion to the prevalence of pests and insects. For example, cotton fields were sprayed on average once a year between 1946 and 1959, and seven sprays a year on average by 1979.[49] The Gezira scheme tenants who raise cattle, sheep, and goats in the vicinity of the scheme to supplement their incomes are made vulnerable to contaminated meat and animal products.

The emergence and expansion of modern agrocommercialism has also served to perpetuate class exploitation and domination. The development of modern irrigation works covering 2 million ha, and of rain-fed mechanized farming of 4.4 million ha, has created a peculiar situation in the Sudan whereby the urban petty bourgeoisie (who are heavily invested in mechanized farming) and the state bourgeoisie (who extract surplus value from the public agricultural sector by virtue of their offices) have created parasitic mutualism. Both classes are northerners and call themselves Arabs. The increasing concentration of agrarian production in the irrigation subsector has allowed the state bourgeoisie to maximize surplus extraction. It is useful to note that farms under irrigation constitute a mere 11 percent of the total area under cultivation and yet they account for 50 percent of the total agricultural output.[50] In addition to total monopolization of the agrarian sector, the urban bourgeoisie control Khartoum's commercial arteries. Indeed, by some estimates, half of the country's wealth is concentrated in Khartoum.[51]

Nothing better illustrates the junction between privileged access to water resources and urban wealth-creation than the Almogran business and residential community development, launched in 2005. This $4 billion massive undertaking is a joint venture between the state and the commercial class, represented by Alsunut, the leading real estate development company with pervasive connections to global conglomerate companies. El Almogran is situated close to the joining of two Nile branches in the heart of Khartoum. When its two parallel phases are finished, El Almogran would cover 1,580 acres, complete with self-contained premium stores, entertainment centers, restaurants, fitness clubs, riverfront promenade and plaza, residential apartments, fire mains, water treatment and waste treatment plants, stormwater drainage, police station, and state-of-the-art hospital. In what amounts to a gated community, there will be 44 commercial plots, 18 hotel plots, two separate 18-hole golf courses, 7,936 apartments, 650 villas, 47,460 residents, 42,000 workers, 109 acres of parks, lakes, and open space, 173 acres of forest reserves, and 15,100 parking spaces.[52]

The Sudanese petty bourgeois class is also a major player in rural wealth-creation. Impressed by the demonstration effect of the Gezira scheme, the urban petty bourgeoisie (largely comprising members of the merchant class) and the religious oligarchy made a foray into the agrarian sector during the interwar years in anticipation of quick profit. The leaders of the El-Hindiyya, Mahdiyya, and the Mirghaniyya religious sects set the example by investing in mechanized farming, using pump stations. After the war, leaders of the major political parties, urban merchants, and local and regional notables rushed capital to the agrarian sector. Entrepreneurial Sudanese, who lacked capital of their own and yet had obtained licenses to begin irrigation schemes, borrowed money from wealthy compatriots on usurious terms. In 1953, a survey group provided further stimulation to private agrarian accumulation when it recommended curtailment of state involvement in capitalist agriculture.[53] Colonial administrators were advised to loosen the reins of state involvement and, consequently, small-scale mechanized operations were allowed to thrive on a private commercial basis. The urban merchant class, native civil servants, tribal leaders, and prominent members of the religious oligarchy jumped on the offer. Within five years, mechanized farms, mostly growing sorghum for the domestic market, covered 1.2 million feddans.[54]

The new symbiosis between the political elites and merchant capitalists allowed the process of privatizing agriculture to continue. National elites began to lease land, ranging from 1,000 to 1,500 feddans, to their supporters, friends, and relatives. By 1968, before things began to fall apart, the government had farmed out a total of 1.8 million feddans to private capitalists, excluding the 1 million feddans that were under unauthorized mechanized cultivation.[55] Rain-fed mechanized farms began to produce sorghum and sesame, largely for home consumption but also for export to the Arab Middle East.[56] In the late 1960s, a combination of internal inefficiencies and low world prices for primary commodities prompted the new agrarian capitalist class to abandon their rural holdings and migrate their capital to the city. Many private owners of mechanized farms sold their holdings to the government. Under the guise of land reform, the government rescued owners of pump schemes from bankruptcy by buying 853 of these schemes on the White and Blue Niles.[57]

The class dimension of access to water resources (and therefore to wealth-creation) is an intractable social problem in the Sudan. The Merowe-Hamdab project currently under construction exemplifies this problem. To make way for the 200-km-long reservoir, over 50,000 people, who made their living in the fertile valley of the Nile, were ordered to resettle in the Nubian Desert where soil is barren, water is scarce, and the climate unforgiving. Dam authorities even refused to recognize the local committees formed for the sole purpose of negotiating with the government. In September 2005, the government confiscated all agricultural land in the Merowe area. The following November, Chinese contractors took over the wells and land belonging to the Manasir nomadic tribe and blocked children and women from accessing the water. Moreover, benefits of the government's promise to provide basic services (seeds, water, etc.) to resettled farmers were undermined by the demand that, in return for the services, the displaced farmers surrender twelve sacks of wheat annually to public authorities. In 2005, the farmers managed to produce less than two sacks of wheat on average.[58]

The harmful ecological consequences of the Merowe-Hamdab project are also incalculable. The findings of an independent review panel from Switzerland, released in March 2006, point to an ecological nightmare. The panel's environmental impact assessment indicates that the project violates every internationally accepted requirement in dam construction. First, the project's standard operations are expected to cause downstream water levels to fluctuate by 4 and 5 m daily, and the surface level of the reservoir itself to fluctuate between 350 and 800 sq km annually. This will cause significant riverbank erosion, complicating local residents' access to fishery and drinking water. Second, the way in which the project is being constructed will make the dam vulnerable to massive sedimentation since up to 130 million tonnes of sediment are expected to be deposited in the reservoir every year. The annual flow deposition of sediment of this magnitude will reduce the storage capacity of the dam by 34 percent within fifty years, thereby undercutting hydropower generation capacity. Third, the dam will likely block fish migration along the river, and the erosion of the riverbanks most likely will destroy spawning areas. Fourth, pollution, contamination, and decomposition of organic matter in the reservoir will compromise the health of area residents who drink water from the reservoir and consume its fish. Finally, the stagnant water in the primary and secondary canals of the project will provide ideal breeding conditions for malaria-carrying mosquitoes, schistosomiasis-causing snails, yellow fever, and water flea—host of the guinea-worm.[59]

The Gezira paradigm has also had important regional dimensions. All major hydropower and irrigation projects are concentrated in the northeast of the country, roughly corresponding with the social morphology of the Sudanese who call themselves "Arab." The correspondence is fundamentally a function of geographic determinants in the northeastern or, more precisely, central Sudan. The area between the two Niles in the north and beyond to the Atbara River is generally flat, composed of rich clay soil. When the British empire builders focused their attention on this region, they were primarily informed by utilitarian and cost considerations. They did not have to invest huge sums of money to level the fields, which could be easily watered with gravity irrigation. These natural conditions, however, proved to have important social implications for class formation and regional disparities in development. The fact that the post-independence elites were drawn from this region led to public bias in its favor, in terms of national priorities and the allocation of national resources. Investments have increasingly been directed to the "Arabized" core of the country, while the periphery (comprising the "other" "non-Arab" Sudanese) has been increasingly marginalized.

To highlight the inequity inherent in the regional dimension of the Sudanese modernization drive, David Roden made the point that 77 percent of all public spending targeted the Gezira district in the late 1950s.[60] In the late 1980s, only 13 percent of Juba (the theoretical capital of the south) residents had drinking water in their compounds, and 79 percent had no access to any sort of sanitation facilities and were forced to the fields or nearby bushes to cleanse themselves. During the rainy season, their excretions and secretions entered the same streams that provided their drinking water.[61] Demands by peripheral formations for equal representation at the center and equitable distribution of development funds have historically been met with determined repression from the "Arabized" elites. Roden is correct when he states that the north/south cleavage in the Sudan must be understood in the context of gross disarticulation of agrarian development, embedded in the Gezira framework.[62]

The progressive relegation of pastoral groups and traditional cultivators to increasingly marginal rural spaces is another lasting consequence of the Gezira paradigm. Unable to support themselves by cultivating marginal lands or grazing their herds on degraded grassland, groups (pastoralists and farmers) began to compete for scarce resources. The resulting impoverishment increased the numbers of traditionally self-sufficient groups who seasonally migrate between farm schemes to eke out precarious livelihoods by selling their labor power. In essence, they are forced to work for the new class for meager wages and on lands they had owned before the alienation of communal land. In the 1970s, private mechanized farms alone commanded between 1.5 million and 2 million seasonal laborers.[63] The increasingly erratic nature of the precipitation regime has further complicated intercommunal and interethnic relations. A recent example is the Darfur crisis, which began in the context of recurrent droughts and desertification. As pasture and water grew scarcer, "Arab" pastoralists began to encroach upon the agricultural possessions of villagers, who happened to be African by descent. In due course, the tensions between the African farmers and the "Arab" nomads have escalated into an all-out genocide with government connivance.

The Sudd and the Jonglei Canal: Twin Crimes Against Nature and Society

No essay, however superbly written, could accurately convey the sharp contrast that exists between the north and south of the Sudan. I say this as someone who has traveled extensively in both parts of the country. In June 1978, I traveled to the south in a company of five, including myself. After five days on a White Nile steamer, we disembarked at Malakal, the capital of the Upper Nile province. To our bewilderment, we were greeted by a raging tribal war that, we were informed, concerned a dead hippo. Two men, one from the Nuer tribe and another from the Shilluk, started fighting when each claimed to have stumbled over the animal first. Warriors from both tribes, armed with swords and bows and arrows, soon joined the fighting. Before tribal chiefs intervened to establish (according to custom) an armistice of sorts, eighty-three men lay dead. Although the issue of who first found the dead hippo may appear to be episodic, it was (and still is) a powerful illustration of the abject food insecurity that pervades the south. The sort of poverty to which southerners are condemned is, in large part, a product of the unjust social relations that define the two regions.

Historically, northern Sudanese and their patrons in the Arab world made no distinction between the humans and the nature of modern-day southern Sudan. Humans were as much articles of trade as the region's ivory and gold. Southerners, perhaps by the millions, were exported to the Ottoman Empire. While open slave hunting might have ended during the colonial era, the southerners' reality has changed little since the Sudan's independence in 1956. The social degradation of southerners has continued without meaningful mitigation. As international denunciation curbed the slave trade and resource exhaustion slowed ivory and gold trading, the northern focus shifted to the south's oil and water resources, well manifested in hydrocolonialism.

The hydrological ecology of southern Sudan is complex and sensitive. Four large swamp regions in the south (the Sudd, Bahr el Ghazal, Bahr El Jebel, and the Machar) are of particular hydrological importance and ecological concern. The Machar marshes occupy a vast area, a no man's hydroecology between Ethiopia and the Sudan. The marsh area varies (from 4,500 sq km to 9,000 sq km.) with the annual rainfall in the Ethiopian highlands; the marshes annually swallow up to 10 bcm of water flowing from the Ethiopian highland via the Sobat River and its tributaries, starving the White Nile of potential resources.[64] The Machar marshes thus represent a technical challenge to hydrologists, a potential "blue gold" for politicians, and a potential nightmare for ecologists should hydrologists and politicians succeed in excavating and draining the Machar swamp waters.

The Sudd is particularly of immediate interest to ruling elites in Cairo and Khartoum. This formidable swamp, the size of Florida, stretching for 450 km, is ravenous in its water absorption. It annually surrenders up to 22 bcm of water to evaporation, water that could otherwise be carried by the White Nile northward to Egypt. Some writers estimate that as much as 41 bcm of water is retained by and evaporated in the Sudd swamp.[65] The seasonal and annual expansions and contractions of the Sudd swamp are associated with Nile flow magnitudes. Before 1961, the Sudd's size averaged 9,000 sq km; since 1964, the Sudd's size has fluctuated between 20,000 and 30,000 sq km, when the average annual flow of the Bahr el-Jabal doubled from 27 to 50 bcm a year, as a result of unusually wet years in the early 1960s associated with the El Niño phenomenon. In response to these precipitation extremes in the high plateau of east Africa, water-holding capacities of Lakes Victoria, Kyoga, Edward, George, and Albert together received 254 bcm of water.

Unable to absorb the torrents coming from the equatorial plateau, the Sudd swamp spilled the additional waters in different directions, killing 130,000 head of cattle and tens of thousands of Sudanese in the south.[66] The Sudd and surrounding lagoons are populated with vertically erect papyrus, ferns, along with thick rotting and breaking plants, which, together with millions of small plants that stretch horizontally, form a complex tapestry of aquatic vegetation. The Sudd and its lagoons are the natural habitat of gigantic Nile perch, crocodiles, and African hippos, and of countless native and migratory birds that are known for gracefully feeding on the fabulous riches of the Sudd.

Before European empire builders succeeded in partially taming the Sudd, the swamp provided natural protection for indigenous communities, animal species, and ecological resources against slave hunters, poachers, and ivory collectors. The initial invasion was directed at clearing the aquatic vegetation to create a year round navigable channel to the interior of east Africa and the source of the White Nile and its ecology. The appetite of British empire builders was not satisfied by making the Sudd navigable: the ultimate aim was to deprive the natural storage of Nile flow in order to enhance Egypt's water security and, by extension, guarantee its stability and agrarian prosperity. As many writers have noted, British preeminence in the area was predicated upon ensuring the security of the Suez Canal and the stability of Egypt. However, these desiderata required the provision of sufficient water to Egypt's peasant cultivators as well as the regulation of Nile flows to shield Egypt against harmful inundation.[67] From the perspective of the empire builders, there was ample water in the plateau lakes of the Great Rift Valley and the Congo-Nile divide. After all, in addition to the massive amount of water that disappears into the Sudd swamp from the Bahr el-Jabal, some ten small rivers from the Congo-Nile divide annually dump 20 bcm of water into the Bahr el-Ghazal River, which in turn feeds the voracious Sudd swamp. Only 3 percent of these water resources is said to eventually enter the White Nile.

Robert Collins calculates that, if these water resources could be harnessed, the Nile flow would increase by 25 percent, or enough to irrigate 2.5 million acres of land and potentially feed 20 million more Egyptians.[68] The empire builders understood that full exploitation of the water resources required massive engineering efforts and adequate storage facilities. William Garstin secured these requirements when he proposed the construction of storage dams in Lakes Victoria and Kyoga and a straight line canal, bypassing the Sudd swamps, to carry the stored water as needed. The hydrocolonialists calculated that raising the level of Lake Victoria by just 1 m would provide an additional 67 bcm of additional storage capacity. They also planned to make Ethiopia's Lake Tana integral to the "century storage" project. By their calculations, heightening this lake by 3.5 m would produce 7 bcm of additional water annually, which Egypt and the Sudan could use for cotton production.[69] Between 1946 and 1950, the Jonglei Committee, tasked with scientific investigation of the proposed canalization scheme, weighed the pros and cons of building long-term storage. Its recommendation, that the Garstin/Hurst idea be put to action, was temporarily waylaid until resurrected in the 1970s by the Equatorial Nile Project.

Egypt and the Sudan agreed in 1976 to conquer the southern swamps once and for all. The first phase of their Jonglei Canal scheme was the excavation of a canal, 50 m wide and 360 km long, to enable the White Nile waters to bypass the Sudd. Digging began in 1978 and was 70 percent completed in 1983, when the Sudan People's Liberation Army (SPLA) disrupted the work. Phase one of the stalled canalization project would add 4.7 bcm of water annually to the Nile flow.[70] After completion of the first phase, Egypt and the Sudan were to initiate Jonglei II, a second canal running parallel to the first. The plan was to realize at least six objectives: liberating more water from the Machar marshes through the modern canalization scheme; widening and deepening the first phase of the Jonglei canal; transforming the east African rift valley lakes into permanent storages in order to smooth out the annual flow of Nile waters and coordinate the release of water with fluctuations in downstream demand; irrigating cropland along the canal to appease southerners; controlling floods; and improving navigation. Realization of phase II would add between 14 bcm and 20 bcm of water annually to the overall flow of the Nile.[71] If Egypt and the Sudan succeed in draining the Kyoga, Bahr el-Ghazal, Bahr El-Jebel, Sudd, and Machar swamps, they might potentially add between 25 bcm and 27 bcm of water annually to the Nile flow, allowing the two countries to equally share net water resources of between 16 bcm and 18.9 bcm.[72] In addition to this anticipated benefit, the Sudan intends to develop four hydropower sites in the south.

The ecological ramifications of such massive canalization projects for the hydrologic regime, geomorphology, climate, and vegetation, and the social implications for the culture, way of life, and material existence of indigenous communities are unknown. We speak of some 37 bcm of water simply disappearing into the lakes, wetlands, and swamps without a clear understanding of the complex ecosystem services sustained by this mysterious process. The question is whether this water really disappears without benefits to humanity or the ecosystem. No one knows how the excavation of 18.9 bcm of water from the wetlands will impact the local ecology. If, and when, the canalization drive materializes, the size of the Sudd alone would shrink to a trifling measure of 360 sq km.[73] Hulme and other hydrologists are perhaps correct in surmising that draining these swamps will probably alter the hydroecology and the precipitation regime over a wide region, including western Ethiopia.[74] To contextualize the potential dangers, it is important to note that the value of wetlands worldwide is estimated at $3.2 trillion per year (in terms of such direct benefits as food, habitats, climate regulation, and related ecosystem services); the comparative value of rivers and lakes is $1.7 trillion annually.[75] The human cost (which the hydrocolonialists neglect to factor into the equation) will be enormous. When the Jonglei canal idea was conceived, it was thought that some 700,000 southerners tending to one million head of cattle would be directly impacted by the canalization drive.[76]

Prior to colonial penetration of the south, southerners perfectly adjusted their social existence to the rise and fall of Nile floods to graze their herds, supplementing their subsistence by shifting cultivation in tropical woodlands and savanna grassland.[77] The coming of the "spoiled world" (as the Dinka would put it), however, interrupted this harmonization of nature and society. Of course, hydrocolonialists regard indigenous communities as expendable. After all, other countries have, to date, expropriated over 1 million sq km of land from indigenous communities worldwide to make way for reservoirs for hydroelectricity, irrigation, and water supply.[78]

The Puzzle

The future hydrological security of the Sudan hinges on whether the country will be able to simultaneously cope with the looming ecological crisis and the widespread injustice perpetrated against the non-Arab indigenous groups. On the first count, in response to the combined effects of unforeseen natural phenomena and hyperacceleration of human activities, the Sudan's ecology is changing. Even though the Sudan has 66 million ha under forest and grass cover, the country is losing its natural endowment fast. Between 1981 and 1985, for example, the country lost half a million ha of forest annually; between 1980 and 1993, the Sudan lost almost 50,700 sq km of forest cover and range land. The amounts of forest resources lost to desertification in northern Sudan in 1989 alone were equal to 25 percent of the country's annual wood needs.[79] Since the Sudan depends on firewood and charcoal for 78 percent of its energy, commercial and household logging is a major factor in forest destruction. In 1994, the country consumed 15.8 mcm of wood products, with households accounting for 89.4 percent of usage.[80] The lack of official protection of ecological resources is undermining the sustainability of the country's forests. Paralleling the country's natural resource depletion is the country's growing rainfall depletion. In keeping with global trends, climatic zones and creeping desertification are rapidly moving southward. Since the 1960s, the long-term annual mean rainfall in the Sudan has fallen steadily. For example, annual rainfall in 1965–1984 was 40 percent lower than the 1920–1939 level. Farmers have suffered as rainfall patterns have also become increasingly erratic. The historically predictable wet season is three weeks shorter, so the dry season has lengthened.[81] Precipitation zones have migrated southward by between 50 and 180 km since the 1950s; the national annual precipitation has declined by 40 to 60 percent. As a result, the growing season in central Sudan, the country's "breadbasket," has fallen from three and half months in the interwar years to just two months in the 1970s and 1980s.[82] Since 1960, desertification has spread southward at an average rate of 5 to 10 km per annum.[83]

Recent events demonstrate the impact of such trends on national food security and human welfare. Thousands died during the 1984–1986 famine, and three million people abandoned their rural dwellings and migrated to urban centers or settled near the Nile River. Since then, the Sudan has become dependent on foreign food aid. In 1993, for example, the country received shipments of 238,000 tonnes of food aid. In 1998, eighteen of the Sudan's twenty-six provinces showed varying degrees of food insecurity as the country's food deficit stood at 1.5 million tonnes.[84] Today, over 90 percent of the population falls below the poverty line.

It is not yet known whether the patterns in rainfall depletion and growing desertification in the Sudan represent irreversible and permanent trends or temporary deviations from the historic norms. In the short run, these trends certainly pose a serious question for the hydrographic configuration of the Nile basin. Since the Sudan represents a transition zone between the expanding Sahara desert and the tropical forest areas of the Nile basin, the growing desiccation of the country's land surface can have major implications for the region's ecology and food production.[85] Indeed, creeping desertification from the north and widespread destruction of critical tropical rainforests in the middle and upper reaches of the Nile can produce a deep ecological crisis and colossal food insecurity throughout the basin. Growing desertification in combination with forest cover removal can alter the radioactive properties of the region. Desert sand has a greater capacity to re-emit sunlight than does land surface covered with lush green vegetation. The destruction of vegetation also results in substantial reduction of water vapor release into the atmosphere, compromising both carbon dioxide sequestration and evapotranspiration processes; the alteration of the radioactive properties of the region's meteorological conditions and air temperature, with the effect of short-circuiting cloud formation, is also possible.[86]

The ethnography of hydrology is another area of concern in the Sudan. For the Sudan to serve as a reliable hydrographic bridge between the major Nile players, the country must promote social equality among its diverse components. Even though, as of this writing, the American-brokered peace deal between the Arab north and the African south seems to be on track, sustainable peace is far from secure. Whether the country can successfully demobilize some 40,000 SPLA fighters and meaningfully integrate them into civil society, repatriate the half a million southern Sudanese refugees, and resettle the four million internally displaced people remains to be seen. Moreover, the willingness of Arab northerners to treat their southern brothers as co-equals and to protect the hydrological balance of their environment and lifestyles is not guaranteed. The next five years are crucial; the Sudan will have to choose between future progress and back to the future.

While the north/south divide remains a major fault line in the country's social morphology, other equally important cleavages exist. One of these concerns the people of the Nuba Mountains. The Nubians, whom the self-professed northern Arabs derisively call infidels, are African by biological inheritance and Muslim by religion; however, their Islam is very much influenced by African traditional practices.[87] As they fought against centralist Arab oppression, the Nubians grew sympathetic toward the SPLA beginning in 1985. Since then, the government has used food deprivation as a major weapon against them, and the Sudanese army has subjected the Nubians to regular air bombardments and ferocious ground assaults. As a result, tens of thousands of Nubians have perished and hundreds of thousands more have been displaced.[88]

As of this writing, another genocidal war (the Darfur crisis) rages on. It is particularly disconcerting to note that the Darfur crisis seems to fit a pattern. Once again, the victims are non-Arab African agriculturalists and the victimizers are "Arab" nomads, with the contexts both ecological and political. The steady deterioration of the ecology compelled "Arab" nomads, seeking water and grazing grass, to encroach upon the biosocial sphere of the settled farmers. When ecological resources failed to meet the demands of both farmers and pastoralists, the two sides began to clash in 1987. In 1989, an intertribal conference was held to reconcile the two groups. However, the central government ignored the recommendations of the conference, thereby allowing the situation to deteriorate.[89] In fact, the pastoral "Arabs" drew on the resources and support of the Islamist government in Khartoum to unleash what Professor Reeves calls "genocide by attrition."[90] This atrocious ethnic cleansing involved burning African villages, destroying wells, and looting livestock. To reverse the balance of forces, the Darfurian Africans created the Sudan Liberation Army, along with the Justice and Equality Movement, to draw governmental attention to their plight.

The government reacted by demonstrably aligning itself with the local "Arab" militia known as Janjaweed. Over 300,000 Darfurians fell victim to a systematic genocide and its concomitant effects prior to December 2004 alone. By then, of the province's 6.5 million people, 1.7 million had languished under dire conditions in camps, and another 230,000 had fled to Chad. Despite international denunciation of the Darfur crisis, which even the Bush administration characterized as genocide, the situation in the region continued to deteriorate. By early October 2005, 3.4 million Darfurians (51 percent of the region's population) were either internally displaced or had become refugees. Of this number, 1.6 million were children under eighteen years old.[91]

Given the voracious vandalization of the country's ecological and hydrological resources by the centralist "Arab" northerners, the Sudan doesn't appear to be prepared to serve as a stable bridge between the various Nile actors. The deliberate policy of internal colonization of non-Arab Sudanese further undermines the country's credibility as a trustworthy player in the hydrographic reconfiguration of the Nile system. As of this writing, the Sudan demonstrates neither the capacity, nor the willingness, to meet the minimum requirements for genuinely secular democracy, social justice, and ecological equity. In its present constitution, the Sudanese state lacks the credibility to supply a much-needed building block for regional hydrological security architecture.

Chapter Four

Ethiopia
Land of the "Blue Gold"

The Hydrological Context

Ethiopia is a country of paradoxes. Poverty in the midst of biotic plenty and thirst in the midst of hydrological abundance define contemporary Ethiopia. Contributing 86 percent of the Nile flow, the country is hydrologically the wealthiest in the entire basin. Yet it ranks among the bottom ten countries globally in terms of its inability to harness water resources to better its citizens' livelihoods. In a given year, Ethiopia receives between 1.3 and 1.6 trillion cu m of water in precipitation, of which 112 bcm of surface water and 2.6 bcm of groundwater are potentially usable. Only 1 percent of these water resources is used internally for purposes of hydropower generation and irrigation, while the country freely exports over 100 bcm of water annually to its neighbors via its nine transboundary rivers.[1] Ethiopia has between 3.6 and 5.7 million ha of potentially irrigable land, of which 2.3 million ha are in the main Blue Nile basin. However, only 160,000 ha of land are under irrigation, including 70,000 ha in the Awash Valley that is entirely unconnected to the Nile hydrologic system. In fact, only 30,000 ha is under irrigation in the main Blue Nile basin, including 8,000 ha of sugar plantations at Finchaa on the Didessa River, a powerful tributary of the Blue Nile. Moreover, Ethiopia's potential hydroelectric generation capacity is estimated at 60 billion kWh annually, or 58 percent of the hydropower potential in the entire Nile basin; a mere 2 percent is currently harnessed.[2]

The Blue Nile, with a mean annual discharge of 59 bcm, is the jewel of Ethiopia's river systems. The Blue Nile basin receives between 1,400 and 1,700 mm of rainfall annually, and covers about 17 percent of the country's total land area. The source of the Blue Nile is Lake Tana in the country's northwest region. Covering an area of 2,500 sq km and containing some thirty small islands, Lake Tana is the largest lake in the country. Since Lake Tana accounts for only 7 percent of its total discharge, the Blue Nile depends on contributions from a dozen important tributaries, among which the Beles, the Didessa, and the Dabus are critical. The latter two are particularly significant for the Blue Nile flow, not only for the water resources they contribute but also for the ethnographic symbols they represent. Both the Didessa and the Dabus rise in the country of the Oromo and other ethnic minorities. Sourced in the region of Illubabor, the Didessa River drains an area of almost 250,000 sq km and donates 13 bcm of water annually to the Blue Nile, or 25 percent of the Nile flow. The Dabus also rises in Wellega with a similarly large watershed. Unlike the Didessa, however, the Dabus donates only 4 bcm of water to the overall flow of the Blue Nile since it surrenders much of its waters to vast swamps where it is consumed by aquatic plants or claimed by evaporation.[3]

Since the Blue Nile and its tributaries all rise in the Ethiopian plateau with elevations between 2,000 and 3,000 m above sea level, the velocity of currents in the main river and its tributaries makes the Blue Nile basin ideal for a range of hydroelectric facilities. The downside is that the topographic features and elevation of the Blue Nile basin enormously increase the amounts of sediments that the river carries, depriving Ethiopian farms of important topsoil while also choking the modern dams in downstream riparian locations. By some estimates, 525 mcm of soupy topsoil are annually lost from the Blue Nile and Tekezze River basins alone.[4] On balance, Ethiopians believe that the Blue Nile and the southwestern basins and the Tekezze watershed together have 900,000 ha of potentially irrigable land, which can play a decisive role in relieving the population pressure in the exhausted highlands.[5]

The Tekezze River rises in the northwestern highlands of the country and contributes 13 bcm of water to the Nile system. Flowing directly northward, this river forms a boundary between Ethiopia and Eritrea before entering the Sudan, where it is known as the Atbara. In fact, the Atbara is the last tributary to join the main Nile River before heading north to Egypt.

Ethiopia is also a major contributor to White Nile flows. In the southwest highlands, home to a number of streams, the Baro-Akobo-Sobat basin is the mainstay of the region's hydrologic system. The waters from the Baro-Akobo and other streams are collected in the Sobat River, which flows from the east to the west to join the White Nile in the Upper Nile province near Malakal. Along the way, the Sobat River and its tributaries lose about 10 bcm of water annually to the Machar marshes, as discussed in the previous chapter. On balance, the Sobat River and its tributaries annually add 14 bcm of water to the White Nile.[6] More important, the Baro-Akobo-Sobat basin is believed to contain 1.5 million ha of potentially irrigable land.[7] Thus, Ethiopians hope that this basin in combination with the northwestern watershed would play a crucial part in poverty alleviation and development-promotion efforts. In fact, in 1981, the regime of Colonel Mengistu unsuccessfully submitted a ten-year development plan to a UN conference in the hope of obtaining investable funds to put 704,000 ha of land under irrigation in both the northwestern and southwestern watersheds.[8]

In addition to irrigation for domestic food production, the Ethiopian elites have a vision, or ambition, to transform the country into a major producer and exporter of hydroelectric energy. The Ethiopian elites are still fixated on the findings of the American Bureau of Reclamation, whose survey identified over thirty potential storage sites in the Blue Nile basin extending over 900 km. Presumably, a series of multipurpose dams stretching from Lake Tana to the border with Sudan could put half a million ha of land under irrigation and harness Ethiopia's untapped electricity generation capacity of 60 billion kWh per annum with 5.4 bcm of Blue Nile water.[9]

The rationale frequently mentioned by Ethiopians to justify this project is the supposition that evaporation rates are much lower in Ethiopia than in either Egypt or the Sudan. A number of commentators do seem to support (at least in part) the Ethiopian position that savings could be realized by shifting storage reservoirs from downstream states with higher evaporation rates to the Ethiopian highlands. According to this view, the 10 bcm of water claimed by evaporation at Aswan High Dam each year could be halved by storing the water in Ethiopia, saving enough from evaporation to grow half of Egypt's annual grain output.[10]

John Waterbury is not impressed by this Ethiopian contention, citing statistics in support of his skepticism. For example, Lake Tana's ratio of average annual precipitation (1,000 to 1,500 mm) to annual surface evaporation (1,200 to 1,300 mm) means that it has very little net gain from rainfall. In fact, the average annual surface evaporation rates for the whole Blue Nile watershed area range between 1,300 mm in higher elevations and 2,000 mm in the lower altitudes. The expected gain from the Tekezze catchment area is even more dubious as the region experiences acute water shortages on a regular basis; its average annual evaporation (2,000 mm) outstrips its annual average precipitation (1,000 to 1,500 mm). In the Baro-Akobo basin, however, the picture is more favorable since the average annual precipitation rate climbs to 2,200 mm while average annual surface evaporation rates remain between 1,000 mm in higher elevations and 1,700 mm in lower altitudes.[11]

However, an important aspect of the problem belies the quantitative argument in support of shifting storage reservoirs from downstream sites to the Ethiopian highlands. While it is easy for commentators to draw up seemingly precise blueprints detailing how to slice the pie into exact proportions for all stakeholders, the problem remains that any quantitative division of resources does not occur in a vacuum. Rather, it requires the presence of the qualitative aspect of human relationship, which is political in essence. Political leaders, who do not keep faith even with their own people, cannot be expected to honor any agreement or treaty they may have voluntarily signed. All material identities of interests do require a corresponding identity of the qualitative determinants of regional relationships. Put simply, a thoroughgoing transformation of the state internally, and the radical redefinition of regional relationships beyond territoriality, are crucial preconditions for "reasonable and equitable" distribution of water resources. Only when these preconditions are fully met can we begin discussions about proper storage sites, which in effect involve technical and administrative determinations.

The Elusive Quest for Food Security and the Modernization Imperatives

Following the 1972–1973 famine, which resulted in 200,000 deaths, a British journalist, Jonathan Dimbleby, documented the circumstances surrounding the famine. His international award-winning documentary shocked the world, not only for the horrific consequences of the famine but also for the callousness displayed by Ethiopian government officials. Until Dimbleby eluded officials in order to visit affected regions and sneak out his slides, the famine was kept completely hidden from the Ethiopian people and the world at large to ostensibly protect the country's international image. During this time, the emperor spent millions of dollars to decorate the capital for the arrival of African heads of state and their celebration of the tenth anniversary of the Organization of African Unity.

This story about drought, famine, and the politics of famine is a perennial metaphor for the history of food insecurity in Ethiopia. In just 38 years, between 1965 and 2006, there have been sixteen major drought years in Ethiopia, of which 1983–1984 and 2002–2003 were the most severe. In light of the almost incessant cycles of drought and famine, Ethiopia has come to be identified with hunger and starvation, along with an embarrassing dependency on international donations. Even in years of bumper harvest, up to six million Ethiopians regularly rely on international food aid. In the 1984–1986 droughts and famine cycle, the international community spent over $1 billion to save more than eleven million Ethiopians from death by starvation; in the 2002–2003 cycle, 1.7 million tonnes of international food aid donations, including $500 million worth of food from the United States, protected thirteen million Ethiopians from hunger and starvation.[12] If anything has been certain in Ethiopia, it is that recurring famine and Ethiopian food politics have remained constant over time. As the world rushed food aid to the hungry and the starving,

Ethiopia's rulers maintained an unfailing presence in the international arms market. During the 1984–1986 famine, the regime of Colonel Mengistu imported billions of dollars worth of Soviet arms to battle the Eritreans. The 1998–2000 war with Eritrea followed the same pattern. Ethiopia's food insecurity is thus largely manmade.

Deforestation, soil erosion, land degradation, and water scarcity are defining features of rural Ethiopia, where over 85 percent of the people live today. Because of harmful traditional practices in farming, and with only 3 percent of its landscape under forest cover (down from 40 percent a century ago), Ethiopia's land is severely denuded and exhausted. The World Bank estimated in the mid-1990s that the annual loss of soil nutrients due to erosion represented a food supply loss of 600,000 tonnes, or 90 percent of Ethiopia's 1993 structural food deficit.[13] The damaged landscape is a direct result of human overpopulation and livestock overproduction; in 2002, over 67 million Ethiopians shared ecological space and resources with 80 million livestock and 53 million chickens.[14] As of 2000, only 180 ha of land per 1,000 Ethiopians were devoted to growing crops; this compares unfavorably with 288 ha per 1,000 in Africa south of the Sahara.[15] The country's runaway population growth will likely further reduce the amount of land devoted to crop production. According to the UN Population Fund, Ethiopia's human population is expected to jump from 77.4 million in October 2005 to 170.2 million by 2050.[16] The rise of the country's human and livestock populations is bound to further exacerbate the degradation of ecosystem services and the structural food deficit.

An estimated 1.5 to 2 billion tonnes of topsoil are annually washed away from the country's land area. Soil loss of this magnitude is the functional equivalent of the loss of between 120,000 and 210,000 ha of fertile agricultural land.[17] To be sure, the crowding of people and livestock populations beyond natural carrying capacities has far-reaching implications for the health of the ecology and, therefore, the welfare of the people. In the 1980s, 250 soil scientists reported that anthropogenic soil degradation was the major threat to sustainable food production worldwide. Removal of natural vegetation, overexploitation of forest resources, overgrazing, industrial pollution, and poor land management were generally seen as the causes of soil degradation. The displacement, and chemical and physical disintegration of soil particles, associated with human activity, produced the permissive conditions for water and wind erosion, loss of important nutrients, subsidence, and compaction of organic soil material. According to the scientists, of the 1,964 million ha that showed marked soil degradation, 56 percent was due to water erosion and 28 percent resulted from wind erosion.[18]

The relationship between human and animal overpopulations, on the one hand, and the consequent fragmentation of agricultural land and deterioration of the ecology and food insecurity, on the other, creates a predictable negative feedback loop. While 66 percent of the country's 112 million ha of land surface is considered suitable for either cultivation or grazing, over 50 percent of this is overgrazed and 80 percent of cultivated areas suffers from soil degradation and erosion. The underlying factor allowing for degradation of this magnitude is the continual annual loss of hundreds of millions of tonnes of soupy topsoil from agricultural lands, which renders expansive tracts of arable land unusable; in 2000, only 11.3 million ha were under cultivation.[19]

The demand for ecological resources appears to grow worse in the near term. Since modern sources of energy are available to only 4 percent of Ethiopians, the majority of the population depends on biomass for 95 percent of the energy needs of food preparation. The dire implication of overdependence on virgin ecological resources was illustrated in 2000 when demand for 58 mcm of wood overshot the market supply of only 11 mcm.[20] Successive Ethiopian rulers rhetorically acknowledged the grim state of the economy and the need to harness the country's water resources for the betterment of the ordinary citizenry. Beginning in the early 1920s, Ethiopia sought to emulate downstream Nile water users by developing modern agriculture and hydroelectric generation capacity. Ethiopia's desire to fully harness its water resources took on added urgency in the second half of the 1950s in the context of the new Egypto-Sudanese agreement. To show its determination to compete with downstream users of Nile waters, Ethiopia requested and received external assistance from the U.S. Bureau of Land Reclamation for a comprehensive feasibility study of the Blue Nile basin. In its seventeen-volume report of 1964, the Bureau identified over thirty projects that could be potentially developed in the Blue Nile basin, including settling four million farmers on almost half a million ha of irrigated land, supported by the generation of 38 billion kWh of electricity per annum. The various schemes (if installed) would have required the detention of up to 51 bcm of water—in effect, almost the entire annual flow of the Blue Nile. However, since most of the water uses in the Blue Nile basin were to be nonconsumptive, the annual loss of water to downstream users would have amounted to only 6.5 bcm of water, representing a mere 8.5 percent reduction in Nile flow.[21]

Whether Egypt would have tolerated a reduction of this magnitude was a counterfactual question, since Ethiopia did not have the means to carry out the projects identified by the American engineers. After all, except for two modest schemes that were implemented, the recommended projects were shelved. One of the two projects was a minor hydropower station on the main outlet of the Blue Nile. The second, a somewhat larger hydropower station and a modest reservoir, was constructed at Fincha on the Didessa River, which is the Blue Nile's largest tributary. Operational for two decades, the Fincha project generates 110 Mw of energy per year and supplies water to 8,000 ha of modern sugarcane plantations from its 1.2 bcm of stored waters.[22] Today, Ethiopia contends that it needs between 5 and 6 bcm of additional water annually to begin to realize the other recommended projects. The enduring legacy of the feasibility study has been the psychological environment it created for Ethiopians to simultaneously wallow in perennial hopes and illusions.

All things considered, Ethiopia's request to use 5 or 6 bcm of water annually from its rivers is by no means exorbitant. After all, between 85 and 88 percent of Ethiopians live in rural areas, suffering from a combination of structural inadequacies, lack of access to food supplies, malnutrition, massive deforestation, and soil degradation. According to an FAO/WFP 2001 survey, 60 percent of Ethiopians were below the official poverty line and 51 percent were undernourished, including two million who were chronically food insecure.[23] The daily calorie intake of the average Ethiopian is 900 calories below the international level for healthy living. In 2000, Ethiopia was ranked 171st on the human development index, surpassing only Burkina Faso, Niger, and Sierra Leone. On the 2004 human development index, Ethiopia ranked 170th out of 177 countries.

It seems as though nature and human mismanagement often conspire to damage the prospect for food security in Ethiopia. Even in years of good harvest, too many go hungry. Despite a relatively good harvest for the 2001 season, for example, the FAO/WFP Mission to Ethiopia forecast that 7.5 million Ethiopians would still be food insecure, requiring 970,000 tonnes of imported food, primarily in the form of food aid. In fact, the FAO/WFP mission prediction was off the mark, since the biblical proportions of the 2002–2003 famine were then unforeseen. The general collapse of the country's agriculture in the 2002 growing season placed over 13 million Ethiopians in danger of grave starvation; food aid dependence continued as the world shipped 1.7 million tonnes of food in 2003 to rescue the hungry Ethiopians. In 2004, 7.5 million Ethiopians relied on 871,000 tonnes of food aid and $85 million in nonfood assistance.[24]

Ethiopia's chronic food insecurity stems in part from an overdependence on rain-fed agriculture, which is vulnerable to dry spells, delayed or interrupted rains, and full-scale droughts. In 1999, agriculture contributed 50 percent to the GDP; employed 80 percent of the people; and generated 89 percent of the country's foreign exchange earnings, of which coffee accounted for 60 percent, and Khat, a mild leafy shrub with psychotropic effects, accounted for 14 percent.[25] On a regular basis, Ethiopia experiences shortfalls of up to 50 percent in basic food requirements. Moreover, in 1997, the per capita income in Ethiopia under the purchasing power parity was $450, compared with $3,820 in Egypt.[26] Over the past half-century, monocrop dependency on coffee for foreign exchange and a discomforting reliance on international food aid have together defined

Ethiopia's international image. These two conditions have made Ethiopia vulnerable to climatic variations as well as to international price fluctuations for its primary commodities. As a result, Ethiopia's one million coffee growers and their fifteen million dependents lead a precarious life.[27]

Under pressure from an exponentially growing population and the consequent overflow of "surplus" people from rural regions to the city, the present Ethiopian regime has made irrigation schemes a priority of its agricultural policy. Like its predecessor regimes, the present government has resorted to externalizing the country's internal inadequacies; it regularly complains that external forces have blocked Ethiopia's effort to harness its water resources.[28] In August 2003, Ethiopia's minister for trade and industry, Girma Birru, blamed Egyptian mischief for his country's inability to harness its natural wealth to alleviate poverty and promote growth. In his words: "Egypt has been pressuring international institutions to desist from assisting Ethiopia in carrying out development projects in the Nile basin. It has used its influence to persuade the Arab world not to provide Ethiopia with any loans or grants for Nile water development."[29] On the empirical level, this may be true, since a mere 160,000 ha is presently under irrigation. At any rate, in the context of the presumed national water abundance and the urgency of poverty alleviation, the present Ethiopian regime appears poised to seek solutions in the rapid development of irrigation and hydropower generation projects. The government has prepared a comprehensive master plan to gradually put 1.5 million ha under irrigation. In the Tekezze basin alone, the government hopes to put 302,000 ha under irrigation, supported by fourteen dams, at a cost of $25.5 billion.[30]

With the intention of achieving food self-sufficiency within three to four years, Ethiopia is presently considering 175 irrigation projects and four major hydropower stations to supply the major population centers with electricity. Ethiopia hopes that a large number will be funded under the East Nile Sub-Basin Action Plan (ENSAP), which is part of the NBI. Under this comprehensive development strategy, Ethiopia has also been seeking funding from individual donor countries. For example, Norway has offered $6 million in aid for the Baro-Akobo hydroelectric power station in the southwestern part of the country.[31] The government's master plan has identified over 606,000 ha of potentially irrigable land in the Baro-Akobo region, to be supported by eighteen dams at a cost of $5.5 billion.[32] Such an ambitious program of modernization of agriculture and energy is bound to generate tension between Ethiopia and downstream users.

At the moment, two irrigation projects are particularly sensitive. The first is the plan to put 50,000 ha of land under irrigation using waters from Lake Tana, the source of the Blue Nile. Even though Lake Tana contributes a mere 7 percent of Blue Nile waters, it is symbolically important for both Ethiopia and Egypt. If Ethiopia were to fully utilize the lake's waters without external repercussions, it might appear as a confirmation of Ethiopian sovereign priority over Nile waters originating within its territory. Egypt views any tampering with Lake Tana as the beginning of the end—namely, the damming of the whole Blue Nile system. This Egyptian apprehension is compounded by Ethiopia's plan to put another 80,000 ha of land under a modern irrigation system using waters from the Didessa River, a major tributary of the Blue Nile.

Lately, however, Egypt seems to have reconciled with reality and has softened its rhetoric on the potential for armed conflict should upstream riparians hamper the natural flow of the Nile. As a result, or in spite of Egypt's posture, international opinion seems to favor Ethiopia's position. For example, a water resources adviser for the World Bank (with the Ethiopian case in mind) opined: "There is no precedent for a country developing without harnessing its rivers and utilizing its water resources."[33] Egypt seems to have realized the shift in international attitude. When the African Development Bank, for example, notified Egypt of its $50 million loan to Ethiopia for the Koga hydroelectric and irrigation scheme, Egypt gave her blessing.[34] In December 2003, Egypt's foreign minister actually flew to Ethiopia to dramatize the importance of dialogue and announced her country's readiness to help Ethiopia develop its water resources for purposes of hydroelectricity generation and food production.[35] It appears that Egypt is seeking to monitor and control Ethiopia's water resources development via cooperation, albeit contorted, rather than risk that Ethiopia embark on unlimited development projects without Egyptian input.

Developments in Ethiopia were also potentially worrisome to Egypt's elites. Beginning in the 1980s, Ethiopia had begun to widen its options; for example, it developed microdams to store water for purposes of putting more land under irrigation. Since microdams require low-tech and modest investment, Ethiopia could potentially carpet the countryside with small-scale irrigated farms. If these patchworks of irrigation were spread over the country, they would virtually become immune to Egyptian military targeting.[36] By the end of 1997, over 200 microdams with an annual storage capacity of 477 mcm were already in place in Ethiopia.[37] The prospect of hydrologically fragmenting Ethiopia's main rivers and their tributaries via the proliferation of microdams, which could significantly compromise Egypt's water security, appears to have been powerful motivation for the partial modification in Egyptian reception of the Ethiopian call for a revision of the present water regime. In this context, despite decades of wrangling with Egypt, the present Ethiopian regime seems to have secured World Bank assistance for and grudging Egyptian acquiescence to the installation of a series of agro-projects.

Western donor countries and multilateral institutions have offered $400 million to back the development of 590,000 ha of irrigated land and the construction of thirteen dams. At the time of this writing, a Chinese company has nearly completed work on another project, the Tekezze hydropower plant near the disputed Ethio-Eritrean border with an installed annual hydropower generation capacity of 300 Mw.[38] The Tekezze project, slated to cost $224 million, will have a storage capacity of 7 bcm of water and is expected to support local irrigation schemes. Another water region, not connected to the Nile system, targeted for national attention is the Omo River, which drains into Lake Turkana. In late 2004, Ethiopia secured a $284 million loan from Italy on easy terms to bring to fruition the second phase of a hydropower project on the Omo River, which will come on stream with a 400 Mw capacity in 2009.

The Politics of Internal Governance

As intimated earlier in this chapter, many Ethiopians believe that they could achieve national food security within a few years, if they were only allowed to use their due water share from the Nile. No doubt, increasing Ethiopia's share of the water budget will help but not solve the country's structural food deficit. So long as the centralist Amhara-Tigrayan ruling circle clings to the antiquated notion of ethnomorphology as the driving force of politics, the country's chronic food deficit and its almost perpetual dependence on international handouts will continue, regardless of increases in its water budget. One problem in the Ethiopian elites' thought process is their tendency to believe that the external world owes them something. To presumably make the international community pay for the country's development, the elites have parasitically become overreliant on language manipulation. However, mastery of the language of donor countries is no substitute for internal self-reliance through hard work.

For example, in early 2005, Prime Minister Meles Zenawi, under the guise of the "poverty reduction strategy" (favored vocabulary of World Bank and IMF bureaucrats), complained that the $2 billion pledged by donors was insufficient; he asked that they double the amount to $4 billion.[39] His argument, a simple reiteration of the familiar Ethiopian approach to foreign aid, was that his country, with its large population, deserved more international aid in order to stimulate national food security.

The "poverty reduction strategy" (banking on foreign donations) is the centerpiece of the so-called safety net program launched in January 2005 to ostensibly move some five million Ethiopians from food donation dependency to self-help activities. The government promised to spend $215 million during the first year for this purpose; the World Bank's initial contribution was $70 million, with $220 million pledged over a five-year period.[40] In an apparent move to actualize the promise, the government issued land certificates to several million farmers in January 2005, supposedly enabling them to exercise de facto control over land so that they could use their land holdings as collateral in the marketplace or transfer land rights to their children. This halfway house between total privatization and complete state control of agrarian properties would encourage farmers to invest in land productivity and curtail rural to urban migration.[41] If all things moved in tandem with the government's strategy, all farmers would be issued land certificates over a period of three years.

However, what the present Ethiopian regime has proposed in the form of a "poverty alleviation" plan is essentially a containment strategy. The government seeks to ground the expanding rural peasant population. If rural to urban migration continues at the present rate, the government knows to expect political upheavals in the cities. Mass unemployment, homelessness, the growing population of street children, and the HIV-AIDS epidemic can easily spark a series of volcanic urban eruptions. The underlying problem for the regime is that a piecemeal approach, such as "poverty reduction" under the guise of certifying land holdings, to the agrarian question will not solve the structural problem. Ethiopia's agrarian sector is so fragmented and overcultivated that only a radical solution can address the issue of rural poverty. Eighty-five percent of Ethiopians live in the rural areas, and over 80 percent of them and 67 percent of the country's livestock population are cramped into the overused highland regions, which account for only 44 percent of the country's total land area. Furthermore, the average land holding in the country is less than 1 ha per farmer.[42] The key to solving Ethiopia's perennial food deficit crisis is not only getting more Nile water, but also establishing the right political machinery.

I alluded earlier to the fact that (despite official rhetoric and revolutionary jargon) Ethiopia is still an empire state, where a tiny circle of Tigrayan-Amhara elites monopolize political power, economic resources, and external diplomacy. The 1974 popular revolution centered on two fundamental issues: the agrarian question and ethnic self-determination.[43] With a promise to resolve these burning issues, the military (under the guise of socialism and with the support of the Soviet Union) highjacked the revolutionary cause. It took seventeen years for the Tigrayan-led armed opposition to dislodge the military junta. The issues always remained the same: equitable land distribution and implementation of ethnic equality in a solidaristic manner.

The Tigrayan-led agglomeration of political groups seized power in 1991, promising to shatter the shackles of empire and establish ethnic democracy within which the land question in particular and the state of economic underdevelopment in general could be overcome. Events of the last fourteen years have, however, proved that the new elites always had an entirely different agenda. Ethnic fragmentation under the guise of "ethnic federalism" was meant to secure the Tigrayan elites' power. Demographically and economically small, the Tigrayans could only displace their traditional rivals (the Amhara) at the center of power, on the one hand, and prevent the solidaristic unity of "other" Ethiopians from different ethnic groups, on the other. Only by fragmenting the empire state into supposed "autonomous" subunits could the present elites entrench themselves in power. However, like all containment strategies, the stratagem of "ethnic federalism" itself proved to be dangerously fraught with fundamental contradictions.

As the idiom of opposition gathered pace (from the center by the displaced Amhara, and from the periphery by the "other" disenfranchised Ethiopians, and spearheaded by the Oromo struggle), the Tigrayan elites undermined their credibility and exhausted their legitimacy. As part of the effort to cope with the legitimation crisis, the Tigrayan elites externalized their gross inadequacies by raising the ante in their demand for more Nile water to presumably harness for purposes of irrigation works and hydropower generation. It was in this context that the country's capital deficiencies forced them to study the language of neoliberal economics. The elites' new language drew accolades from their supporters in global institutions and in academia; Joseph Stigletz, Nobel Prize winner for economics and former World Bank economics chief, and Jeffery Sachs of Columbia, now head of the UN Millennium Development project, paraded Ethiopia's Prime Minister, Meles Zenawi, as the "latter-day saint" of neoliberalism. Meles's stature became such that prime minister Tony Blair recruited him as one of the seventeen commissioners who composed the Commission for Africa, intended to promote and demonstrate the African capacity for self-governance as the prerequisite condition for the inflow of foreign aid and capital.

Eager to establish internal credulity and to buttress his international stature as Africa's "brilliant visionary," Meles unwittingly placed himself under compulsion to first demonstrate his own capacity for self-governance. The May 2005 national elections were presented with huge fanfare as a test case. International poll-watchers were officially invited to monitor the electoral process, heralded as exemplary for the rest of Africa. However, the outcomes, meant to impress Western donor governments and global institutions, shocked Meles and his allies to the core. The opposition camp appeared to strike a coup de grace to the regime. The opposition swept all twenty-three seats in the Ethiopian capital, regarded by observers and the regime itself as the bellwether for the other regions. The government, in full control of public media, went on the offensive as the electoral victor. Long before the ballots were counted, the regime's minister of information announced that the ruling party had won more than 300 of the 547 parliamentary seats, or twenty-six more than it needed to form a government. To suppress the political tinderbox, the electoral commission postponed official results accounting for two months, giving the ruling party sufficient time to weigh its options and establish containment mechanisms. The vexing conundrum, which will perhaps remain indefinitely unsolved, is that the opposition won the majority of seats in polls where international monitors were present, while the ruling party claimed to have swept virtually all rural votes where foreign poll-watchers were absent.

To express frustrations with what they considered a stolen election, Ethiopians took to the streets in large numbers in early June 2005. The brutality of the regime's response echoed the practices of the outgoing military dictatorship. Security forces opened fire on demonstrators, using live munitions; at least forty-two were killed by official count, over a hundred were injured, and over 3,000 were herded away to prisons. In a second wave of confrontations between demonstrators and security forces in late October and early November, security forces killed fifty-one and injured 300 civilians. By some counts, between 40,000 and 50,000 protesters were imprisoned in various concentration centers.[44] In retrospect, what was expected to be a public exhibition of Meles's commitment to governance turned out to be a signpost of his public disgrace.

Ethiopia's experience under the present regime (under all previous regimes, for that matter) veritably demonstrates that poverty alleviation and growth promotion are functions of politics, not of economics or abundance of natural resources. From a theoretical viewpoint, a classic growth strategy and the ecological economics paradigm are now competing to grab the attention of policy makers to address Ethiopia's external dependency and internal inadequacy.

The growth paradigm, water by neoliberalism, presupposes the likelihood that Ethiopia can grow out of poverty by adhering to the principles of market fundamentalism. Removing the impediments to free trade and foreign investments, cutting public spending, privatizing public assets, and deregulating the market are understood to be conducive to internal capital accumulation and international capital inflow. Insofar as the conventional argument goes, if these principles are strictly adhered to, Ethiopia can not only outgrow poverty but also effectively compete with other capitalist countries on equal terms. At the risk of overstating the obvious, the growth paradigm has historically proven itself to be an ideology of penetration and domination. Different versions of the growth paradigm have been on display in the past fifty years; none has lived up to its promise. Despite the billions of dollars that poured into Ethiopia, and despite a relatively rich natural endowment, Ethiopia has made little progress under the growth regime. Citation of a few facts will suffice to punctuate this point.

After a half-century of belated modernization drive, Ethiopia's economy is still dependent on a primitive mode of agrarian accumulation. In 2000, there were only 3,000 tractors and 100 harvesters in the entire country.[45] The agrarian sector still employs 85 percent of the population and generates 90 percent of export earnings; coffee by itself accounts for

65–75 percent of total foreign exchange earnings. In 2002, the country barely managed to earn $400 million from exports while it spent $1.6 billion on imports, the national literacy rate was 35.5 percent, and primary school enrollment was 46 percent. The central government's annual budget was $1.76 billion for a nation of 70 million people, and the $110 per capita income was the second lowest in sub-Saharan Africa.[46] Moreover, only 24 percent of Ethiopians had access to safe drinking water, and 47 percent of children under the age of five were malnourished.[47] A review by Rajan and his associates of the macroeconomic performance of the present Ethiopian regime provides further evidence that the growth model is not working. Prime Minister Meles and his coterie of pro-marketers came to power pledging to usher in a new era marked by political accountability, poverty eradication, macroeconomic balance, and freedom from the shackles of external debt. Yet, in 2003, 81.9 percent of Ethiopians lived on less than a dollar a day. Although the government officially installed a privatization regime in 1994 by selling 225 state-owned enterprises to private undertakers, the policy made no dent on the country's state of under-development, poverty, and unemployment. The composition of the country's basket of exports and imports showed no change in the post-privatization period. As a result, the structure of trade and budget deficits as well as the external debt remain unaltered.[48]

In fact, the state of poverty and social degradation among Ethiopia's masses has worsened in the post-reform period. The issuance of reports (almost simultaneously) by UNICEF, the International Migration Organization (IMO), and the UN Population Fund (UNFPA) in October 2005 exposes the state of human tragedy in Ethiopia. According to UNICEF, 6,000 girls between the ages of thirteen and sixteen fell victim to commercial sexual exploitation. In 1996, there were over 150,000 street children, whose number has been growing by 5,000 annually. By the time UNICEF issued its report in October, there were 4.6 million orphans in Ethiopia. In the absence of a meaningful state of social existence, women and children are always the first victims of unemployment, poverty, hunger, and maltreatment. In its report, the IMO notes there were over 130,000 Ethiopian women in the Arab Gulf States and other countries of the Middle East who were generally treated as slaves, subjected to a cascade of emotional, sexual, and physical abuses; this prompted the IMO to appeal to the Ethiopian government for action.[49]

In its annual report, the UN Population Fund also gave a grim assessment of the state of gender inequality and the unacceptable level of reproductive health services in the country. According to the report, only 6 percent of Ethiopian women give birth in hospitals and clinics with a skilled nurse in attendance. As a result, over 25,000 women die each year from maternal complications, and another 50,000 become disabled after having given birth. The maternal mortality rate in Ethiopia is 871 per

100,000 births compared with 24 per 100,000 births in Mauritius. The life expectancy of women in Ethiopia is 41.1 years; the global average is 54.8 years. Furthermore, 94 percent of Ethiopian women are subject to domestic violence, while the global average is 33 percent. It is ironic that Ethiopia and Egypt (the two biggest Nile states) share the dubious distinction of being in first place in spousal abuse.

The second road, which Ethiopia's elites can elect to follow if they are serious about poverty eradication and social justice promotion, is ecological economics or even a variant of ecosocialism. This author is fully aware that the very mention of "socialism" in any context evokes a negative connotation, although an authentic "ecosocialism" has not been tried anywhere on a meaningful scale. So ecological economics (which seeks to achieve the goals of sustainable scale and social justice within the framework of capitalism) is a moderate approach to issues of poverty alleviation and environmental equity. The Scandinavian countries may have made significant strides to approximate the essence of ecological economics. Indeed, their collective experiences appear to demonstrate that genuine democracy, social justice, and ecological integrity intrinsically touch each other at all critical junctures. Small wonder that the Scandinavian countries are widely known for having the most rigorous environmental regulations in conjunction with an enviable social safety net and fair political representation, even though these sources of justice and equity seem to be under stress lately due to the dark side of globalization.

The presupposition here in favor of social justice and ecological integrity (stemming from the notion of ecological economics) rests on the recognition that, under the prevailing social order, neither internal growth nor equitable sharing of national wealth is possible. Even if Ethiopia were to monopolize the entire flow of Nile waters, it could neither reduce poverty nor establish social equity without prior transformation of the state, and without radically altering the existing mode of production.

The Eritrean Dimension of Nile Waters

From the perspective of some analysts, Eritrea is perhaps the least significant co-riparian state in the Nile system in terms of the hydrological contribution it makes to the overall hydrographic configuration of the Nile basin. Its status as a co-riparian state within the Nile basin is marginally related to the Tekezze and Gash rivers. As noted earlier, the Tekezze, rising in the northwestern Ethiopian plateau, assumes the name Setit and forms a common border between Ethiopia and Eritrea before entering the Sudan as the Atbara. The extent to which Eritrea can influence the flow of the Setit River to the Sudan is not clear. It may be able to draw water from the river to develop a limited hydropower station as well as agricultural schemes.

The Gash River rises in Eritrea, then ceases flowing once inside the Sudan but before reaching the Atbara. One suggestion holds that some water flows can possibly occur from the Gash River to the Atbara via underground channels. When in season between June and September, the Gash can be very rough because of the enormous volume of water it carries to eastern Sudan. In fact, the volume of the river led the British to hope that it could be harnessed for purposes of irrigating some 300,000 acres of cotton fields in eastern Sudan. The British built a 100-feet-high weir across the river to slow down the flow of the river and raise its waters. However, the violent river swept away the weir in 1906. Undismayed, the British built another weir the following year, which was able to withstand the flow of the Gash River.[50]

In addition to the waters that Eritrea generates via the Gash and Setit rivers, the country seasonally supplies eastern Sudan with good amounts of water resources via the Barka River. All told, Eritrea's annual contribution of water to the Nile system probably reaches 1.7 bcm.[51] Thus, Eritrea's place in the reconfiguration of the Nile system and its potential to become agriculturally self-sufficient cannot and should not be underestimated. Near and around these rivers, Eritrea may be able to develop a modest system of irrigation works. The nation's cultivable area is estimated at 1.6 million ha, even though the total cultivated area in 2002 was 503,000 ha. At the upper end, the country's irrigation potential, independent of water availability, stands at 567,000 ha; given the country's hydrological determinants, financial resources, and technology, Eritrea may be able to put 187,000 ha under irrigation. In 1993, Eritrea had 4,100 ha under perennial irrigation using water from wells, springs, and dams.[52] Moreover, Eritrea has the potential to be self-sufficient in hydropower generation. The Setit, Mereb-Gash, and Barka rivers together have 16,890 Gwh, of which about 5,600 Gwh can be harnessed with modest investment to make the country relatively self-sufficient in energy production. Perhaps it is here where Eritrea may play an important role that may be of major consequence for the Sudan if, and when, Eritrea chooses to aggressively tap its water resources. Historically, the Gash River, which originates in Eritrean territory, has been an important hydrological meeting ground for the two countries. In 1925, Italy and Britain (on behalf of their respective colonies) entered into an agreement by which Eritrea would refrain from obstructing the seasonal flow of the Gash River. In return, the Sudanese government would share the benefits from the cultivation in the Gash delta by annually paying Eritrea 20 percent of the sale of crops above and over 50,000 pound sterling.[53]

Several contingencies are likely to prompt Eritrea to pursue an aggressive water policy. In the first instance, Eritrea is located in the Sahelian rainfall zone, comprising savannah, steppes, and semidesert regions. More than 90 percent of the country's total area receives an annual rainfall of

450 mm; only 1 percent receives more than 650 mm, and rainfall averages vary by region from 50 to 1,000 mm. Moreover, extreme evapotranspiration rates, ranging from 1,700 to 2,000 mm, play a crucial role in water resources depletion. Thus, the context of periodic droughts and dependence on foreign food aid may leave the Eritrean regime with no option other than to harness as much water as possible from the Barka, Gash, and Setit rivers to foster irrigation-based agriculture. The period 2000 to 2004, for example, witnessed unprecedented recurrence of drought, erratic distribution of rainfalls, complete crop failure, huge losses in livestock production, and chronic water shortages. To capture the full picture of Eritrea's worsening food insecurity, it is useful to note that Eritrea produces only 50 to 60 percent of its food needs even in years of good harvests, leaving a huge gap that must be regularly filled with food imports or food aid. In January 2005, the FAO/WFP reported that the 2004 cereal production was a mere 85,000 tonnes, or only 24 percent of the country's annual cereal requirements of 347,000 tonnes. In line with the January 2005 projection, the international community was asked to ship 352,900 tonnes to feed 2.3 million Eritreans (or more than 60 percent of the population) during 2005. In fact, the FAO/WFP estimate was far short of the actual requirements, prompting the United States to pledge 200,000 tonnes in food aid on June 22, 2005, in addition to the 142,705 tonnes already pledged by the Bush administration for fiscal year 2005.[54]

Even with such massive infusion of foreign food aid, the malnutrition rate in the country is intolerably high by global standards. For example, the rate among pregnant and lactating mothers runs between 40 and 60 percent.[55] Over 70 percent of the general population was classified below the minimum international living standard in 2002; since the prevalence of malaria incidents among the general population is 67 percent, women and children in particular suffer from high morbidity and mortality rates.[56]

The poor state of the national economy worsened general living conditions for rural as well as urban dwellers. Between March and September 2004, for example, the inflation rates for pulses, cereals, and all food items soared to 178 percent, 112 percent, and 78 percent, respectively.[57] It is in the context of this grave food insecurity that the Eritrean government has lately focused its attention on the Setit-Gash-Barka triangle in the southwestern region of the country. At the time of writing, a network of microdams and diversion canals had been either under operation or construction to provide irrigation water to a series of sesame, sorghum, corn, onion, cotton, watermelon, citrus fruits, and sugarcane plantations. This network will certainly improve the food security situation; however, the long-range implications of fragmenting the region's seasonal rivers for Sudanese-Eritrean relations remain to be seen. Moreover, the Gash-Barka region of the country, generally regarded as the breadbasket of the country, is sensitive to political events inside and outside the area. The fact that the Ethiopian elites targeted the area for military devastation during the 1998–2000 war with Eritrea demonstrates how vulnerable this important food-growing region is to external mischief. According to the World Bank, Ethiopian troops destroyed, consumed, or drove across the border into Ethiopia a large number of cattle worth $225 million. The devastation that the Ethiopian occupation caused to the 3.5 million livestock population in the area is incalculable.[58]

Second, conducive conditions for the growth paradigm are not in prospect internally and externally. Eritrea appears less well positioned than its immediate neighbors (at least for the moment) to grow itself out of poverty through industrialization. The opportunity for its two seaports to serve as a major source of public revenue and employment seems to have receded into the past as Ethiopians are less keen to depend on Eritrea for goods transit. The irrationality embedded in the regime's authoritarian policy has further weakened the prospect for internal capital accumulation or external inflows. It is useful to note that, for all practical purposes, Eritrea has been dependent on the diaspora Eritrean community for fungible resources, both before and after independence. However, because of the regime's heavy-handedness in matters of internal politics and its contemptuously repulsive attitude toward the diaspora community, remittances from Eritreans abroad have substantially declined in recent years. In 1999, for instance, Eritrea received over $400 million in remittances, which dropped to $276 million in 2004.[59] Diminution of inflows of this magnitude (representing 32 percent of GDP) is substantial in light of the chronic macroeconomic and trade imbalances of the country. It is worth noting that, in 2003, Eritrea's total exports amounted to $12 million compared with $456 million in imports.[60] Thus, given the absence of any tangible economic growth, contextualized by a poor agricultural base and gross governance deficit, Eritrea's food security situation is very precarious.

The Puzzle

All things considered, Ethiopians have a legitimate basis for repudiating the existing Nile water regime. The extent to which they complain about the external obstacles they face in trying to harness their water resources also has merit. However, Ethiopians tend to overlook their own internal weaknesses. The country is poor and underdeveloped not because downstream states overuse Nile waters but because the country's ruling elites have historically failed to provide the country with a vision of progress, self-reliance, and ethnic equality. Successive Ethiopian regimes have misplaced their priorities. Given the history of maladministration and ethnic discrimination in the country, the fundamental question is whether Ethiopia can put its house in order to address issues of social justice, national self-determination, and ecological integrity by which it can buttress its demand for a "reasonable and equitable" water regime.

The other terrible conundrum is the extent to which present or future regimes are committed to stabilizing the country's human and animal populations. Predetermination of an optimal balance between the carrying capacity of the ecology and population sizes is a requisite condition if Ethiopia is to genuinely attain poverty eradication and food security.

To pull the threads of my argument together, I propose that four contingencies bear close watching if Ethiopia is to embark on the road to genuine development. The first is the geopolitical contingency. The Amhara-Tigrayan circle of elites and the major opinion holders in the country have not given up on Eritrea. Still wedded to the antiquated notion of territoriality and empire building, they continue to see Eritrea as a mere extension of the Ethiopian empire state. Using the recent border dispute, the present regime has opted for a "no war, no peace" strategy to ruin the Eritrean economy, and with it the Eritrean regime. Ethiopia has a 200,000-strong standing army, one of the largest on the African continent, which is intended to keep the peace process at bay, despite the standing decision of The Hague arbitration court. Under the terms of the 2000 Algiers peace treaty between Eritrea and Ethiopia, whose practical effectuation was guaranteed by the United States, the European Union, the United Nations, and the African Union, the arbitration court issued its verdict in April 2002, calling upon the two governments to cooperate with the boundary commission in giving finality to the boundary delimitation and demarcation tasks. Although both Eritrea and Ethiopia agreed in Algiers that the commission's decision would be final and binding without recourse to appeal, the verdict has yet to be implemented. The hundreds of millions of dollars that Ethiopia spent to procure all sorts of weapons to prosecute the war on Eritrea between 1998 and 2000 and to perpetuate the "no war, no peace" policy could have gone a long way toward poverty reduction and economic progress. Furthermore, the United Nations had by September 2005 already spent over $2.6 billion to keep an uneasy peace between Eritrea and Ethiopia; in early 2001 it inserted a token force of two blue-helmet battalions between the belligerent states. This money, too, could have been used constructively to advance the cause of progress and poverty alleviation in both countries.

The indifference of the guarantors of the Algiers peace treaty toward Ethiopia's defiance of The Hague verdict has given aid and comfort to the Ethiopian elites. The underlying reasons for the guarantors' indifference are, of course, geopolitical and geoeconomic, pure and simple. The major power, the United States, still views Ethiopia as a geopolitical ally against global terrorism; the recent Ethiopian military intervention in Somalia (with American endorsement and backing) is a lucid illustration of the relationship. Washington invested billions of dollars (mostly in food aid) in Ethiopia between 1991 and 2006 to ensure the survival of the Zenawi regime. For its part, the European Union had aid projects in Ethiopia by the end of 2005 worth over one billion Euros, in addition to the generous assistance funneled to Ethiopia from individual E.U. member countries.[61] The World Bank had thirty-one ongoing projects in Ethiopia as of January 2005 worth $2.25 billion; the bank's annual assistance to Ethiopia also accounts for 37 percent of the $1.2 billion the country receives from donor countries.[62] Ethiopia's large standing army, large population, geostrategic location, and respectable status in sub-Saharan Africa are understood as important attributes of its power. Ethiopia's large market of 77.4 million potential consumers, compared with Eritrea's tiny market of four million poor consumers, provides additional motivation for the guarantors not to offend Ethiopia by threatening it with international sanctions. The national and international presentation of Ethiopia in geopolitical terms is, however, delusional in the long run. It can only serve the gross misplacement of priorities and, by extension, the perpetuation of the status quo of structural poverty, degradation of ecosystem services, external dependency, and potential political implosion.

The second contingency has to do with the prevailing ethnopolitics. Ethiopia still represents a congeries of diverse ethnic groups. Historically, power has been centered in the Amhara-Tigray axis, which together account for 35 percent of the total population. The remaining 65 percent of the population belongs to over seventy ethnic groups, which have historically been marginalized with their cultures devalued and their identities degraded. Even in the supposed present ethnic federalism, the Amhara-Tigrayan elites essentially remain the strategic power brokers. The armed resistance by the Oromo Liberation Front, among others, is an important signification of the yet unresolved question of national self-determination. The electoral fraud perpetrated by the ruling party in May 2005 was in part meant to maintain the status quo and preempt the peripheral ethnic groups from participating at the center. Without ending the ignoble cause of empire, including its concrete manifestations in ethnopolitical control of the state as well as the ethnosocial domination of the major arteries of the economy by the Amhara-Tigray axis, it is improbable that Ethiopia will make progress toward meaningful political representation, economic equality, and ecological integrity.

The demographic question is the third contingency facing any serious regime. Gaining access to more Nile water resources is not a satisfactory answer to Ethiopia's structural poverty. No amount of diverted Nile waters can satisfy a booming population. Ethiopia must make a hard choice between managing its population size in a sustainable and immediate way and postponing the issue until the demographic bomb explodes. After all, to divert Nile waters in sufficient quantities to realize irrigation-based agriculture and hydroelectricity-based industrialization will require massive quantities of fungible financial resources and the surmounting of enormous geological challenges presented by the country's physiography. The demographic contingency takes on added urgency in light of the growing influence of the Sahara Desert, which is rapidly advancing southward. According to the report of the Famine Warning Network, issued in August 2005, Ethiopia was among the seven countries on the fringes of the Sahara that would likely be severely affected by recurrent famine and food insecurity. Half of the twenty million people expected to experience hunger in that region in 2005–2006 were Ethiopian.[63]

This grim forecast comes five years after the UN secretary-general, Kofi Annan, appointed the director-general of the FAO, Jacques Diouf, to head a group effort to overcome the problem of hunger in seven African Horn countries: Ethiopia, Eritrea, Djibouti, Kenya, Somalia, Sudan, and Uganda. According to the task force report, in the year 2000, seventy million people, in these countries suffered from chronic food insecurity, hunger, and malnutrition. Mr. Diouf and his group correctly note that mere food shortages are not the root causes of the food insecurity identified in the report; rather, underlying causes have always included the lack of accountability and access to education, structural poverty, stagnant conflicts, and demographic explosion. The report adds that gross misplacement of priorities is another daunting challenge. This is exemplified by growing militarization in the region; in 1997 alone, the Horn of Africa countries devoted $2 billion to their militaries.[64]

The search for more food in response to the demographic puzzle further encroaches on virgin ecological resources regardless of the impact on the ecohydrological regime. Alan Dixon's study on the status of wetlands in the administrative zone of Illubabor in southwest Ethiopia highlights the dilemma. Historically, indigenous communities in the zone sustainably used the wetlands for construction material, drinking water, medicines, and growing vegetables and food crops on the wetland margins. In recent years, however, the wetlands have come under a serious threat from massive migrations and political interventions. In order to boost overall food production, the government encouraged commodification and commercialization of wetland cultivation. Instead of traditional seasonal cultivation, drainage and cultivation of wetlands were made permanent. Consequently, Illubabor's wetlands have faced the brunt of widespread degradation and erosion, and many have already become wastelands.[65]

The destruction of forests and the substantial diminution of wild animal habitats are also altering the trophic state for many members of the natural ecology. The confrontation between the rural populace and wild game-hunting animals is sharpening. During the third week of September 2005 alone, for example, a large band of lions devoured twenty and wounded ten people, and consumed seventy cattle in the Hadia zone, some

400 km north of the Ethiopian capital. Terrified by the ferocity of the lions, over 1,000 villagers fled the area in search of safety.[66] This is not an isolated episode, in number or geography. According to observers, human overpopulation, deforestation, and overhunting by humans are substantially reducing the ecological resources available to the wild animals, forcing them to aggressively compete with humans for space and resources.

The socioeconomic question is the final contingency on whose resolution all other contingencies hinge. The fundamental question is: what socioeconomic system will enable the country to promote social justice and ecological integrity? Regurgitating manufactured neoliberal economic principles, sugarcoated with high-sounding terminology, is not sufficient. Without prior resolution of the socioeconomic contingency, the rush to construct dams for purposes of irrigation water and hydropower generation may do more harm than good in the long run. Recall the history of the Awash project since the late 1960s when the Ethiopian government, reliant on foreign aid, targeted the Awash River valley for a series of sugarcane, cotton, and banana plantations on the basis of forceful expropriation of expansive land. Over 20,000 indigenous Afar nomads and their livestock were literally evicted from the area without compensation to make way for irrigated cultivation.[67] In search of space and ecological resources, the Afars descended upon areas belonging to other ethnic groups, triggering interethnic warfare. Today, most of the Afars in the area subsist on international food handouts. The enduring lesson from the Awash River valley experience, which must not be lost in Ethiopia, is that more water and more dams will not solve the country's structural difficulties unless the Ethiopians first learn to construct an economic system that is conducive to human freedom, social justice, and ecological equity.

Chapter Five

The Middle Nile "Squatters"
Kenya, Tanzania, and Uganda

The Historical Context

Key to understanding the place of the three east African states in the overall hydrographic configuration of regional interests is the nature of the precipitation regime and the presence of a constellation of lakes in the area, naturally considered convenient water reservoirs for downstream users. British empire builders saw the great rift valley lakes in particular as ideally suited for use as "century storage" where waters from the equatorial region would be collected and stored to meet Egypt's needs. Having such water storage capacity in east Africa, a region characterized by much lower evaporation rates compared to North Africa, would obviate the need for building huge dams in Egypt itself. Because of their proximity to the intertropical convergence zone in the equator, the interannual rainfall in Kenya, Tanzania, and Uganda is generally regarded as relatively stable. In the past, this situation created permissive conditions for rain-fed agriculture to develop in the region. Traditional cultivation and the popularity of pastoralism in many parts of the region relatively shielded the rift valley lakes from human encroachment for irrigation water, even though the indigenous communities regularly accessed the lakes and rivers for fisheries and transportation; those activities, however, did not impede the natural state of the lakes or the regular flows of the rivers.

It was in this context that, during periods of colonialism, both Great Britain and Egypt viewed the east African rift valley lakes simply as convenient water storage from which the flow of White Nile waters would be regulated in line with Egypt's water needs. Because the economies of the east African colonies were embedded in rain-fed agriculture and pastoralism, British and Egyptian hydrologists assumed that the equatorial lakes could be developed and protected for the benefit of Egypt. In keeping with this imperial orientation, Britain signed a number of protocols and treaties on behalf of its African colonies with the Congo Free State in 1889, with Italy in 1891, with Italy and Ethiopia in 1902, and with Egypt in 1929. The end result of these agreements was to affirm Egypt's appropriative rights to east African waters.

Under the principles of *uti possidetis* and state succession, Kenya, Tanzania, and Uganda were expected to live up to all international obligations that were assumed by Great Britain prior to their independence. In practice, this meant that the water regime that Great Britain and Egypt supposedly erected through international treaties would remain operative even after Britain gave up its colonial possessions. Contrary to conventional wisdom, however, the east African states immediately questioned the legitimacy of the bequeathed water regime. Following independence, Julius Nyerere quickly asserted a version of the Harmon doctrine, hence the Nyerere doctrine, which holds that the east African colonies, by virtue of their outright exclusion from all matters affecting them, were under no obligation to accept the colonial relics left behind by Great Britain. African independence was a repudiation of colonialism, including all its legacies. In July 1962, Julius Nyerere's government officially announced that "the provisions of the 1929 agreement, purporting to apply to the countries under British Administration, are not binding on Tanganika."[1]

This doctrine informs the present position of the east African states on the existing hydrographic reality. This view was made categorical as recently as March 2004 by Tanzania's water resources minister, Edward Lowassa, when he told a conference of government delegates and water experts: "We do not recognize what happened in the past. We want equitable and reasonable use of the Nile waters for mutual benefits in all the riparian states."[2] Incidentally, the ministers and experts were gathered in Nairobi to explore new ways of sharing Nile waters. Although Uganda's position on the Nile question has relatively been softer, Kenya's orientation is close to that of Tanzania. Kenya's Vice President Moody Awori made his country's view clearer in these terms: "The Nile is the most important single asset that is shared by all the ten countries that lie within its basin. As such, the Nile River is not the property of any one state."[3]

The east African states call into question not only the legality of past colonial treaties, but also the morality of the present distribution of water resources. For example, 98 percent of Egyptians today have access to electricity generated by the Nile while only 10 percent of Kenyans are connected to the electric grid. The three east African states differ in their vulnerability to resource scarcity and contributions to the water regime. In addition to controlling a large chunk of Lake Victoria, Uganda has four satellite lakes wholly or partly within its territory. Moreover, Uganda contributes over 50 percent of Lake Victoria's water, while Kenya and Tanzania contribute 30 and 18 percent of the lake's waters, respectively.[4] The foregoing provisional remarks suggest that the nature and texture of the future role of the three east African states in the hydrographic race for Nile waters will be determined by the objective material conditions internal to each state. This chapter examines how the internal dynamics of the east African states are likely to shape their hydrological orientations and strategies in the coming years.

The Elusive Quest for Food Security and the Modernization Imperatives

As elsewhere, the three east African states (some 80 percent of whose labor force is engaged in agriculture) are seeking to harness their streams and lakes to achieve self-sufficiency in food and energy production. In addition to pressure from growing populations, precipitation shortfalls have weakened the regional food security situation. The regularity of inadequate rainfalls and the almost permanent requests for international food aid by all three states have become increasingly disconcerting to both donor and recipient countries. For example, in 2000, long grain maize production (1.4 million tonnes in Kenya) was 22 percent lower than in 1998, and 36 percent lower than in 1999. As a result, Kenya was compelled to import 1.4 million tonnes of maize until September 2001.[5]

Furthermore, a severe drought in the 2003–2004 growing season caused complete failure in crop production in five of Kenya's eight provinces, exposing four million people to potential starvation. In September 2004, the Kenyan government appealed to the international community for 156,000 tonnes of food to feed the hungry until the next harvest.[6] Again in July 2005, the World Food Program reported that Kenya would require 79,000 tonnes of international food aid between September 2005 and February 2006 alone for the 1.6 million Kenyans expected to need food assistance.[7] A comprehensive assessment of Kenya's food insecurity presents an even bleaker picture, since by early June 2005 the country's maize reserves were 1.1 million bags short of the required yearly stock. According to the World Vision report, 3.6 million Kenyans required food assistance during the 2005–2006 period. Moreover, according to the WFP report, 33 percent (10.3 million) of Kenya's population was undernourished.[8] This is partly due to the government's inability to garner and effectively distribute food. For example, between September 2004 and August 2005, the government managed to distribute only 131,191 of the 291,825 tonnes of food requirements.[9] As of this writing, Kenya appears to have lost its grip on the food security situation in the country since widespread drought and famine have continually worsened. In early January 2006, Kenya's president declared the famine situation a "national disaster" and asked for $263 million in emergency donor aid to feed four million Kenyans on the verge of starvation.[10] The recurrent problems of drought, famine, and food insecurity have indeed led to growing poverty, since the proportion of the Kenyan population defined as "poor" progressively rose from 11 million (48 percent) in 1990 to 17 million (56 percent) in 2003.[11]

Naturally speaking, Kenya shouldn't find itself in the present situation in terms of food security. Almost on all counts, ranging from precipitation to soil fertility and forest endowment, Kenya has historically been a nation with excellent prospects for prosperity. With more than 35,000 plant and animal species, the country possesses an enviably deep biodiversity. Before sheer neglect allowed it to disintegrate, a relatively well-developed infrastructure made commerce a thriving reality. In fact, Kenya and Egypt are the only two of the ten Nile states that have so far avoided being categorized as least developed countries.[12] In the last three decades, however, Kenya has eroded its natural endowment through official corruption and land grabbing, population pressure, massive timber harvesting, and climatic factors. Unrestricted exploitation of forest products has, for instance, reduced available timber by more than half since independence. In addition to the vast areas cleared for cultivation, Kenya has lost 5,000 ha of virgin forests every year to wood fuel production.[13]

The salient features of Kenya's land tenure system and the pattern of forest exploitation were cast during the colonial era. To induce European immigration to east Africa, the British colonial administration glowingly depicted Kenya's potential for quick wealth accumulation with minimal investment and made the best lands in Highland Kenya available to newcomers at extraordinarily cheap concessions.[14] Land accumulation under settler colonization quickly acquired a special dimension; at independence, the large estates in European hands stood at 2.6 million ha.[15] Having secured the best lands, the settlers soon specialized in cash crop production. At the beginning of the twentieth century, the settler farmers introduced coffee and tea into Kenya. Although natives already grew maize as a staple, new commercial estates also adapted their farms to grow maize for the home market. By 1929, over 1.2 million ha were devoted to maize production under market conditions.[16] To be sure, the colonial settler sector of the economy accounted for two-fifths of Kenya's agricultural production and for 85 percent of total exports by value.[17]

Alongside the granting of land for commercial farming, new settlers were also offered forest resources. Particularly known for generosity in this area, Sir Charles Eliot, the British high commissioner in Kenya from 1900 to 1904, granted forest concessions covering tens of thousands of ha without even consulting with the colonial office in London. Timber companies were given free rein over Kenya's forests. War requirements after 1939 accelerated the destruction, as timber production in Kenya soared from 19,750 hoppus tonnes in 1938 to 116,500 hoppus tonnes in 1945.[18] Without a regulatory regime in place, the timber companies freely abused the forest by engaging in selective logging of the luxuriant trees or by leaving substantial amounts of felled trees to rot. In the words of a horrified forester, "the forest work carried on in the felling area here is almost beyond conception. No one seems to be in charge of the boys who are doing the forest work, and they go along cutting and felling in any way they like."[19]

Following the colonial pattern of land appropriation, Kenya's national elites embarked right after independence on a rapacious agrarian accumulation, which furthered land fragmentation and deforestation, on the one hand, and the growth of personal ranches and estates, on the other. Land accumulation in postindependence Kenya became a function of tenure of office. Nicholas Biwott, one of President Moi's powerful ministers, for example, simply declared ownership in January 2002 of 1,000 acres of forest, claiming that he needed the land to erect a monument in memory of his mother.[20] Such official behaviors facilitated encroachments on virgin forests and pastures that were historically used in a sustainable fashion by indigenous communities. The massive alienation of land from the Maasai and Ogiek peoples is instructive in this regard.

The Maasai and Ogiek peoples are neighbors in the 250,000 ha Mau forest complex, which straddles six Kenyan districts while graciously extending into northern Tanzania. During colonial times, the cattle-herding Maasai people lost 15 million acres (75 percent) of their inherited lands to colonial developers; between 1978 and 1999, the Maasai again lost over 1 million acres to politically well-connected land speculators, tourism developers, tea plantation owners, and other commercial interests.[21] Today, the Mau forests, which traditionally provided the Maasai people and other ethnic groups with water, food, timber, and forage for themselves and their livestock, have come under serious threats from the same forces. The watershed of the Mau forests is fabulously endowed with permanent water supply, extraordinarily dense vegetation, medicinal herbs, and forage. Nakuru, Bogoria, and Natron, the main rivers that flow into Lake Victoria, rise in the Mau forests. The Mau forests are also home to many endangered species, like red and blue monkeys, colobus, giant wild hogs, yellow-backed duiker, bongo antelopes, and elephants.

The official land grab began in the Narok district in the 1970s. It was so widespread that, as one commentator observed, virtually every politically connected person or rich foreigner in Kenya had property in the Mau forest of the Narok district; this includes the 4,000 ha purportedly claimed by the family members of Moshe Dayan, former defense minister of Israel. Since the inauguration of the land grab, the area under forest cover has decreased from 400,000 ha to 135,000 ha today.[22] The forests have been shrinking at 10 percent annually. Since 1995 alone, 77 square miles of Mau forests have been set aside for economic development, ranging from all sorts of plantations to tourism concessions.[23] The massive loss of forests will affect not only the Maasai and Ogiek peoples, but also the more than three million people from other ethnic groups in the area who depend on the Mau forests for food, wood, and water.

Since landlessness in Kenya is increasing exponentially, forests and watersheds are likely to suffer more damage. Unable to count on the government for equitable agrarian land reform, many Kenyans are taking matters into their own hands. The episode surrounding the 47,000-acre farm of Basil Criticos is emblematic of the sorts of land problems that Kenya is likely to face on a national scale unless radical steps are taken to address the land issue. Mr. Criticos, a second-generation Kenyan of Greek origin, was a member of parliament in 2001 when 3,000 landless Kenyans in the Coast province invaded and occupied his farm. Despite Mr. Criticos's pleas to the government for the return of his farm, the invaders have yet to leave.[24]

When Mwai Kibaki ran in 2002 to replace Arap Moi, whom Kenyans regarded as an irredeemable kleptomaniac, the land issue and corruption topped his campaign planks. After several years in office, President Kibaki has yet to address the land issue beyond asking Kenyans to patiently wait for a comprehensive land reform. The problem is that Kenya may follow the Zimbabwean model before the promised land reform sees daylight. Lilian Njenga, a senior official in the Ministry of Lands, expressed this fear:

> The situation in Zimbabwe has made our work more difficult, as landless Kenyans who have learnt from the events in other countries are piling pressure on the government to settle them. People are now talking of getting back their ancestral land that is in the hands of multinationals. They are testing the waters trying to find out if the government can give in to their demands.[25]

The senior official's observation is supported by prevailing circumstances in Kenya, which suggest that things are likely to get worse before they get better. The rise of the landed native bourgeoisie and the presence of a small (yet rich) white settler population in the midst of land hunger can create a highly explosive environment, and any episode (like the killing of a game warden in early June 2005) can serve as a rallying event. Thomas Cholmondeley, a white settler who owns a 100,000-acre colonial estate in Kenya's rift valley, shot and killed one of the wardens who approached the estate's slaughterhouse to investigate for illegal activity. The attorney general apparently believed Mr. Cholmondeley's claim that he mistook the wardens for poachers, and exonerated him from the murder charge. More than the act of killing, the fact that Mr. Cholmondeley was released scot-free raised the blood pressure of most Kenyans. In the context of growing urban and rural poverty and unemployment, such episodes can certainly catalyze chaos.

The struggle for resources will not be limited to the one between the haves and the have-nots; it will also involve a fierce struggle among the poor themselves. Competition among the nation's diverse ethnic groups can easily lend itself to a rising temperature in intercommunal relations, which may eventually challenge the country's territorial integrity and political stability. A case in point is the recent bloody feud between the Gabra and Borana ethnic groups in northeast Kenya. Competition between the two groups for water and pastures culminated in what amounted to a massacre. On July 12, 2005, some one hundred armed men from the Borana group descended upon the Gabra village of Turbi and opened fire indiscriminately on school children and villagers. At the event's end, seventy-six people were dead, including twenty-two children.[26]

Difficulties involved in the land issue in Kenya are directly connected to the way in which favors have been farmed out since independence. Eager to replicate the colonial model of land accumulation, Kenya's postindependence elites used their offices to manufacture documents to falsely establish land titles. The manufacturing of bogus title deeds usually peaks during national election seasons. During the 1997 national election season, for instance, President Arap Moi himself reportedly issued 700 such titles. Again, in the 2002 election cycle, the president's party farmed out almost 170,000 acres of forest land to its supporters, including 150,000 acres in the Mau forests.[27] They used these false deeds as collateral to borrow money from banks to develop the falsely acquired urban and rural properties. In fact, by mid-2005, some 54 percent of the bank asset portfolio in Kenya was said to be tied to land, held as collateral, exposing $3.4 billion of bank assets to potential loss.[28]

The land issue in Kenya remains unresolved precisely because the challenge of governance also remains unaddressed. The bad governance expresses itself in the pervasiveness of corruption. For all practical purposes, every public office in Kenya, and therefore any public service, is for sale. Capitalizing on popular outcry against official corruption, the opposition political leaders promised a clean break with the institutionalized culture of nepotism, corruption, and authoritarianism of the past. Together with the land issue, the anticorruption campaign swept the opposition to power in December 2002. The opposition blocs were centered upon the two dominant ethnic groups: the Kikuyu and Luo, supporting Mwai Kibaki's National Alliance and Raila Odinga's Liberal Democratic Party, respectively.

Kibaki and Odinga's jump on the popular bandwagon served to blur the class character of the anti-Moi movement. It is instructive to bear in mind that, before their falling out with Moi, the seventy-three-year-old

Kibaki was Moi's vice president while Odinga was energy minister in the same government. By appropriating the idiom of popular opposition, the self-styled opposition political parties highjacked the authenticity of the mass movement. Long before the eggs of power were hatched, Kibaki and Odinga struck a secret deal to share power by creating an office of prime minister for Odinga while allowing Kibaki to keep the presidency.[29] To accommodate this change, the political leaders and countervailing civic movements saw the urgency for drafting a new constitution.

During his presidential inauguration in January 2003, Kibaki promised to deliver a new constitution within one hundred days and to reduce the powers of the president by transferring certain powers to the new office of prime minister. In the end, though, Kibaki and his allies got what they did not wish for. The new draft constitution startled the political class by envisioning a substantial reduction in the authority of the presidency and the creation of a powerful office of prime minister. From the perspective of the framers of the draft constitution, the new political configuration would sufficiently decentralize power by making the apex of public administration genuinely pluralistic, allowing the potential tension between the two offices of the executive branch of government to counteract corruption.

Because the national elites did not deem the draft constitution to be consistent with their class interest, Kibaki and his allies moved to obstruct its adoption. The one hundred days came and went without a new constitution. Then, in response to international pressure and a series of domestic demonstrations, Kibaki's government allowed the introduction of the draft constitution in parliament for a vote in early July 2005, two and a half years after the promise for a new constitution was issued. However, the regime mobilized its parliamentary supporters to amend the original draft in such a way as to keep most of the powers in the presidency. Parliament adopted this watered-down version on July 22, 2005, by a margin of 102 to 61. A nominal office of the prime minister was to be established to satisfy the demands of some counter-elites. To the chagrin of the political class, however, on November 21, 2005, Kenyans decisively defeated the draft constitution by a 57 to 43 percent referendum vote.

Meanwhile, government officials continued to prosper from a bonanza of corruption under Kibaki's government. By some estimates, official corruption has cost Kenya $1 billion, or a fifth of the government's budget, in the two and a half years since Kibaki assumed office.[30] In fact, rapacious corruption under Kibaki's administration became so widespread that Sir Edward Clay, the British high commissioner to Kenya, pointedly characterized the level of corruption as "massive looting" and bluntly accused Kenyan ministers of "eating like gluttons (and) vomiting on the shoes of foreign donors."[31] To show the gravity of the matter, Sir Edward produced twenty cases involving dubious contracts worth hundreds of millions of dollars, awarded without public bidding and transparency. One of these involves passport-making equipment, awarded to a French firm without public tender; the price tag for the equipment was $34 million, even though the originally publicized price was just $10 million.[32]

In short order, the Kibaki administration distinguished itself as a champion of "business as usual." Disillusioned by the administration's promise to stamp out corruption, major donor countries and global institutions began holding back aid. The United States, Great Britain, Germany, and Norway moved to slash their assistance to Kenya by $20 million, after John Githoni, the anticorruption czar, resigned from his post in frustration in February 2005.[33] Hoping to impress upon the Kibaki administration, Great Britain actually revoked the visa issued to Chris Murungaru, then minister of transport, barring him from entering or passing through the United Kingdom. Even the minister of justice Kiraitu Murungi openly admitted that Kenya was losing the battle against graft. On August 10, 2005, the justice minister told an anticorruption conference:

> In January, I declared 2005 the year of action. We promised more arrests, more prosecutions, and more asset recoveries. Eight months down the road, very little seems to be happening. There has been very little change in the mentality, attitude, and behavior of our civil servants. They believe nothing will happen to them. Everyday there is talk of bribery, embezzlement, fraud, extortion, nepotism, vote-buying, abuse of power, conflict of interest, judicial corruption, and misappropriation of public funds.[34]

Since urban sources of wealth accumulation are milked dry, the object of resource extraction and expropriation is now the country's forests. To put the problem into perspective, it is useful to consider that, in 1980, only 9.2 percent of Kenyan land was under forest cover, a proportion that has since dropped to just 1.7 percent of the country's total land area. Of the 2.4 million ha under forest cover, 1.6 million ha is gazetted. The remaining 800,000 ha is ungazetted, or registered as trust land, and fragmented into 273 units.[35]

There is a powerful economic rationale behind the new wave of forest expropriation. Informed by neoliberal economics, the Kibaki administration sees the answer to Kenya's underdevelopment in the privatization of nature for the generation of exportable products. According to the government's blueprint, 10 percent of all areas under forest cover will be open for cultivation by outsiders in order to ostensibly improve the country's food security.[36] During the 2005–2006 growing season, 250,000 ha of additional land was put under maize cultivation. According to the U.S. Department of Agriculture, this would raise Kenya's total maize production by 800,000 tonnes over the 2004 harvest of two million tonnes.[37] While the government uses the environmental protection label to deny the poor access to forest resources, it exempts logging companies from any restriction, invoking a bogus argument to justify its decision. For instance, two giant logging companies, among the exempted firms, are said to provide employment to 30,000 Kenyans, considered reason enough to permit them to ransack the forests.[38]

The long-term impact of deforestation on Kenya's general ecology and economy is unmistakable. Five of the six rivers that originate in the Mau forest complex have increasingly become seasonal, and the sixth has dried up. The frequency and severity of droughts have impacted small farmers, herders, and large tea plantation owners alike. The denudation of the country's landscape has exponentially increased the incidents of floods and landslides, affecting millions of Kenyans. What makes the prospects of further ecological degradation particularly worrisome in Kenya is that the prospects of proper governance are dim. In the absence of a functioning political machine, people will look to the forests for subsistence. Even worse, the government is bound to encourage such activity as a way of coping with its legitimation crisis. Regardless of who does it, whether government officials or dispossessed and desperate individuals and groups, the end result is the same: total collapse of ecosystem services.

The present state of Mount Kenya, the headwaters of the River Tana, is instructive in this respect. Because of official development projects and encroachment by individuals who illegally clear its forest to make way for marijuana plantations, the mountain's ecosystem is rapidly degrading. Its unique giant forest hogs, sunbirds, giant lobelias, and other mountain forest species are endangered. The River Tana itself, one of Kenya's vital rivers, is severely affected by the ecological deterioration. In the words of Mark Collins of the UN Environmental Protection Agency, the River Tana

> is important for drinking, for cities, for hydropower. With seven dams on the river, it is vital for irrigation and transportation. But the ecological damage is doing more than threatening species or inhabitants. It is destroying the lives of people downstream who depend on those ecosystems hundreds of miles from where they are living. We are seeing the river dry up, we are seeing siltation of the dams, we are seeing flash floods, we are seeing irrigation schemes that are failing, despite millions of dollars in development aid.[39]

In addition to the gross governance deficit, Kenya suffers from the fact that agriculture remains the chief anchor of the country's economy. Not only do primary commodities define the sector, but also a mere six commodities account for 68 percent of agriculture's GDP and 17.5 percent of aggregate GDP. Furthermore, the farming sector still employs 75 percent of the workforce. If one includes such agriculture-associated activities as processing and transportation, then the sector accounts for 50 percent of all national economic activities.[40] The enigma inherent in reliance on primary commodities is that they are highly vulnerable to climatic factors and price fluctuations, whether internal or global.

Since Kenya relies on the export of cash crops to generate foreign exchange earnings, the volatility in global prices for primary commodities has a negative multiplier effect on the country's economy. In response to external shocks and price fluctuations, agricultural producers must either increase production volume to make up for lost revenue, which can only depress prices further, or substantially reduce investment in the sector. If they choose the first course of action, they can boost production only through increased acreage, which means more destruction of virgin forests. The recent government decision to enclose important portions of previously protected forests illustrates this dilemma. If farmers adopt the second course of action, people will flock to the city. Unforeseen climatic factors, such as drought and crop failure due to infestation of diseases, may further set limits on the agrarian sector. In the context of the demographic boom that Kenya is experiencing, these can be huge problems.

The dismal performance of Kenya's agriculture in the 1990s, when liberalization and privatization were in full swing, lends substantial credence to this point. During the first decade after independence, Kenya's agriculture registered an impressive annual growth rate of 6 percent, which declined to 4 percent in the 1980s, and then dropped to 2 percent in the 1990s.[41] There is an ironic twist with the neoliberal regime here.

To impress donor countries, the Moi government set up the Free Export Processing Zone (FEPZ) in 1990, allowing investors to enjoy all the privileges of tax holiday and exemption from import duties. The aim was to stimulate technology transfer, diversification of Kenya's export crops, and job creation. The FEPZ not only failed to live up to its purpose but also became parasitically dependent on child labor. According to the report of the International Labor Organization, there are 1.9 million child workers in Kenya, 1.3 million of whom have no access to school. Equally deplorable is the fact that wages in the "free zone" are as low as a dollar a day.[42]

Predictably, investors and donor countries alike blame the poor performance and the poor working conditions in the "free zone" on poor governance, bad infrastructure, and the high cost of energy and transportation. As a demonstration of open displeasure with corruption, and in the hope of positively influencing the business environment, the IMF in 1997 actually froze its disbursement of loans to the Moi government. When the Kibaki administration expressed its commitment to deepen the liberalization process and to eradicate corruption, the IMF resumed disbursement of $252.8 million in loans in November 2003. The IMF example was followed by donor countries and by the World Bank, which together provided over $500 million annually in loans and credits.[43]

Despite promises for clean government and the expression of a commitment to the neoliberal regime, Kenya's economy remained stagnant. International assistance began to flow, but it represented a mere 20 percent of the 700 billion Kenyan shillings required to jumpstart the development trajectory.[44] Liberalization and privatization are generally presented as crucial providers of growth stimuli through internal and external competition, forcing producers to become efficient innovators. The problem with this strategy is that similarly situated countries generally imitate each other and compete for the same markets with the same products. Even worse, global corporations with huge financial resources, scale economies, and a long learning curve can, and always do, easily undersell newly liberalizing economies.

In Kenya, for example, imports of wheat, dairy products, maize, sugar, and rice have increased substantially since liberalization.[45] Rather than stimulating domestic production, such import penetration strategies by foreign firms inevitably lead to the opposite result. For example, the area devoted to sugar plantations in Kenya peaked in 1980; since then sugar production has been declining steadily. In 2002, Kenyans consumed 600,000 tonnes of white sugar per annum, of which domestic producers supplied 400,000 tonnes while the remainder was imported. At the present rate of growth, demand for sugar in Kenya is expected to reach 1 million tonnes per annum by 2012, making the country one of the biggest sugar importers in the world.[46]

As Otieno Odek and his associates note, because sugar is both a strategic and political commodity, Kenya's increasing dependence on sugar imports could have far-reaching adverse implications for the country's economy. In view of the fact that sugar is widely used in confectionary, beverage, pharmaceutical, chemical, and wine and alcohol industries, its multiplier effect on the economy is immeasurable. For this reason, the livelihoods of over one million Kenyans are attached to the sugar subsector.[47] The problem for Kenya is that the sugar subsector has not been cost-effective in relation to international competitors. The factors often cited as reasons for the lack of competitiveness include lack of irrigation works, technological lag, poor scale economies among growers, and milling inefficiencies. Moreover, Kenya's sugar firms are handicapped by heavy indebtedness, with debts representing 91 percent of their total assets.[48]

In the context of growing liberalization, the subsector is likely to face further setback. Removal of barriers to sugar importation in the name of liberalization could swamp Kenya with cheap imported sugar from low-cost producers. The policy dilemma for the Kibaki administration is that, were the country to put tariffs back in place to protect domestic producers, it would be hammered by WTO rules or retaliation by sugar-exporting countries, especially Egypt, which is one of Kenya's chief tea export markets.

Kenya has also lost ground in the global coffee market, as coffee exports plummeted from 130,000 tonnes in 1988 to 50,000 tonnes in 1998.[49] The collapse of Kenya's coffee export has been due to the increase in the number of coffee-growing countries. Vietnam, for example, a newcomer on the block, surpassed Columbia as the second largest coffee exporter after Brazil. Cost of production also matters. Brazil has doubled coffee production in a decade; production cost there is half that in Kenya. More important is that just five global corporations control 50 percent of the world's coffee purchasing, affording them the ability to influence prices.[50]

The two areas that pro-marketers conveniently present as shining examples of neoliberalism in Kenya are tea and horticulture. Tea production steadily rose from 200 million kg in 2002 to 328 million kg in 2005, making Kenya one of the biggest black tea exporters in the world, capturing 22 percent of the global market share.[51] However, the boom in tea production has resulted from horizontal expansion, which involves putting more land under cultivation. Kenya has also shown a marked improvement in horticulture, such as cut flowers and fruits. In 1992, Kenya exported 57,363 tonnes of horticultural products, which climbed to 84,143 tonnes in 1998.[52] Contrary to assertions by pro-market liberalizers, the boost in tea and horticultural exports is due to international demand conditions rather than the virtues of private initiatives.

The economic stagnation in Kenya must be understood in the context of two crucial dimensions. The first is that in order to contain its legitimation crisis, the government is more likely than not to accelerate the vandalization of ecological resources by allowing the commercial enclosure of more forest land or by settling dispossessed peasants on forested areas to keep them away from the city. However, allocation of and competition for land and water resources only sharpens the social contradictions and interethnic tensions. The vexing dimension of the problem is that since the regime will be unable to keep the 80 percent of Kenyans who still live in rural areas where they are, the landless and the destitute rural people will continue to flock to the city.

The growing congestion of Kenya's capital illustrates the dilemma. Nairobi's population increased by 800 percent between 1963 and 2005 (from 266,000 to 2.8 million people).[53] However, there are neither adequate housing facilities nor enough jobs to satisfy the needs of the urban unemployed and the new arrivals. According to estimates of the late 1990s, at least 10,000 new housing units are needed each year in Nairobi alone to accommodate the needs of those who have the means to buy their own homes.[54] But those Nairobians who could afford to own homes are a small number. More than 60 percent of the city's dwellers live on less than $.50 a day, an amount insufficient for securing food and proper shelter. The option is to erect shacks or sleep in the streets. Nairobi's Kibera slum (the largest of its kind in Africa) houses over

800,000 people, cramped in just 1 square mile. As a result, Nairobi has become a metropolis of burgeoning slums, carjackers, burglars, child prostitutes, and beggars. By some estimates, there are 25,000 street children in Nairobi. In the false hope of forgetting the world of darkness surrounding them, the street children sniff glue and become vulnerable to addictions of all sorts, respiratory infections, sexually transmitted diseases, and malaria infestations.[55]

To return to the central themes of this work, the absence of genuine democratic governance, social justice, and ecological integrity has important internal political and regional hydrographic implications. In the midst of resource depletion and ecological collapse, Kenya's politicians are likely to look more and more to Lake Victoria for irrigation waters and hydropower generation. During the 2002 national election cycle, Raila Odinga had attempted to make the Victoria waters a campaign issue as he positioned himself to challenge his rivals for the presidency. The invocation of Lake Victoria waters was both natural and opportunistic. Odinga regards himself as, and the Luo people see him as, the natural representative of Luo interests in Nairobi. The Luo, who inhabit the region on the Lake Victoria shores, see the lake as vital to Luo development. In this context, Odinga openly challenged the 1929 Nile water agreement as "outdated and unfair." He contended that:

> it (the treaty) was signed on behalf of governments which were not in existence at that time. We are bound by an agreement to which we are not party and we are saying this is an unfair agreement that we should negotiate afresh. If you want to use that water for food production, why should you be prevented from doing so, and you are conserving it for Egypt to go and use it for production, we think this is not fair.[56]

Odinga's statement was made against the backdrop of the government's refusal to issue permission to an American aid group who offered to help Luo farmers revive their rice cultivation by drawing water from Lake Victoria. Since Odinga made the waters of Lake Victoria a campaign issue several years ago, the political pendulum in Kenya has swung in his direction. In fact, Kenya appears similar to Ethiopia in its rhetorical militancy regarding the distribution of Nile waters as it actively solicits international support for Kenya's right to use Victoria's waters for irrigation and other commercial purposes. In a well-rehearsed keynote address on land policy and management delivered on March 15, 2005, Kenya's assistant minister for culture and sports, Alicen Chelait, lashed out at Great Britain and Egypt for imposing a cruel treaty on Kenya and its sisterly neighbors without their participation in the matter. She characterized the 1929 treaty as:

repressive, obsolete, selfish, and unrealistic. . . . It is a shame that almost all catchment areas of Lake Victoria are managed and sustained by governments and citizens of Kenya, Uganda, and Tanzania, yet they are barred by the treaty from using its waters for irrigation purposes, a move that has locked out a huge agricultural potential in the region. Downstream Egyptians who have nothing to contribute in managing the lake's catchment are busy tapping River Nile waters for commercial activities.[57]

The assistant minister's denunciation of the 1929 Anglo-Egyptian treaty is certainly just. The danger is, however, that there is a false assumption that underlies the demand for more Victoria waters. Out of its total estimated irrigable land area, Kenya has, to date, managed to put 80,000 ha under irrigation. The prevailing assumption in Kenya is that the country could overcome its food insecurity by putting more and more land under irrigation by drawing water from Lake Victoria. Even if Kenya were to be given the entire waters of the lake, the country's food security situation is unlikely to improve much. In fact, if the three east African states were to exploit their combined irrigable land using Victoria waters, the ecohydrological consequences of extensive irrigation works could be far larger than they anticipate. Kenya's half-century experience with irrigation-based rice production supplies ample evidence to substantiate this point.

In 1966, Kenya enacted an irrigation law to encourage and regulate rice production on a large scale. The model was the colonially inherited Mwea irrigation scheme, composed of 450 sq km of rice paddy fields and the hamlets for the tenant farmers, dependent on the Thiba and Nyamindi tributaries of the Tana River. Following the 1966 Irrigation Act, Kenya launched three irrigation schemes in western Kenya to grow rice. While the Mwea scheme accounted for 70 percent of rice production over the decades, the newer schemes accounted for the remainder. However, due to mismanagement, corruption, the increasing shortage of water, and land disputes, all rice paddy fields in the country are in total disrepair. Sections of the Mwea Dam's wall are crumbling, water canals are clogged with vegetation, the population of vector snails is rising, malaria infestation is growing, and crocodiles are threatening the rice growers. Rice production in western Kenya has fallen by more than 50 percent in recent years. The plan to make Kenya self-sufficient in rice production has come to naught. As a result, Kenya has not only become a net rice importer, but also the volume of imported rice is rising year after year, as domestic production fluctuates between 35,000 and 50,000 tonnes annually. In recent years, the country has spent Sh 7 billion annually on imported rice. In 2002, Kenya imported 128,438 tonnes of rice, which since then has been steadily rising to an average of 220,000 tonnes a year.[58]

In addition to Lake Victoria, Kenya has begun looking at its own major rivers with an increasingly possessive eye. In its "National Water Resources Management Strategy" report, issued in January 2006, Kenya's ministry of water and irrigation warned of a catastrophic water shortage in Kenya unless the country developed a comprehensive plan to protect and sustainably use its rivers.[59] In an apparent effort to buttress Kenya's claim to the water resources originating in its territory, the document highlighted the fact that 45 percent of the water flowing into Lake Victoria and the upper Nile originates in Kenya and that nine Kenyan rivers together carry huge amounts of water to Tanzania, Uganda, and Ethiopia. The document also noted the increasing diminution of the quantity, quality, and availability of water resources owing to widespread degradation of watershed ecology. Lake Baringo in the Rift Valley, for example, which measured 15 m deep in the 1920s, is only 1.8 m deep today, resulting from massive deforestation of the catchment area and the consequent siltation of the lake. By implication, Kenya's ministry of water and irrigation sees the urgency to intensify the competition for water resources either by receiving due share from Lake Victoria or controlling the flow of its rivers. The objective reality of burgeoning population and drought cycles is likely to contextualize this urgency to capture more resources. After all, Kenya's population of 32 million today is expected to rise to 45 million by 2015. Presently, Kenya has 7.4 bcm of surface water and 1 bcm of ground water.[60]

Of the three east African states, Tanzania appears to have not only more expansive areas of potentially irrigable land than its neighbors, but also an ambitious plan to exploit its agricultural potential. In several important respects, Tanzania is actually the mirror image of Ethiopia. Like Ethiopia, it has relatively abundant water resources from its nine river basins and three important freshwater lakes: Victoria, Tanganika, and Malawi; the first two are the second largest and the second deepest lakes in the world, respectively. Tanzania's portions of these three lakes cover 7 percent of its total land area of 947,000 sq km. There are also four important inland lakes. In addition, the country has five extensive wetlands, covering 439,000 ha or 5.8 percent of the country's total area, excluding the seasonally flooded vast plains. However, like Ethiopia, Tanzania faces a number of difficult challenges to meeting its future water requirements.

The first challenge stems from a growing population. If present projections hold, Tanzania's population will grow from 36 million today to 60 million by 2025. Such demographic growth is likely to put enormous pressure on the country's water resources; by 2025, Tanzania will be in the water-stressed category as the water resources available per person will be reduced by 45 percent.[61] The second challenge stems from the uneven distribution of the country's water resources. Important regions of the country are not only far from the main water centers, but are also drought-prone;

dry spells frequently exacerbate the situation. Bringing water from resource-rich regions to resource-poor areas has proved prohibitively expensive. Infrastructure for the transfer of vital resources from one region to another is either extremely poor or nonexistent. In consequence, more than 50 percent of Tanzanians in rural areas have no access to safe drinking water, and in some areas the proportion of people with access to clean potable water is lower than 12 percent. In areas where there are water projects, 30 percent is in total disrepair; even in the country's capital, low-income neighborhoods are not served by water utilities.[62]

Changes in the climate of the region can only further complicate matters for Tanzania. Changes in climatological conditions are affecting the sources of its vital resources. For example, the ice cap on Mount Kilimanjaro in Tanzania is said to have lost 80 percent of its original size in the last eighty years. If this trend continues, by 2020, Mount Kilimanjaro will have no ice left.[63] In the hope of meeting these challenges, the Tanzanian government issued a water blueprint in 2002, promising to radically overhaul its priorities from a focus on resource development to resource conservation, protection, and management. Central to this shift in orientation was privatization of water utilities and sewage services.

Mediated by the World Bank and IMF structural adjustment program, presumably intended to promote public–private partnership in water resource management, the British water company, Biwater, and its German partner, Gauff Ingenieure, and the Dar es Salaam Water and Sewerage Authority entered into a ten-year joint venture to run the city's water and sewage services. The World Bank, the African Development Bank, and the European Investment Bank together supplied 86 percent of the $164 million initial capitalization. However, Tanzania terminated the contract in late May 2005, two years into its operation, and deported three British senior operators of the contract. Biwater then accused Tanzania of breach of contract and demanded restitution of its investment. In a rare moment, bureaucrats of the global financial institutions sided with Tanzania in citing the European partners in the contract of maladministration. Only one out of five of the total three million city dwellers had actually been connected to the water mains, and services had worsened since the public–private partnership contract had been in force.[64]

Tanzania's disenchantment with privatization appears to have compelled the government to look to Lake Victoria for more fresh water. The government has the intention of implementing the old colonial idea of drawing water from Lake Victoria to the interior of the country. The plan would entail the construction of a large canal leading all the way from the shores of Lake Victoria to the central plains of Tanzania to put 600,000 ha of arable land under irrigation at a cost of $6 billion.[65] As a significant prelude to realizing this vision, the government announced in 2004 its decision to construct a 170-km-long canal from Lake Victoria to supply one million people with water in the northwest of the country. When completed, this artificial channel being constructed at the cost of $178 million will supply water from Lake Victoria to households and herders in the drought-prone regions of northern Mwanza and Shinyang. In fact, this project is a small instalment of the country's ambitious long-term $27.6 billion national water resources development plan.[66]

It is an understatement to say that this plan has rung an alarm bell in Cairo. Egypt is more concerned about the precedent-setting implication of the project than about the quantity of water resources required under the plan, since the amount of water diverted will not be much at this point in time.[67] What makes Tanzania's decision to go ahead with the unilateral construction of the canal particularly interesting is that it occurred as the Nile states continue negotiations on how best to share the resources of the Nile. Tanzania had long made it clear that it did not recognize the 1929 Nile water agreement between Britain and Egypt. Pointing to Egypt's raised eyebrows, water resources Minister Lowassa didn't mince words in repudiating past colonial treaties. He rhetorically asked, "Can we deny our people the right to have water just to keep people happy abroad? . . . Will it be right for the people of Shinyanga to continue walking for over 25 km looking for waters when the Nile is just a step away?"[68]

Egypt has every reason to worry about Tanzania's move, since Kenya also has plans to use Victoria waters for irrigation. Furthermore, Tanzania seems to possess a large area of potentially irrigable land. Of the 94.3 million ha of tillable land in mainland Tanzania, only 5 million ha were under cultivation in the 1980s. By 1997, there were only 190,000 ha under irrigation in small holdings, dependent on "run-of-the-river" irrigation methods. According to the World Bank, Tanzania could potentially irrigate up to 850,000 ha.[69] There are certain objective factors that are likely, in the long run, to impel the government to proceed with large-scale irrigation schemes in order to bolster the country's food security.

The first factor involves the nature of Tanzania's agriculture. Not only does agriculture account for 50 percent of the country's GDP, but it also employs two-thirds of the economically able-bodied Tanzanians. In 1996, there were almost 3.9 million small landholders, the majority of them holding between 0.2 and 2 ha of highly fragmented cropland. Even a radical shift in Tanzanian economic orientation doesn't seem to have improved the country's food security. Almost two decades after liberalization, for example, growth in agriculture has remained sluggish. The country's tea production in year 2000 was the same as in 1995; outputs of coffee, cotton, rice, and maize were actually down. As a result, the country's maize deficit in 2000 was 680,000 tonnes. Second, the subsistence crops, such as cassava, plantain, maize, pulses, sorghum, and millet are highly vulnerable to drought.[70]

The World Bank and the IMF blamed the poor state of Tanzania's agriculture on the country's brand of Afrosocialism. In their view, the presence of the state in all sectors of the economy stifled price signals with the result of perpetuating agrarian fragmentation and stagnation. The evidence was the country's dependence on the international grain market to feed its people. Between 1972 and 1985, Tanzania's net average annual imports of maize and rice (the country's two staple crops) were 105,800 tonnes and 51,000 tonnes, respectively.[71] The prescription for the agrarian ills was the installation of a neoliberal market regime under which land accumulation could take place to achieve scale economies, increased yields, and high labor productivity. When Tanzania hesitated to swallow the bitter neoliberal pills, the World Bank slashed its aid disbursement from $97.9 million in 1982 to $28.5 million in 1985.[72] Under circumstances of no option, Tanzania fully embraced the neoliberal economic regime, decontrolling prices, slashing subsidies, and commodifying land holdings so that landholders could buy and sell land titles.

The results are disappointing, however. Labor productivity in the food production sector actually dropped in the post-reform era, as maize production in terms of per capita fell by 22.5 percent between 1985 and 1998. Likewise, per capita GDP in agriculture declined by 5.5 percent during the same period.[73] One of the dark sides of liberalization has been the corporate penetration of selective sectors of the economy at the expense of small producers. The tea sector exemplifies this paradox.

Tea growth began in Tanzania in 1902 on colonial estates. After independence, following nationalization of the tea plantations, Tanzania had encouraged small holders to engage in tea production. Consequently, by the early 1980s, small producers accounted for over a quarter of the total tea production. With the installation of the neoliberal regime, however, foreign capital flowed into the large estates, capturing majority shares of previously state-owned estates. The small producers were then pushed aside since they could not match the technological prowess and financial resources of multinational corporations.

Thanks to rationalization of production and the injection of fresh capital into the rehabilitation of the large tea estates, tea production rose from 20,000 tonnes in 1990 to 26,000 tonnes in the 2001–02 season, but only at the expense of small tea farmers. Many small producers were driven out of business. By 1998, small producers accounted for a mere 5 percent of the total tea production.[74] The dismal performance of Tanzania's agriculture under the neoliberal market regime thus belies the superiority of privatization to other forms of economic order. In fact, two fundamental structural factors accounted for the stagnation of Tanzania's economy in general, whether before or after liberalization.

The first factor involves the way the international division of labor is structured. Condemned by historical circumstances to specialize in the production of primary commodities, the international market severely handicapped Tanzania by depressing prices for primary commodities while at the same time pushing prices for finished goods upward. A study by Skarstein shows that during the period 1977–1985, Tanzania's terms of trade in primary commodities fell by 50.8 percent, and the general income terms of trade dropped by 64 percent.[75] Second, population growth in Tanzania appears not only to have outstripped growth in food production but also to have contextualized the further fragmentation of agrarian holdings. Since independence, the country's population growth (at over 3 percent per annum) has been among the highest in Africa. In a nutshell, the neoliberal prescription has failed to address the structural impediments to resolving the fundamental problems of Tanzania's underdevelopment.

Unable to feed its people, Tanzania invited the FAO/WFP mission in January 1999 to assess the country's food security situation. According to the FAO/WFP assessment, Tanzania's food deficit for 1999 was 909,000 tonnes, out of which 561,000 tonnes had to be imported. This was due to a 60 percent reduction in the Vuli maize harvest because of poor rain. It is useful to note that an FAO/WFP mission had (in August 1998) estimated the number of Tanzanians in need of food assistance to be 300,000; in light of the new reality, the mission revised the estimate for 1999 to one million in need.[76] To be sure, food insecurity has continued to bedevil Tanzania's effort to overcome its dependence on foreign food aid.

As in Kenya, Tanzania's nine river basins are under enormous stress and strain from competition among farmers, pastoralists, household consumers, fish harvesters, hydropower generators, and game reserves. The drive toward greater use in irrigation and hydropower generation for purposes of ensuring national food security and energy independence is further straining allocation of water resources.[77] Conflicts among various stakeholders over water allocations, especially in the Pangani and Rufiji River basins, are already rife. Since Tanzania produces 90 percent of its electricity by hydropower, mainly in the aforementioned basins, the rise in violence over water use has become of major concern to the government, which is particularly sensitive to the Pangani and Rufiji River basins since Tanzania historically depended on them for water resources and hydropower generation.

The two river basins cover an area of almost 220,000 sq km, where most of the country's water storage reservoirs are located. Not only are the water levels in the storage reservoirs dropping, but the increasing degradation of water quality in the basins is also of major concern. It is worth recalling that between 1986 and 1992, 38,600 Tanzanians were struck by a cholera epidemic; 4,344 died. In fact, waterborne diseases regularly account for more than half of the diseases that affect the country's population.[78] The lack of a coherent and integrative approach to the various components of national development has simply served to worsen the situation. For example, the government haplessly approved 2,300 ha in the Pangani River basin for rice cultivation as part of the Lower Moshi

Irrigation Scheme. However, none had anticipated the demonstration effect of the project; rice cultivation stimulated further expansion with 3,000 additional ha put under rice irrigation by abstracting water from existing use. The resulting water shortage led to widespread commotion and violence.[79] In response to the worsening situation, the government set up regional water offices in the Pangani and Rufiji River basins for purposes of mitigating water-related conflicts, regularizing water allocation, and monitoring the flow and quality of water resources.[80]

Tanzania's water resources are also threatened by massive deforestation. The country's endowment of endemic plant and tree species ranks Tanzania among the twenty-four most forest-rich countries in the world. It has 44 million ha under forest cover, constituting 45 percent of its total land area. But large sections of its moist rainforests in critical catchment areas are rapidly disappearing. The country is losing between 130,000 ha and 500,000 ha of forest cover annually. Illegal loggers alone destroy over 91,000 ha of forest cover per year; the forest products are exported to the advanced countries where they are processed for musical instruments, furniture, and perfume.[81] Forest destruction of this magnitude is likely to compromise the integrity of the precipitation regime as well as the availability of water resources. After all, as noted earlier, Mount Kilimanjaro has lost most of its glaciers since 1962 because of extensive deforestation.

Of the three east African states, Uganda represents a critical hydrological nexus in the Nile system. In addition to providing the bulk of Victoria waters, Uganda represents the choke point in the Nile River. The country is ideally situated to provide strategic locations for large storage facilities to smooth over the annual flow of the White Nile for the benefit of Egypt and the Sudan. It was with this strategy in mind that British empire builders conceived of the "century storage" plan. Although the plan never materialized, the idea nonetheless resulted in the construction of the Owen Falls Dam on the outlet of Lake Victoria, operational since 1954. This 762-m-long and 30-m-high dam was supposed to be the prototypical project for the century storage plan, supplying energy to Uganda while at the same time storing some 20 bcm of waters for Egypt and the Sudan. Today, the Owen Falls Dam generates 150 Mw of electricity for Uganda. Even though the dam does not have the storage capacity originally envisioned, Egypt and the Sudan enormously benefit from the dam since it helps to regulate the flow of the river. Moreover, in order to ensure that Uganda's use of Lake Victoria waters remains nonconsumptive, Egyptian engineers and hydrologists are permanently stationed at Jinja where the hydroelectric plant is located.

A new ambitious and yet controversial project is the Bujagali Dam. This hydroelectric plant, with 200 Mw (doubling Uganda's hydroelectricity generation capacity), is being built on the Nile River just 10 km from Lake Victoria in Uganda, with $550 million from the World Bank and other investors. When completed, the Bujagali Dam will be 750 m long, 30 m high, with 100 km of power transmission lines. The project is contentious on two grounds. First, the World Bank, by sponsoring the collection and disbursement of funds for the construction of the dam, is violating the central tenets of the World Commission on Dams report that calls for the full consultation of indigenous communities. After all, the dam will obliterate the Bujagali Falls, which has hitherto been regarded as a pristine national landmark. Second, the benefits to Ugandans at large are dubious, since only 3 percent of the country's population will actually be connected to the hydroelectric grid.[82] The World Bank, while admitting that the facility was environmentally bad, nonetheless justified it on the grounds that Uganda could receive $18 billion annually by exporting surplus energy to Kenya and Tanzania.

From the perspective of downstream users, Uganda could install hydropower stations without affecting the overall flow of the White Nile. After all, Uganda has been considered a water-abundant country in light of regular and heavy annual rains. However, the situation is changing. Uganda's population is rapidly rising and the country's subsistence agriculture is unable to provide needed food supplies. While agriculture's share of GDP is only 39 percent, the sector still employs 80 percent of Ugandans. Most of the country's 2.5 million subsistence farmers on average cultivate 2 ha of cropland per person. The country supplements its food stock with 220,000 annual fish catch.[83] In view of the growing population and degrading ecology, the prospects for further stimulation of food production under the prevailing primitive methods of traditional farming and maintenance of the current level of fish catch do not look rosy. Per capita food production has been declining steadily since the mid-1980s, resulting in a rural poverty rate of 75 percent in 1992.

The quantity of food that the country produced in 1993 was equal to the amount produced in 1985.[84] As a result, Uganda has become precariously dependent on foreign food aid. In 2004, the World Food Program distributed 115,000 tonnes of food to 2.8 million Ugandans. One veritable consequence of rural poverty is that people have begun descending upon the country's forest reserves, for both commercial logging and settlement. Mayuge National Park, for example, has already lost 76 percent of its area, and Mabira National Park (the biggest reserve system in the country) has lost 7,000 ha of its 29,570 ha in recent years. Moreover, following the drought that hit the country in late 2005, more than 180,000 displaced Ugandans invaded the forest reserves, rummaging the forests for food and water, rendering the forest agencies helpless to protect the reserves.[85] It thus stands to reason that the growing deterioration in ecosystem services, degradation of Uganda's lakes, and overexploitation of its fish stock are likely to add pressure to the effort to modernize the country's agriculture. A glance at the country's basket of exports shows that Uganda is not in a position to export manufactured goods to pay for food imports. In fact, coffee, tea, and fish products are the country's chief exports. This means that the country is likely to look to Lake Victoria to provide water for irrigation and hydropower generation.

The row among the three east African states in early 2006 over Uganda's withdrawals of water from Lake Victoria presages intensification of the hydrographic race in the Nile basin. Although climatic changes in the region and the decline in precipitation are partly responsible for the 2 m drop in Lake Victoria's water levels, Uganda is said to have contributed to this precipitous drop by taking 55 percent more water than its share from the lake.[86] In the face of acute water shortage in Kampala, Uganda's water corporation was spending $14 million in early 2006 to expand its supply capacity by producing 80,000 cu m of additional water daily for Kampala. This involved extending the pumping station by 2 km deep into Lake Victoria.[87]

The general discussion in this section illustrates that in order to shield themselves against the vagaries of nature and to enhance their relative food security and energy independence, all three east African states are about to follow the example of downstream users—namely, increasing reliance on their lakes and rivers to develop irrigation-based agriculture and hydro-based energy sources. Kenya, Tanzania, and Uganda together can potentially put 1 million ha of land under irrigation using Lake Victoria waters. Irrigation of this magnitude would require, and would thereby reduce the White Nile flow by, 10 bcm of water annually; Egypt and the Sudan would not view this favorably.[88]

A comprehensive review of the development orientation in the three east African states suggests that the focus of attention still remains on agriculture. This presupposes that the search for national food security and cash-generating crops is likely to intensify the quest for more water. In what appeared to be a demonstration of a commitment toward inter-state cooperation in this area, the finance ministers of Kenya, Tanzania, and Uganda read their 2005–2006 budgets on the same day (June 8). A cursory glance at all three budgets shows that agriculture is still considered the cash cow of development. In effect, this means modernization of agriculture, simultaneously embedded in irrigation works and aggregation of fragmented traditional farms.

Jointly reading budgetary figures from a podium as a show of solidarity is not a substitute for real consideration of other options, however. Three fundamental issues are glossed over by the finance ministers. First, since agriculture in all three countries still provides employment to more than 75 percent of their populations, a sheer focus on the sector will not solve the structural problem. Modernization and rationalization of agriculture actually involve removing a substantial number of those still engaged in farming from the sector and providing them with alternative opportunities for incomes in the nonfarm sectors. In light of the fact that unemployment rates in all three countries are already too high, shifting a large number of people from the agrarian world to the nonfarm sectors is a daunting challenge. It is instructive to note that 52 percent of Kenyans and 35 percent of Tanzanians and Ugandans are below the official poverty line.[89]

Urban dwellers, unable to find jobs or to index their incomes to rising inflation, are already putting the central governments under pressure. Kenya's health workers, for example, demanded a 600 percent pay raise to make a modest gain in their incomes; when the government refused to give in, they went on strike in early June 2005, paralyzing the country's health care system for six days. This happened at a time when the donor countries and the World Bank thought that Kenya's expenditure on its civil service population of 250,000 was already too large to be sustained for much longer.

The second danger inherent in the agrarian orientation is the growing desire to enclose more and more forest lands for commercial cultivation. Such a move will, in the long run, compromise watershed integrity and, by extension, the precipitation regime. In the view of ecologists, it is essential that at least 10 percent of the total land area in Kenya, for example, should remain under undisturbed forest cover to make the precipitation regime sustainable. Economically, too, commercial enclosure of forest land will be self-defeating. It is worth noting that ecotourism is a major source of foreign receipts for all three east African states. In Tanzania, for example, revenue from tourism steadily increased from $65 million in 1990 to $725 million in the 1998–1999 season; revenue from tourism now accounts for 40 percent of Tanzania's total foreign exchange earnings and provides employment to over 200,000 persons.[90] For its part, Kenya collected $540 million from foreign tourists in 2004.[91] At the risk of overstating the obvious, foreign tourists do not flock to east Africa to visit modern monuments, statues, or skyscrapers, but rather to seek the company of nature. If the countries fail in their stewardship of nature, they are bound to lose the enormous contribution that their fabulous ecological resources make to their collective economies. Contextualized by unprecedented drought and human and livestock overpopulation, the forest reserves in all three east African countries are currently under enormous threat from widespread degradation. In early 2006, for example, livestock animals and their owners invaded Kenya's Tsavo East National Park, which attracts over 150,000 visitors annually, generating employment for a large number of people and handsome incomes for the national park system. The human and livestock invasion of the park has pushed half of the 10,000 elephants off the Tsavo East National Park, causing them to search for forage and water elsewhere, killing and injuring people in the process.[92]

The third problem involves the continued reliance on foreign aid as a major source of development. The combined budgets of the three countries for 2005–2006 were less than $10 billion, over 40 percent of which was expected to flow from donor countries and international institutions.[93] If such aid is to continue, the countries must adhere to the fundamentals of neoliberal economics. In an ostensible effort to provide an investor-friendly environment, Kenya promised to review its regulations governing some 600 trade and investment licensing requirements.[94] The problem for both donors and recipients of aid is that a disease cannot be cured by simply increasing the dosage of the same bitter pill if the diagnosis is already faulty. Uganda offers an excellent illustration in this respect.

Museveni's Uganda had been the "darling" of the West since 1987 because of his embrace of neoliberal economics. Crafty that he was, Museveni quickly mastered the language of the new ideology, emphasizing the importance of privatization, deregulation, and the removal of barriers to free trade as the essential conditions for the flow of foreign dollars. Inspired by his rhetoric, donor countries and the global financial institutions sought to transform Uganda into a premier model for the rest of Africa. Between 1993 and 2003, they poured $11 billion into Uganda, regularly accounting for over 50 percent of the country's annual budget.[95] Since the supplied medicine failed to cure the illness, despite some seeming improvement in the country's economic health, the patrons began having second thoughts about the "darling baby."

In June 2005, Great Britain pulled back some $9 million already in the pipeline for Uganda; the United States, the Netherlands, and Ireland followed Britain's lead. The reason was simple: the "prodigal son" turned his back on democracy and left home again. Not only had between $100 and $175 million been disappearing from the budget into the wrong pockets each year, but Museveni also slipped back into his real self, practicing the familiar big-man politics. From the perspective of his international patrons, he had the audacity to tamper with the 1995 constitution that term-limited the tenure of the presidency; his amendments to the constitution allowed him to run for a third term and beyond.[96] Signs persently indicate that Uganda is drifting toward hard authoritarianism. For example, in order to preordain his election victory, Museveni ordered the arrest of his formidable challenger (Dr. Kizza Besigye) on trumped-up charges of treason, rape, terrorism, and possession of weapons. Although Besigye was released from prison and allowed to run for the presidency because of domestic and international pressure, the challenger was no match for Museveni's superior propaganda machinery and party organization. Museveni won the presidential election by almost 60 percent of the votes, although even the U.S. Department of State found the election to be marred by irregularities. The presidential brigade of praetorian guards, already 10,000 strong, is primarily tasked with protecting Museveni and ensuring regime survival.

A distillation of the analytical arguments advanced in this section suggests two essential points. First, the degree to which recent east African voices decry the inherently undemocratic nature of the present water regime is something that bears serious consideration. These voices do indeed echo the legitimate concern that colonial arrangements placed the east African countries under onerous obligation to conserve and nurture the watershed ecology and the hydrological determinants of the rift valley lakes, simply to safeguard the "acquired rights" of downstream users. "Acquired rights" are products of history, made at a particular time and under specific circumstances.

In this case, the east African states were colonies when Egypt and Britain agreed to negotiate away their natural rights, which neither Egypt nor Britain owned. The present reality is that these societies have now reclaimed their voices to represent their rights and interests, and their demand is not out of the ordinary. What the new voices are simply saying is that what history crafted unjustly ought to be undone. After all, history is a living force that surges forward through a wearisome process of negations and affirmations. Egypt can do right by the east African societies when it recognizes the detrimental impact of the colonial injustice that Egypt together with Britain visited upon them. It thus goes without saying that these voices ought to be heard. It is here when integrative discourse becomes a useful medium in resolving the dilemma involved in the hydrographic competition in the Nile basin. The east African states can only become active players in the preservation and protection of the watershed ecology and hydrology of the region when there is something in the effort for them. The alternative to the integrative approach to the general question of food security can be unilateral vandalization of ecological and water resources to the equal detriment of upstream and downstream users.

The second point meriting a focused attention is the issue of governance. A mere recognition of the existence of the identity of interests in the Nile basin is insufficient to build a self-sustaining water regime; nor is the piling up of quantitative studies and recommendations enough to produce a regional consensus on the sharing of Nile water resources. A meaningful integrative discourse cannot take place among kleptocrats in the context of a gross governance deficit. This observation applies to all ten Nile states in equal proportion. Only when the right political framework is put in place can actors freely, and meaningfully, negotiate the proper modalities of a just economic order, social equity, and ecological integrity.

Aquatic Resources and the Search for More Food Security

The future food security of the east African countries is inexorably bound up with how they sustainably use their lakes, and how they harness the waters of those lakes for irrigation and hydropower development, without risking open confrontation with downstream users. Indeed, the state of the east African rift valley lakes will provide either the permissive opportunities for inter-riparian cooperation to ensure the biological conservation of the lakes or the context for a race among riparian states for water resources. In short, the state of the lakes will be determinative of the sort of relationship that the east African states are bound to cultivate with Egypt and the Sudan and among themselves as well. For purposes of prefatory presentation, I will argue that the future state of the east African lakes will be integral to the effort to achieve food security as well as to the hydrographic relations between upstream and downstream users.

To make the point, suffice it to say that the bodies of freshwater cover 20 percent of Uganda's total surface area from which 350,000 directly employed and 1.2 million indirectly employed Ugandan fishermen produce an average of 220,000 tonnes of fish annually. Likewise, Kenyan and Tanzanian fishermen together produce approximately 350,000 tonnes of fish per year.[97] Whether these countries will be able to sustain such levels of fish harvest over time will shape the character of the food regime. Indeed, a 2002 research survey showed that the fish stock in Lake Victoria had already fallen by one-third due to a combination of the overfishing of undersized fish using illegal mesh net, the introduction of exotic species, and the discharge of municipal as well as industrial effluents into the lake.[98] The growing threat to the ecological health of the lake was such that the Swedish International Development Agency (SIDA) was prompted into action in 2002 to set up a Lake Victoria Directorate to manage a $100 million program to rehabilitate and protect the lake and its watershed area.[99]

In light of combined population growth and ecological degradation, it is safe to assume that the east African states are very likely to intensify their lake water uses for purposes of irrigation to bolster their food security. This section is intended to provide some suggestive insights as to the nature of future relations among the three east African states and their relations with downstream users.

The east African rift valley is home to a number of ecologically productive lakes, formed over a long geological time. Lake Tanganika, 677 km in length and with an average width of 50 km, is the longest lake in the world. With maximum depth of 1,470 m and mean depth of 572 m, it is the second deepest lake in the world, after Lake Baikal in Russia. It holds one-sixth of the world's available freshwaters. It is so deep that the retention year or residence time of water in the lake (the amount of time the original water stays in the reservoir before mixing or leaving the lake) is 5,500 years. The fact that the water remains in the reservoir for so long before it mixes or flashes out through evaporation makes the lake vulnerable to pollution and degradation. According to recent studies, Lake Tanganika has up to 1,500 species of fish, invertebrates, and plants, including:

    I.   350 fish species of which 200 are endemic haplochromine
         cichlid species
   II.   Another 67 species of fish of which 47 are endemic
  III.   60 aquatic snails of which 30 are endemic
   IV.   Seven endemic crabs
    V.   13 bivalve mollusks of which five are endemic
   VI.   33 copepod crustaceans of which 11 are endemic
  VII.   A large number of gastropod mollusks, half of which are
         endemic.[100]

Ten million people from Tanzania, Zambia, Burundi, and the DRC share the lake's resources for revenue, food, drinking water, and transportation. However, a combination of factors including climate change, overpopulation in its watershed area, overfishing, and growing economic and human activities in and around the lake are threatening its ecological integrity so much so that the UNDP is prompted into action to develop a rescue program at a cost of $10 million.[101] Whether such a small program will contain the level of degradation, limit human activities, and find sustainable alternatives for the people of the region remains to be seen.

One of the difficulties involved in the restoration effort is that global warming is a crucial factor exogenous to the lake region. According to a group of researchers, warming temperatures and reduced regional wind velocity appear to have contributed to the decrease in fish yields by 30 percent in Lake Tanganika in recent years, although the total annual catch is still estimated at between 165,000 and 200,000 tonnes.[102] Widespread deforestation in the littoral states and global warming have combined to reduce the water levels of Lake Tanganika. On the Burundi section of the lake, for example, a 1.5 m drop in the lake's levels has rendered 300 m of docking space unusable, forcing vessels to unload their contents far from the shores and then use small boats to carry the goods ashore. As a result, this landlocked country, which depends on Lake Tanganika for 90 percent of its exports and imports, finds its economy in serious jeopardy.

The crown jewel of the east African rift valley lakes in terms of productivity and ecological services is Lake Victoria. The annual fish catch in Lake Victoria ranges between 400,000 and 500,000 tonnes, generating some $3.4 billion in gross annual revenue.[103] While Tanzania controls 49 percent of the lake, Uganda's share is 45 percent and that of Kenya is only 6 percent. The size of Ireland with a surface area of 69,000 sq km, a shoreline of 3,500 km, and a watershed area of 284,000 sq km in five countries, it is the largest tropical lake and the second largest freshwater lake in the world. The lake holds approximately 2,760 bcm of water, or only 15 percent of the water stored in Lake Tanganika. Lake Victoria, with a maximum recorded depth of 84 m and mean depth of 40 m, is generally considered shallow in relation to other lakes.

The hydrological balance between precipitation and evaporation in the lake is relatively stable, as the lake receives 85 percent of its water directly from precipitation and loses 85 percent of its water to evaporation. The lake, however, supplements its storage capacity by 7 bcm from six Kenyan rivers and by another 7.9 bcm of additional water per year from the Kagera River, which rises in the highlands of Burundi and Rwanda. Although there is great controversy among hydrologists and geographers as to the actual source of the White Nile, it is in Lake Victoria where the White Nile begins its arduous journey to join the mighty Blue Nile in Khartoum. After settling accounts between precipitation and evaporation, the lake releases 15 percent of its water to flow under the name of the Victoria Nile in the direction of the Owen Falls, Lake Kyoga, and the Murchinson Falls, and then joins another outflow from Lake Albert, bearing the name of Albert Nile. The Victoria and the Albert Nile acquire the name of White Nile until the river adopts different names upon crossing into the Sudan.

The Lake Victoria ecosystem is biologically unique in many ways. Its highly convoluted 3,500-km-long shoreline is punctured by a series of quasi-autonomous shallow lakes, inlets, and bays, buffered with vast tapestries of swamps and wetlands, providing home to hundreds of endemic species. The relative geographic isolation of the lake over a long geologic time provided permissive opportunities for diverse biological species to establish themselves in the lake and its surroundings. The biological complexity of the lake is exemplified by the remarkable resilience and adaptability of the haplochromine cichlid species of fish. In the midst of complex evolutionary interactions and co-evolutionary relationships with other species in their physical and biological environment, the cichlids exhibit a rare propensity for extraordinary genetic transformation and propagation through rapid speciation. Before the introduction of invasive species into the lake, over 500 endemic haplochromine cichlids shared Lake Victoria with over fifty noncichlid species of fish, of which twenty-nine are endemic.[104]

However, the permissive environment of the lake and its basin for a vast array of economic activities, including human settlement, cultivation of maize, beans, sugarcane, tea, coffee, cotton, livestock production, fisheries, forest harvesting, and hydropower production, have raised human demands on the lake for energy, water for drinking and irrigation, shelter, transport, and biotic resources, threatening the lake's carrying capacity. The lake is also a major repository for the basin's industrial, agricultural, urban, and human waste. Thus, a sequence of human activities and events, such as the introduction of nonnative species, overexploitation of fish stocks, and the rapidity with which the eutrophication process is occurring, is alarming ecologists.

The introduction of invasive species of fish, particularly the Nile perch, appears to have compromised the integrity of the aquatic ecosystem. To make up for the dwindling commercial fish stocks in Lake Victoria, British colonial administrators drew up plans to introduce the Nile perch into Lake Victoria in the 1950s. When scientists vigorously questioned the wisdom of doing so, a British colonial officer was ordered to sneak out the Nile perch from Lake Albert into the Ugandan portion of Lake Victoria. In keeping with the law of natural selection, the Nile perch flexed its muscles to compete for space and food with the native species and radically altered the structure of the lake's food web. In due course, the population of this predatory fish exploded as cichlid populations declined by a factor of 10,000.[105] Prior to the introduction of the Nile perch, the endemic haplochromine cichlids accounted for anywhere between 80 percent and 99 percent of the biomass in Lake Victoria, whereas by the early 1980s the Nile perch contributed over 80 percent of the biomass in the lake.[106]

The immediate casualties are the native species of some 500 cichlids on which the Nile perch thrived as a major source of food. In a matter of two decades, 200 of the 500 haplochromine cichlid species became extinct, an episode of mass extinction rarely paralleled in history. The populations of the remaining cichlid species have also dramatically declined; at this rate, ecologists believe that no cichlid species will be left in Lake Victoria sixty years hence.[107]

The deoxygenation of the deep portions of the lake associated with the growing eutrophication of Lake Victoria seems to have given the perch an added advantage over the native cichlids because the Nile perch is known to function well in dim light compared to cichlids. With relatively low vision, the cichlids cannot maneuver well in dim light and thus become an ever-present prey for the predatory perch. For example, researchers discovered that there were up to six cichlid species per genus in portions of the lake where the water was transparent, compared to only one cichlid species in parts of the lake characterized by high turbidity.[108] To be sure, the growing human population in the Lake Victoria basin, overfishing with fine mesh nets, Nile perch predation, habitat destruction, fluctuations in lake levels, and the high turbidity and anoxic conditions in the lake have decimated the native fish species.

Paradoxically, the enormous loss of biodiversity in the lake notwithstanding, fish landings increased fivefold after the introduction of nonnative species. In the late 1970s, the annual fish harvest was around 100,000 tonnes per annum, which rose to 561,000 tonnes by 1990. In the Kenyan section of the lake alone, the fish harvest rose from 25,000 tonnes in 1978 to 175,000 tonnes in 1990.[109] Today, commercial fishing in Lake Victoria is dominated by three fish species: the Nile perch, the Nile tilapia (also nonnative), and the dagaa. Whereas, in 1978, the Nile perch represented only 5 percent of the commercial catch, by 1990, it accounted for 60 percent of the total; the tilapia and dagaa or omena shared most of the remaining 40 percent between them.[110]

In monetary terms, the Nile perch brings in over $250 million in foreign exchange earnings annually to the three east African states.[111] Because the Nile perch is huge, the fish yields in Lake Victoria increased fourfold during the last two decades of the twentieth century, leading to the popularity of gill net fishing for the Nile perch and the tilapia as well as to the proliferation of fish landings and fish processing facilities on the entire shore of the lake; by 2000, there were thirty-four fish processing industries in all three zones of the fishing regime.[112]

One of the paradoxes of the popularity and productivity of the predator perch has been the integration of Lake Victoria into Western fish markets. The promise of gains from international fish exports has not only drawn a large number of fishermen but also led to the modernization of fishing gears, often to the detriment of the traditional artisanal fishing regime on which the livelihoods of millions of people depended for centuries. This in turn has led to the fear that the propagation of gill net meshes and beach seines, along with the modernization of the fishing regime characterized by open access without transparent regulation, might lead to the collapse of the aquatic ecology.[113] This fear is exemplified by the very fact that the Nile perch itself is losing ground to over-exploitation. The gap between labor investment and productivity is widening. By some estimates, 70 percent of Nile perch currently caught are immature. This is not only the result of the growing international market for the perch, but also in part due to local demand for smaller fish, including juvenile Nile perch, since low-income people could not afford to pay for big Nile perch.[114] Moreover, because of the radical alteration of the trophic state of the lake, intraspecific competition has intensified as larger perches are eating smaller ones of their own kinds.[115]

The present state of the fishing regime in the lake, yielding 500,000 metric tonnes per annum, only suggests that the sustainability of fisheries in the lake has come under serious jeopardy. In 1990, Uganda alone harvested 132,400 tonnes of fish from the lake, which declined to 106,000 tonnes in 1995.[116] Yet Uganda is still planning to generate $1 billion from fish exports over the next decade; to ensure that this target is achieved, the government ordered six speed patrol boats to monitor fish production and export. The other riparian states have similar plans. To maximize gains from fish exports, Tanzania announced in early January 2005 that it was using three modern speedboats to patrol its lake waters against illegal fishing and smuggling. The speedboats would be aided by newly acquired surveillance planes. According to reports, 36,000 tonnes of Tanzania's 175,000 tonnes of fish are smuggled out of the country annually. Since 70 percent of the Tanzanian catch consists of the highly priced Nile perch, smuggling of this magnitude has proven problematic for many of the country's fish processing plants, and the 550,000 Tanzanians who are directly or indirectly dependent on the fishing sector face grim uncertainty.[117]

The race to exploit aquatic resources in Lake Victoria is causing alarm regionally and internationally. A research group carried out a survey between 2000 and 2004 to assess the state of the fishing regime. The group discovered that the reason for the dwindling of fish in the lake was the growing number of fish harvesters. According to the survey, the number of fish harvesters in Lake Victoria rose from 129,305 in 2000 to 175,890 in 2004, and the number of fishing vessels rose from 42,483 to 52,479 while gill nets increased from 655,053 to 984,084 over the same period.[118] Meanwhile, illegal beach seines on the lake and gill nets of different mesh sizes have been increasing at alarming rate.

The impact of the invasive perch is not limited to the fate of the cichlids. It has had profound implications for the local economy, the way people have come to lead their lives, and the aquatic ecology of Lake Victoria. Because cichlids naturally feed on algae, their disappearance means blue-green algae bloom. When the algae die, the dead organic matter falls to the bottom of the lake, magnifying the eutrophication process. By the same token, because an adult Nile perch measures over two m long and weighs between 100 and 200 kg, the fishermen could no longer use sun to dry the fish as they did with the cichlids. They began to smoke or refrigerate the perch in order to preserve it, which is expensive compared to free solar energy.

A resort to smoking as a preservation method entailed cutting the woods in the area for firewood. Thus, a combination of natural processes and cultural eutrophication, reinforced by a sequence of human activities throughout the basin associated with removal of riparian vegetation, deforestation, soil erosion, drainage of wetlands for agriculture and fish landings, agricultural runoff, industrial waste, and urban sewage, have profoundly affected the integrity of the aquatic ecology. In addition, 33 million people of the 90 million combined populations of Kenya, Tanzania, and Uganda are in the Lake Victoria basin, turning over $5 billion in gross annual output, thereby substantially modifying or altering the physical character and biotic morphology of the environment. In the context of the growing population in the area, a large number of industrial plants and food processing-related facilities are also springing up in the area, all dependent on the lake for energy, commercial navigation, supply of water, and drainage; they will likely follow the example of Uganda's largest beer brewery, which has been dumping its effluents and untreated sludge into Lake Victoria for the past fifty years.

Ntiba notes that major point and nonpoint sources of pollution and contamination (which magnify the problem of external overloading of inputs) are proliferating throughout the basin. These industrial establishments include breweries, sugar factories, coffee and tea processing facilities, fish processing plants, tanneries, soft drinks and food processing plants, livestock operations, soap making or oil processing mills, and abattoirs that discharge with impunity their waste untreated into streams, rivers, and lakes.[119] Metallic contamination is another growing problem associated with the establishment of industrial facilities. Researchers have identified mercury pollution as a major source of potential health problems in Lake Victoria.[120] Mercury-laden effluents pouring into the lake from old and new gold mines are of major concern.

Burning of biomass is also considered a source of mercury since plants naturally absorb mercury from the soil as a mineral nutrient. During burning of the biomass, through forest fires or shrub fires, the mercury is released into the air and soil in the lake's watershed area and, during precipitation, enters and pollutes the lake. Unlike terrestrial ecosystems that drain excess inputs by water movements, lakes are particularly susceptible to external loading of inputs from streams and rivers. Over time, because of the complex processes of bioaccumulation and biomagnification, the levels of metallic substances and trace elements in the lake become such that the fish bioconcentrate them, in the process becoming contaminated and affecting the health of those who depend on them as a protein source. Although they have not yet reached levels high enough to cause an immediate health concern, traces of such metals as lead and chromium are steadily accumulating in the lake.[121]

Thermal stratification is another emerging problem in Lake Victoria. Because of the relative constancy in the annual average temperature and solar radiation in the tropics, as well as the rapid nutrient regeneration and relatively uniform distribution of nutrients in tropical lakes, limnologists have historically regarded lakes in tropical zones as less vulnerable to stratification. Lake Victoria has been no exception. In light of the effective penetration of solar radiation in combination with the wind-induced mixing of Lake Victoria's waters, the waters in its bottom portions used to be well aerated and well oxygenated year-round, making all portions of the lake productively livable for all species. This positive reality appears to have been a major factor in the ability of the haplochromine cichlids to comfortably segregate themselves into different groups, a condition that allowed them to undergo an extraordinary speciation and genetic transformation in relative isolation. Not anymore; the waters of the lake do not mix well and the bottom waters remain anoxic year-round. In order to fully capture the enormity of the problem associated with eutrophication, having long-range implications for the quantity and quality of water, food security, and public health in Lake Victoria's basin, a brief discussion on the general limnological conditions that lead to the problem of stratification seems warranted here.[122]

Naturally, solar radiation always warms the surface of a lake long before penetration of its deeper portions. This creates temperature differentials between the various layers of the lake. In a naturally undisturbed and unstratified lake, the differential input of sunlight in time would not affect the limnological conditions since the regular vertical mixing of top and bottom layers of the water will equalize the temperature and circulate oxygen and other nutrients in the lake. Since sedimentation of organic matter and nutrient regeneration generally take place at the bottom of the lake, vertical mixing of water is critical to internal loading, which acts as a regulator and distributor of essential nutrients by causing the resuspension of nutrient-rich sediments and transporting oxygen from the surface to the bottom of the lake.

In a stratified lake, an intermediate zone known as thermocline is created between the surface water, or epilimnion, and the bottom layer, or hypolimnion. Once formed, the thermocline works to block the mixing of the oxygen-rich surface water with the sediment-rich water of the hypolimnion; because the water column in the thermocline zone is colder and denser than the water above it, the surface water simply floats without mixing. This phenomenon creates two important conditions. First, the epilimnion becomes well aerated, warm, and less dense; as a result, primary production associated with photosynthesis takes place here. Second, because the warm and less dense surface water is easily moved horizontally by wind currents, the condition for upwelling or upward movement of water from the hypolimnion, usually anoxic, is created and anoxic water takes the place of the surface water temporarily moved by wind. Since biological energy transformations in aquatic systems occur as a result of the chemistry, composition, quantity, and cycling of elements, the segmentation of lakes for a long period of time is bound to have serious consequences for the aquatic ecology.

In order to extract energy from carbohydrates in the aquatic environ, microbes or bacteria in deeper layers of lakes use oxygen heavily. The resulting respiration process produces excess carbon dioxide. Microbial respiration during the decomposition of organic matter then creates anoxic conditions in deep aquatic zones. Photosynthesis (which relies on sunlight and carbon dioxide as energy sources) and respiration (which depends on oxygen as a source of energy) stand in opposition. In a stratified lake, photosynthesis takes place almost exclusively on the surface of the lake where sunlight is plentiful. In contrast, since sunlight cannot penetrate the thermocline and, by extension, the hypolimnion of the lake, photosynthesis cannot occur in the hypolimnion in the absence of solar energy. The veritable result is that dissolved oxygen is either sharply limited or depleted by microbial action and decomposition, accentuating the process of respiration and creating anoxic conditions that are harmful to aquatic animals.

The phenomenon of stratification as a function of eutrophication threatens Lake Victoria today. Kaufman notes that the alarming long-term consequence of the human-induced process of eutrophication is the stratification of Lake Victoria, associated with the destruction of littoral vegetation, conversion of forests for agriculture and human habitation, poor land use, mining, pollution, and overfishing of the native haplochromine cichlids.[123] The limnological conditions in Lake Victoria and its satellite lakes are increasingly characterized by high turbidity and fundamental alteration in the water column structure, significant reduction in oxygen levels and water clarity, high phytoplankton productivity, increased accumulation of plant litter, and explosion of microphytes and toxic blue-green algae. For example, the Secchi transparency index, which measures algal abundance from a distance, has dropped from 5 m in the early 1930s to less than 1 m in the 1990s.[124] Algal blooms have increased by a factor of ten in the past decade or so, in part owing to the depopulation of the cichlids that fed on algae and partly due to a marked rise in phosphorus concentrations in the deeper portions of the lake, along with nitrogen accumulation on its littoral edges.

It is here where the critical importance of cichlids looms large. In addition to providing livelihoods to traditional fishing communities, haplochromine cichlids perform crucial biological services in removing nutrient or biomass overloads during their lateral and vertical migrations, thereby assisting wind circulation in mixing the lake's waters. Moreover, cichlids remove large quantities of algae through consumption and have a unique biological capacity for decelerating the accumulation and rotting of nutrients in the deeper portions of the lake.[125] Thus, the collapse of the haplochromine cichlid species means blue-green algal bloom, accompanied by the accumulation of biomass and organic matter that sink to the bottom of the lake, accentuating the thermal stratification of the lake and creating anoxic conditions. Fish species intolerant of eutrophic conditions naturally face the Hobbesian choice between making a vertical descent into the deeper portions of the lake, escaping predation by the Nile perch but risking asphyxiation under hypoxic conditions, or moving to shallow waters in search of nutrition and oxygen but at the risk of becoming prey to the Nile perch. In either case, the result is mass extinction.

In the absence of the crucial biological services of the cichlids coupled with the continual additions of nutrient inputs from agricultural and urban sources, Lake Victoria's water transparency has steadily decreased. So long as the accumulation and sedimentation of dead organic matter continues unabated in the lower reaches of Lake Victoria, thermal stratification for most of the year is unavoidable. Even in the thermocline zone (the region between 25 and 50 m in depth) in the case of Lake Victoria, deoxygenation is proving to be problematic.[126] This means that so long as water mixing through wind circulation cannot occur, then exchanges of nutrients, including oxygen, between the epilimnion and the hypolimnion of the lake will be permanently inhibited. Because the bottom portions of the lake are becoming increasingly anoxic, the prospect for sustainable fish harvest will diminish, threatening the two million people who directly depend on Lake Victoria's fisheries.

Researchers have observed massive fish kills as a result of periodic upwelling, which is the upward movement of hypoxic water; because of the deoxygenation of the deep portions of the lake, upwelling of hypoxic water has become a serious threat even to fisheries in shallower portions of the lake.[127] In sum, unless the factors that lead to the depletion of dissolved oxygen available for living organisms are somehow contained, and the natural oxic conditions are restored, the growing stratification of Lake Victoria will certainly make it biologically less productive and it will lose its biodiversity completely.

As of this writing, the prospects for reversing the eutrophication process in Lake Victoria do not inspire optimism. Weak environmental regulations, designed to influence the migration of dirty factories from the global north to the region, and the increasing reliance on chemical fertilizers are likely to compound the problem by causing external loading of nitrogen and phosphorus, which encourage blue-green algal blooms. The potential loading of nitrogen and phosphorus is proportional to the acceleration of their use by humans for a variety of purposes. One source of the problem involves the modernization of agriculture and increased dependency on fertilizers. Since nitrogen is not biologically available, it has to be fixed or bonded with carbon, oxygen, and hydrogen to be usable. Humans play a significant role in the fixation process. Industrial fixation in the form of fertilizers, biological fixation by plants, and circulation of previously fixed nitrogen via precipitation and dry deposition are the major vehicles by which nitrogen becomes an active component of the general nutrient cycling process. Estimates of nitrogen loading due to anthropogenic agency are in the range of 50 percent, causing significant damage to rivers and lakes. If the east African states continue to cling to the Western model of modernization (increasing dependence on nitrogen fertilizers and manufacturing plants), they are likely to increase the nitrogen loading of Lake Victoria and its feeding rivers.

It is instructive to note that Europe and North America are responsible for 70 percent of the total pollutional nitrogen input into the waters of the world's rivers.[128] The role humans play in influencing phosphorus cycling is no different from the one they play in the overproduction of nitrogen. Through deforestation, removal of riparian vegetation and the consequent erosion, the use of phosphorus fertilizers and detergents, and the dumping of industrial waste and municipal sewage, humans greatly influence the productivity of algae. In Europe, 70 percent of phosphorus pollution in rivers and lakes is due to municipal sewage. It is reported that the phosphorus concentration levels in many North American rivers are ten times greater than the natural concentration levels.[129]

Water hyacinth is another invasive plant species introduced into the lake region from Rwanda, floating on the Kagera River. Although native to South America, this attractive plant showed up in Lake Kyoga in 1988 and made its way into Lake Victoria in due time. By 1995, green carpets of the plant blanketed an area of 12,000 ha, infesting 90 percent of Uganda's 300-km-long shoreline, which is shallow with a muddy bottom and therefore suitable for hyacinth growth. The ecologically delicate bays and inlets of the lake are now choking from thick masses of hyacinth, destroying the natural habitats of many species. Mats of water hyacinth, sometimes reaching up to 1,000 ha in size, began floating between the Ugandan and Kenyan sectors of the lake, threatening the destruction of the aquatic ecology. Hyacinth is so resilient that it can double its coverage area in a few days and can stay dormant for fifteen to twenty years.

In the mid-1990s, it blocked commercial navigation, disrupted fishing operation by tangling nets, reduced the water supply and quality, began to destroy fisheries by deoxygenating water and exhausting nutrients in the bays and inlets of the lake that fish use as breeding ground and nursery, threatened Uganda's principal hydroelectric facility at Owen Falls by interfering with running turbines, and provided a comfortable habitat for snakes and an ideal breeding ground for disease vectors such as malaria-carrying mosquitoes and schistoma-hosting snails. The hyacinth scourge became so alarming that the World Bank provided funding and expertise and, in a rare demonstration of solidarity, even Egypt got involved in the containment effort.

In 1999, Uganda and Egypt signed a cooperative relationship to fight the hyacinth by establishing forty landing sites and clearing waterways. Under the Ugandan-Egyptian collaborative effort, over 70,000 tonnes of hyacinth were mechanically removed.[130] Regular application of herbicides to the lake was considered and then ruled out because of the potentially harmful effects on human and environmental health associated with the likely accumulation of dead hyacinth in the lake.[131] Then mechanical control was tried, which proved laboriously time-consuming, expensive, and ineffective. Every time an area was mechanically cleared of the hyacinth, it returned promptly to the same area. Eventually, bioremediation was tried and seems to be working. As of this writing, 90 percent of the hyacinth was destroyed using two types of weevils, imported from Benin. Since the weevil program started, some six billion weevils have been released to fight the hyacinth.[132] The weevils proved to have voracious appetites for the nasty plant. The war on the plant is by no means over, however, since the remaining 10 percent has now provided the basis for resurgence. Indeed, by the end of 2006, the water hyacinth was back in full swing, prompting Egypt and Uganda to extend the Aquatic Weed Project until 2009 with Egypt providing $5 million to fund the effort; Egypt had committed $13.5 million to the project since 1999.[133]

The problems of water degradation, pollution, and contamination and the deterioration of aquatic ecosystems are not confined to Lake Victoria; all rift valley lakes are experiencing similar conditions. Lake Nakuru, one of Kenya's centers of ecotourism and a favorite destination for migratory birds, has undergone major changes in recent years. The lake is known for its pretty pink flamingos, two million of which take over the entire lake, swimming on the lake's waters with spectacular orderliness to consume its rich supply of algae, crustaceans, mollusks, and aquatic plants. However, workers from Kenya's Wildlife Service have spent the last decade doing daily removal of hundreds of dead flamingos from Lakes Nakuru and Bogoria. Ornithologists estimate that several million flamingos live in or visit the east African rift valley lakes, where over 30,000 died annually during the 1990s.[134] Many suspect that heavy-metals contamination of the alkaline lakes is responsible for the birds' deaths.

The town of Nakuru has been undergoing rapid changes for quite some time, both in terms of demographics and economics. The town's population grew from just 30,000 some forty years ago to 360,000 in the mid-1990s. By the mid-1990s, the town had twenty-five major industrial plants, ranging from bottling companies to textile manufacturing plants, all of which dump discharges directly into the lake.[135] Examination of tissue from the algae-consuming flamingos showed the presence of nine metallic substances, including mercury, copper, zinc, chromium, arsenic, lead, cadmium, selenium, and iron. Residues of organic chlorides, DDT, and other pesticides were also found in the lake. Because the lake is a closed system, every metallic or toxic substance deposited remains there indefinitely. In addition, the groundwater flowing into the lake is being depleted, perhaps a major reason for the shrinking of the lake's size.

Lake Turkana is also threatened with desiccation. Lying in the northern section of the rift valley on the Kenya–Ethiopia border, 240 km long and 40 km wide with an average depth of 35 m and covering 70,500 sq km, Lake Turkana is the largest of its kind in the world. When the lake's surface water was 80 m higher than its present level, Lake Turkana was linked to the White Nile via several natural channels. Today, the lake has no outlet except through evaporation, a major cause of its shrinkage. Moreover, receiving 80 percent of its waters from the Omo River in Ethiopia, the lake was once freshwater; today, its waters are hardly potable because of exceptionally high levels of alkalinity.[136] Between 1973 and 1989 alone, the lake's delta expanded by 380 sq km as its water level dropped. The growing shrinkage of Lake Turkana is due partly to recurrent drought and evaporation, and partly to water diversion from three smaller rivers to irrigation schemes.[137]

Another body of water threatened by pollution and contamination from the extractive sector is Lake George in western Uganda, which is linked to Lake Edward in the rift valley via a 30-km-long channel. Until some two decades ago, a mining company operated a copper mining and processing plant in the watershed of the lake. Years after the company left the area, metal-rich soils continue to wash into the lake and its wetlands. Covering an area of 500 sq km, Lake George and its wetlands are biologically rich, hosting fifty-seven species of fish.[138]

Another little known treasure of biodiversity facing utter desiccation is Lake Jipe on the border between Tanzania and Kenya, sandwiched between Mount Kilimanjaro and the Pare Mountains. This 12-km-long body of water provided important food and freshwater to thriving riparian communities in the area for centuries. In recent years, over 120,000 people have depended on Lake Jipe and its environs for their livelihoods, combining fishing with farming and animal husbandry. In addition to the livelihoods it provided to the indigenous communities, the lake offers natural habitats for countless animal species, including prolific varieties of fish, hippos, crocodiles, pigmy geese, waterbucks, amphibians, reptiles, the lesser jacana, the purple gallinule, and other waterbirds. Lake Jipe is actually the only habitat in the world for the endemic tilapia, known as Oreochromis Jipe; this unique fish now on the brink of extinction.

Due to harmful anthropogenic causes, such as increased turbidity and alkalinity of the lake, growing siltation of feeder rivers, and reduced lake runoff, the near collapse of Lake Jipe is threatening the livelihoods of humans and the existence of animal species. In the last ten years, Lake Jipe has lost 50 percent of its water mass, and its water storage capacity declined from 60 mcm to 20 mcm during the same period as over half of the lake's area was overtaken by invasive waterweeds. At the current rates of siltation of the lake's feeder rivers and its wetlands as well as the degradation of its catchment area, this important body of water may not exist ten years hence.[139]

The immediate ecology of Lake Jipe, the Lumi River, rising in Mount Kilimanjaro, and the Mbaro River, which flows from the North Pare Mountains, have all succumbed to the combined weight of increasing human numbers, expanding cultivation, extensive deforestation, and growing livestock population. Moreover, the diversion of 450,000 cm of freshwater per day from the Lumi River into the Ruvu River, which is the outlet for Lake Jipe, in order to promote irrigation-based farming in Tanzania, has eroded the hydrological foundation of the lake. As a result, Lake Jipe has become increasingly alkaline, forcing freshwater species to migrate or become extinct and humans to travel further in search of fresh drinking water.

The indigenous communities have (in the past few years) been either following the receding lake to drain its wetlands for farming or abandoning the area altogether. At the time of this writing, the governments of Tanzania and Kenya, with the help of donor countries, are tentatively moving to save Lake Jipe from complete desiccation through such activities as desilting the watercourse of the Lumi River, removing water obstruction canals, rehabilitating existing water schemes to provide drinking water to the local communities, increasing the flow of freshwater into the lake, strengthening the banks of the rivers, and promoting afforestation programs in the lake's watershed area. In 2004, the European Union and the UNDP joined forces to inject $416,000 into the effort to salvage Lake Jipe, while the government of Tanzania adopted a three-year awareness raising and restoration program to give momentum to the effort.[140] Whether these efforts will halt the disintegration of Lake Jipe's ecology and preempt the death of the lake itself is uncertain.

The Puzzle

This chapter has shown that the three east African states have to meet a number of hydrological, environmental, political, economic, and social challenges to improve the prospects for internal progress, regional stability, and environmental sustainability. If they can put in place the right institutional, economic, and legislative frameworks, they seem to have sufficient water resources. However, two questions must be raised to appreciate the enormity of the challenges facing the east African states. First, do these states have the political will, institutional capacity, legislative framework, programmatic vision, and adequate resources to conserve and sustainably use their water resources and biotic riches? Second, to what extent can the east African states offer their citizens alternative opportunities in the nonfarm sectors?

On the surface, the first question appears to be answered positively by the cooperative agreement reached by the governments of Kenya, Tanzania, and Uganda in 1994 to form the Lake Victoria Environmental Management Project (LVEMP). With the assistance of the FAO, the three littoral states drafted a comprehensive program to promote the conservation, restoration, and protection of Lake Victoria and its environs. To effectuate the program's vision, the Global Environment Facility (GEF) led an effort to collect $70 million from international donors, and the east African states themselves supplied another $7.8 million for the execution of the first phase of LVEMP, which began in 1996.[141] The catalog of steps and tasks planned under the LVEMP include control of such heavy-metal concentrations as chromium, mercury, and lead in the lake; promotion of sustainable fisheries; conservation of the lake's biodiversity and genetic resources; regeneration of the lake's trophic state; protection of wetlands; promotion of sustainable agriculture in the lake's catchment area; monitoring of water quality; control of the spread of water hyacinth; provision to riparian communities of a disease-free environment, safe drinking water, employment, and predictable incomes; and harmonization of national environmental programs to reverse ecological degradation.[142]

The three countries have also created the Lake Victoria Fisheries Organization (LVFO) to strengthen the fishing regime within the context of broader regional environmental orientation. To demonstrate the apparent seriousness of the matter, and to make prominent the LVFO, the governments of the three countries agreed to establish a Council of Ministers composed of senior officials responsible for fisheries as the highest organ of the new fishing regime. The council will be assisted by a permanent secretariat in carrying out the daily affairs of the fishing regime. The latter, in turn, will be aided by a number of scientific, executive, and administrative committees made up of senior persons with expertise in such matters as biology, finances, fishing technology, fish harvesting, and fish processing technology. The new fishing regime would promote better and sustainable fishery as part of the overall effort to promote biodiversity conservation, control of nonnative species, ecological efficiency, and ecological balance.[143] The regional efforts subsumed under the LVEMP and the LVFO will be further supported by specific projects undertaken in each country.

The World Bank's International Development Association (IDA) agreed in 1998 to supply $75 million for Kenya and $80 million for Uganda to provide for safe drinking water supply and sanitation in Lake Victoria's basin. In addition, the World Bank was positively considering giving Kenya another $55 million to promote soil conservation.[144] On paper, the governments of the three countries and their international sponsors have reached a global consensus that the various disturbance regimes throughout the catchment area of the lake, such as habitat destruction, deforestation, damage to wetlands, land degradation, and water pollution, could resolve themselves only in the context of broader harmonization of national programs, comprehensive cooperation among all stakeholders, and regional integration.[145] All told, under the envisioned integrated management system (supplied by both the LVEMP and the LVFO), the grassy wetlands and papyrus swamps of the lakes will be protected from human activities, such as those that cause deforestation, soil erosion, agricultural runoff, and urban effluents. Human population movements around the lakes will be monitored to reduce the impact of deforestation, land degradation, and deterioration of water quality. Additionally, farmers will be assisted in promoting sustainable farming consistent with the caring capacity of the catchment area. The lake and its watershed will be cleaned up of industrial, urban, and human waste.

Evaluating the feasibility of both the LVEMP and the LVFO is difficult for a number of reasons. First, there are positive normative sides. The extent to which both programs have holistic orientation is inspiring. The recognition given by the framers of the programs to the interdependence of the lakes, the biotic resources in them, and the living ecology of the catchment area is a very progressive step forward. Second, the regional approach embedded in the agreements, emphasizing the indispensability of comprehensive coordination of efforts and of regional integration, is equally laudable. Third, the framers of the programs have done a very good job in identifying the problems and proposing the steps needed to resolve those problems.

The great puzzle that remains untouched is whether such ambitious projects can be achieved within the prevailing ideology of neoliberalism and existing political structures. The major flaw of the programs lies in the mismatch between the broadly outlined steps that must be taken and the resources needed to realize the vision of the programs. As drawn by the planners, potential realization of the various components of both the LVEMP and the LVFO would require billions of dollars in investment. A few millions here and there will not enable the stakeholders to make the ecological and fishing regimes sustainable. Because local, national, and regional agencies and stakeholders expect resources to flow from without, attainment of the target goals of the programs is likely to be illusory. Note that the annual per capita incomes of the thirty-three million people who live in Lake Victoria's basin range between $90 and $270.[146] Raising the incomes of the people already living in the basin as well as accommodating additional newcomers to the basin will require lots of investment.

Second, the integration of Lake Victoria into global markets, which may appear beneficial to the local and national economies in terms of short-run generation of foreign exchange earnings, is likely to have long-range dislocating effects on inhabitants. Foreign firms are already surveying the fish resources of the lake with covetous eyes. Three firms from France, Belgium, and Spain have been vying for access to Kenyan waters of the lake. The French firm reportedly offered Sh 2.4 billion to introduce cage fishing into Lake Victoria. For its part, the Belgian firm sought to build a modern fish processing factory at a cost of Sh 1 billion on the condition that it would have a five-year monopoly right to export Kenya's fish and fish products.[147]

The most aggressive firm to date has been Redicon International, a South African company. In an apparent effort to create the political conditions for a takeover, an official from Redicon International reportedly treated a number of Kenyan parliamentarians to a sumptuous luncheon in Nairobi in early January 2005. The company had been (for quite some time) trying to penetrate the fishing sector in Lake Victoria. The company offered Sh 1 billion in investment in Kenyan fishing waters in exchange for the exclusive rights to harvest fish in Kenyan waters for ten years. Under this proposal, only twenty-six of the 304 landing beaches on the lake's shoreline would remain operational and the rest would be closed to fish harvesters, meaning that the 37,348 artisanal fishermen (operating 12,248 fishing vessels and catching over 105,000 tonnes of fish annually) would be out of business at a stroke of a pen. To prevent what the company considered illegal artisanal fishing, and to ensure monopoly harvesting by the firm, the landing beaches and the lake's shoreline would be policed by patrol boats and surveillance aircrafts. Moreover, all fish caught in the Kenyan portion of the lake would be auctioned at cold storage centers owned and operated by Redicon International.[148]

These moves by European and South African companies have raised many eyebrows locally and regionally. Despite stern police denunciation and warning, thousands of Kenyan traditional fishermen vowed to continue with planned demonstrations in mid-January 2005, accusing politicians of gambling with their livelihoods by planning to lease the Kenyan section of the lake to a foreign firm for ten years in exclusive fishing rights. In challenging the police warning, a spokesman for the fishermen daringly declared, "We do not care about threats from police because this is a matter of life and death. We want to be told exactly what the government thinks about the lake which is the lifeline of the Nyanza people."[149] The Kenyan fishermen were not alone in challenging what amounted to the corporatization of the fishing regime. Official and nonofficial voices in Tanzania and Uganda questioned Kenya's right to unilaterally contract with foreign entities for any project prior to consultation with the other littoral states. The dissident voices contended that, since Lake Victoria is a shared resource, no single country could willy-nilly privatize its portion of the lake.[150] After all, in 2004, Tanzania and Uganda together had over 91,000 fishermen operating 30,000 fishing boats on Lake Victoria.[151]

In light of local and regional opposition, the Kenyan government is embarrassingly compelled to distance itself from the idea of leasing its portion of the lake, at least for now. Yet, sooner or later, not only Kenya but also the other littoral states are likely to succumb to international finance capital in the name of modernization requirements of the fishing sector. To put it bluntly, the three east African states are likely to continue ransacking their ecology and water resources. The terrible conundrum of poverty, ecological degradation, and water resource depletion can resolve itself only when the present political obstacles are removed, the prevailing mode of production is vigorously contested, and an alternative social order is ushered in.

A viable alternative model already exists in Kenya in the form of the Green Belt Movement (GBM), founded in 1977 by the Nobel Peace Prize winner, Wangari Maathai. As Professor Maathai acknowledged in her acceptance speech, her movement came into being in response to the problems associated with the lack of firewood, balanced diet, safe drinking water, income, and shelter, all problems already identified by rural women. Since its creation, the GBM has planted over thirty million trees that serve multipurpose functions, ranging from providing fruits, food, wood fuel, income, shelter, female empowerment, soil restoration, and watershed protection.

By using tree planting as a segue into emancipatory politics, the GBM has succeeded in grassroots mobilization not only to secure the emancipation of women but also to promote ecological sustainability, biodiversity conservation, and capacity building. At present, the GBM commands more than 600 women-centered community networks throughout Kenya, tending over 6,000 tree nurseries.[152] Now tree planting has come to symbolize the fermenting social struggle between the haves and the have-nots, since the movement has cast its net far and wide to address issues of equality and equity, poverty eradication, social justice, self-determination, community empowerment, sustainable development, and ecological integrity.

The class character of the movement manifested itself in the confrontation between the Moi government and the greens. When the government announced a plan to build a sixty-story office tower at the center of Uhuru Park in Nairobi, Maathai and her foot soldiers resorted to grassroots mobilization to oppose the plan. Sensing the heat, President Moi scaled down the proposed building to thirty stories. The grassroots movement would not go for it, however. Foreign investors, standing by to funnel in money for the tower, pulled back from the project. This was an implicit recognition of the growing salience of popular pressure from below.[153] The new context supplied by the GBM to communalize ownership of natural resources, production, and consumption of resources and services represents an embryonic form of ecological economics.

Will the green movement in Kenya evolve into a larger movement to challenge the prevailing social order and to demand a radical transformation of existing political institutions? The answer to this question will determine both the future status of the water regime and the evolving order in east Africa.

Chapter Six

The Uppermost Riparian States
Rwanda, Burundi, and the
Democratic Republic of Congo

Problematizing Watershed Integrity

The Democratic Republic of Congo (DRC), Rwanda, and Burundi are generally treated as peripheral to the formation of a water regime in the Nile basin. For this reason, they are not given weighty attention in the emerging literature on regional hydrology. I would argue that they are as important as the other co-riparian states for four reasons. First, their contributions to the Nile system are by no means negligible. Rwanda and Burundi contribute close to 8 bcm of water annually to Lake Victoria via the Kagera River, representing 20 percent of Lake Victoria's water balance. The Kagera River crisscrosses both Rwanda and Burundi, collecting a good amount of water from a number of streams in both countries before traveling for several hundred km in Tanzania to join Lake Victoria. The DRC also contributes close to 5 bcm of water annually, directly from precipitation and via the Semleki River, which flows into Lake Albert. The DRC also shares Lakes Albert and Edward with Uganda.

Second, the massive deforestation taking place in the three uppermost riparian states can certainly have significant harmful consequences for the region's biodiversity and climate and precipitation regimes. The three southernmost co-riparian states are part of the moist African tropical rainforests that stretch eastward to Tanzania and parts of Ethiopia, and westward to Gabon and Sierra Leone. In fact, the DRC and Gabon are two of the nine countries that house 80 percent of the total global tropical rainforests. The biological complexity and diversity of moist rainforests are captured by the fact that a given hectare of moist tropical rainforest on average contains between 100 and 250 species of trees, reaching up to 80 m in height.[1] The role that the moist tropical rain-forests play in the ranges of temperature and humidity, biomass accumulation, organic matter production, soil development, energy transfer, precipitation, water retention, nutrient cycling, and gas and climate regulation is immeasurable; forest canopies capture up to 90 percent of the solar energy that strikes them and then release this energy during evapotranspiration to the atmosphere where it plays a critical role in the stabilization of regional and global climate.[2]

> The forest canopy filters out about 98 percent of the sunlight at ground level, dramatically reducing daytime temperatures. It traps air and insulates increasing night temperatures under the canopy and maintains high and constant humidity. Trees absorb the energy of tropical storms, aerate the soil to allow water absorption and slow water flows, all of which prevent soil and nutrients from being washed out of the system. Trees create the microclimate and habitats essential to the soil fauna that help recycle nutrients, facilitating their reabsorption by the system.[3]

It is useful to note that the co-evolutionary dependence of animal and plant species is essential to healthy ecosystems. Different insects and animal species play essential roles in the propagation and growth of trees and flowering plants by circulating seeds and pollens within the system. In fact, naturalists tell us that tropical rainforests globally produce essential ecosystem services worth $3.8 trillion per annum; bats, bees, birds, beetles and other insects are hard-working pollinators and pest eaters that make farms thrive.[4] But to perform important ecosystem functions, animal populations require a stable climate and a stable ecosystem that supplies continuous flows of nutrients. The animals that make their home in these uppermost riparian states are integral to the health of the moist tropical rainforests.

The Ruwenzori Mountains, rising 16,000 feet and covered with a variety of high-elevation cloud forests, are both important climate regulators and food sources. Acting as hydrologic towers in the equator, these mountains intercept air and force it into precipitation. They are covered with clouds three hundred days of the year and their summits are blanketed with glaciers, snow, and ice caps. The locals call the Rwenzori Mountains "rain giver" to note the perenniality of their hydrological significance. However, increasing human encroachment and deforestation are threatening degradation of the important ecosystem services that the mountains and their moist tropical forests and animal species provide. Africa as a whole has already lost 42.3 percent of its original moist tropical rainforests and the annual percentage loss today is 0.53 percent; between 2000 and 2005, Africa lost four million ha of forests annually.[5] In addition to playing critical roles in biodiversity conservation, soil formation, water generation and retention, climate regulation, and provision of wood and nontimber food products, forests are the green lungs of the earth. For instance, the forest biomass alone stores about 283 gigatons of carbon. In fact, the amount of carbon stored in forest litter, biomass, dead wood, and soil is 50 percent more than the quantity of carbon present in the earth's atmosphere.[6] Therefore, the conservation, regeneration, and protection of the tropical rainforests are as important as the Nile flows. It is also useful to note that the three uppermost Nile states represent a hydrological and ecological bridge between the Nile and the Congo river basins. Indeed, the DRC, Rwanda, and Burundi together account for 61.7 percent of the total area of the Congo river basin; 98.7 percent of the DRC's total area of 2,344,000 sq km lies within the Congo river basin.

Third, the pollution and contamination produced in the uppermost riparian states can accentuate the degradation of water quality in Lakes Victoria, Albert, Edward, and other minor lakes as well. In light of this negative potential, it will be in the best interest of all Nile states to be concerned about events and developments in the uppermost riparian countries.

Fourth, the ecological collapse in the southernmost co-basin states, now in the making, can create propitious conditions for interethnic conflicts with tragic consequences, as seen in Rwanda and in its two neighbors. Since 1993, all three uppermost riparian states have been engulfed in devastating internal strife worsened by the mutual support they have been giving to their respective local proxies and allies. One aspect of internal instability is refugee formation with profound implications for the ecology, economies, politics, and sociocultural identities of neighboring countries. For example, the two million Hutu refugees from Rwanda have been major players in the destabilization of the DRC. In light of the potential consequences of these factors for Nile basin integrity, all downstream or middle-stream states should have a stake in the well-being of the uppermost riparian countries.

The Ethnography of Hydrology and Food Security

One positive characteristic of nineteenth-century empire building (however self-serving that might have been) was the long time horizon with which the colonizers approached the issue of hydrological integrity of the Nile basin. British empire builders, in particular, understood early on the magnitude of harm that uppermost riparian states could do to downstream states in the distant future. Cognizant of this potential, the British sought to prevent future confrontations among riparian states over hydrographic arrangements by putting in place a series of interconnected treaties. They even included what is today the DRC in their long-range vision for establishing a unitary water regime in the Nile basin by ensuring the integrity of important tributaries to the hydrological stability of the west Nile basin. In 1889 and 1906, for example, Great Britain brought the Congo Free State under the canopy of British imperial design by well-crafted agreements. A portion of the 1906 instrument reads that: "The government of the Independent State of the Congo undertakes not to construct or allow to be constructed any work on or near the Semleki or Isango rivers that would diminish the volume of water entering Lake Albert except in agreement with the Sudanese government."[7]

The British were particularly looking for suitable sites for reliable storage facilities. The first site that British hydrologists identified as an ideal storage reservoir was Lake Albert, shared by Uganda and the DRC for fishery and navigation. What makes Lake Albert ideal is that it lies between two parallel escarpments. The lake, with maximum depth of 56 m and mean depth of 25 m, is about 150 km long and 35 km wide. The lake covers an area of 5,300 sq km and holds up to 280 bcm of water. The original plan was to expand both its surface and water-holding capacity. The old imperial vision hasn't died. When Egypt and the Sudan agreed in 1974 to propel the Jonglei Canal plan into motion, they had every intention of transforming Lake Albert into a storage site. Since such an undertaking would certainly flood large areas of land, significant incentives to bring both the DRC and Uganda on board are necessary. It is here where the hydrographic significance of the DRC looms large. The Semleki River, which rises in the vast Ituri rainforest of the DRC, provides almost 5 bcm of water annually to Lake Albert. In addition, several streams from the slopes of the Rwenzori Mountains regularly make a modest contribution of water to Lake Albert. It goes without saying that preservation of the great Ituri rainforest and protection of the mountain slopes are central to the ecological health of Lake Albert. Removal of the rainforest and mountain vegetation will not only modify or alter the precipitation regime in the area, but also accelerate sediment transport to Lake Albert.

The increased levels of human activities around Lake Albert are already taking on troubling dimensions. In fact, the overexploitation of fish has recently become so worrisome that the local fishermen have voluntarily suspended fishing to allow the regeneration of the fish stock. Sarnowski documents that the factors behind the depletion of fish in Lake Albert are widespread pauperization among the communities around the lake, lack of economic alternatives, and lack of proper fishing gears leading to the widespread use of small mesh net. The growing conflicts between natives and migrants, on the one hand, and between the poor and rich fish harvesters, on the other, are exacerbating the ecological degradation of the lake. Sarnowski's research further documents that traditional artisanal fishing regime in Lake Albert historically depended on subsistence activity. Now, in the absence of alternative economic outlets and contextualized by growing poverty and overpopulation of both natives and new arrivals to the lake region, incomes from fishing activity must cover the cost of virtually everything, including food, clothes, education, consumer goods, medicine, and taxes. In consequence, boys as young as six years old are deployed to the lake to contribute to family incomes. The natives told Sarnowski that, in the past, only young adults fished when they established families, usually after age eighteen.[8]

On the ecological ledger, Lake Albert is said to be increasingly eutrophic. The waters of the lake are becoming progressively anoxic in response to the growth of algal blooms and toxins. There are fears that petroleum prospecting activity in the area will make things even worse. If discovered, future hydrocarbon exploitation will only accelerate the lake's contamination and eutrophication.

As underscored by the preceding discussion, it will be a crucial necessity to pay greater attention (than previously given) to the DRC if the conservation of aquatic resources and the restoration of Lake Albert are to occur. In terms of food security, the DRC is poorly endowed, not because the country lacks the natural basis for self-sufficiency in food production but because it lacks a functioning political system. Minerals, water resources, agriculture, and forests can be major sources of national wealth. If properly run, mined sustainably, and equitably distributed, the country has abundant mineral resources that can be pivotal for internal development. Additionally, these endowments can be used to empower an agenda promoting conservation and restoration of its ecological resources. However, since the country's mineral resources have fallen to foreign corporations, internal kleptocrats, and regional bandits, the masses have to increasingly rely on the forests, lakes, and rivers to eke out a living.

More than 70 percent of the population depends on subsistence farming or on forests for nontimber production such as food, charcoal, construction materials, and medicines. Moreover, although the Inga hydroelectricity grid has an installed capacity of 1.8 GW, only 550 MW of this is being used; most of the population is not connected to this important energy source. Instead, they rely on the forests. According to a 1994 report, the people of the country were harvesting 42.6 mcm of wood annually for charcoal production.[9] The DRC's arable land is estimated at 63 million ha, which can be raised to 80 million ha by converting some of its forests into farmland. Before the current upheavals, however, only 6 million ha, including 15,500 ha under irrigation, were actually under cultivation, supporting 58 million people.[10] Estimates of the DRC's potentially irrigable land range between 4 million and 20 million ha. Realistically, the country can put 7 million ha under irrigation of which 6,980,000 ha are in the Congo river basin, while 10,000 ha are in the Nile basin, and another 10,000 ha are found in the west-central coast of the country. The annual water requirements to irrigate 7 million ha and to begin a sustainable process of modern industrialization will be 108.5 bcm, which will not be problematic since the country internally generates 935 bcm of renewable water resources per year.[11]

The DRC has 170 million ha of virgin forests, covering 75 percent of its total land area; 139 million ha of these forests are regarded as economically productive, capable of supplying 700 mcm of industrial wood per year, of which only a half mcm are actually exploited annually at present.[12] The modest commercial exploitation of forest products is not due to the beneficence of the national elites and commercial loggers, but rather to the undeveloped infrastructure to transport the harvested forest products. From an ecological point of view, the development of modern infrastructure can pose a serious threat to the country's virgin tropical rainforests. Even now, without good infrastructure, the DRC's forests have come under serious threats from commercial logging companies and shifting cultivators who are deprived of their basic livelihoods by the ongoing internal war.

When the logging firms selectively cut down the luxuriant trees, and when the broad masses fell the remaining trees for farmland or to sell timber, the value of the cleared land quickly reaches diminishing returns. Tropical soils by definition are poor in nutrients and thinly anchored. When the soil loses its fertility after two or three harvests, people must clear more forests to start afresh. This vicious cycle destroys the forest ecosystems with profound implications for the region's biosphere. As noted in chapter one, the biosphere is an interacting aggregation of all living things. In interaction with the natural driving forces, primarily originating with solar activity, human-induced perturbations can strongly influence the composition and density of vegetation, the patterns of atmospheric circulation, the processes of evapotranspiration and cloud formation, as well as the precipitation and climate regimes. Removal of vegetation, for example, can strongly affect the degree to which the geographic area can absorb the incoming solar radiation and regulate the outgoing terrestrial energy. Such an exchange of energy fluxes between the sun and the earth determines the radioactive properties of the region and defines soil moisture, air temperature, wind speed, relative humidity, and the processes of evapotranspiration and cloud formation.[13]

One veritable consequence of this kind of human-induced perturbation is soil desiccation, which may undercut the region's agricultural potential. Even worse is the problem of laterization (associated with clear-cutting). When the forest is severely logged or clear-cut, the heavy precipitation characteristic of tropical ecosystems washes away the poorly anchored soil. What is left is a hard, impermeable surface known as laterite, which accentuates the leaching of soil with exposure to heavy rain and wind.[14] In addition to the threats from internal forces, the

DRC's forest destruction has recently been associated with the refugee formation from Rwanda.

In 1994, approximately two million Rwandan Hutu crossed into the DRC and congregated in Ngoma, just 50 km from the impressive 790,000-sq-km Virunga National Park (shared by the DRC, Uganda, and Rwanda). On average, 40,000 (and at times, up to 80,000) refugees descended daily upon the park, taking up to 1,000 tonnes of forest product each day for hut construction and firewood. Commercial logging for charcoal making also thrived. In less than six months, approximately 300 sq km of Virunga Park were completely or partially deforested. Moreover, of the 23,000 hippopotamus known to live in the park, only 11,000 were left by November 1995; the fear of mass species extinction compelled UNESCO to change the classification of Virunga Park from world heritage to endangered world heritage.[15] The Virunga forests are the natural home of the 670 mountain gorillas remaining in the world, giant forest hogs, forest elephants, golden monkeys, chimpanzees, buffalos, and the breathtaking biological diversity exemplified by endemic reptiles and amphibians.

The virulent internal war in the DRC has also created similar threatening conditions to other forested areas of the country. The case in point is the 7.7-million-ha-wide Maringa-Lopori-Wamba forests in the north-central DRC, known as the world's second largest contiguous moist tropical rainforest. Traditionally, the indigenous communities in the area subsisted by growing maize, yams, cocoa, palm oil, and coffee. Now, the civil war has completely shattered the livelihoods of the communities, forcing them to seek refuge in the forests. Even more damaging is the new practice of illegal commercial logging. As a result, the little-known bonobob ape, forest elephants, Congo peacock, sitatunga, other incredible species are under real threat.[16]

Similarly, the Kahuzi-Biega National Park in eastern Congo has come under threat from a host of poachers and loggers; 30,000 sq km of this world heritage site and home to east lowland gorillas is being rummaged by unscrupulous commercial loggers, local inhabitants, and refugees for survival. The raging civil war provided the context for unrestricted access to the tropical forests by these forces. In consequence, the number of east lowland gorillas fell from about 17,000 in the early 1990s to 5,000 in 2004.[17]

The threat to the well-being of all riparian states from the widespread destruction of the moist tropical rainforests is predictable. Both upstream and downstream states will suffer in equal proportion from the twin problems of forest destruction: widespread soil erosion in upstream states and choking sedimentation in downstream states. Ecologists tell us that clear-cutting of a forest area can increase sedimentation by as much as 7,000-fold, causing havoc in streams and lakes.[18] It is instructive to note that the Congo river basin is only second to the Amazon river basin in the size of the moist rainforests that it contains, and that the DRC contains

12.5 percent of the world's remaining moist tropical rainforest; only Brazil and Indonesia possess more rainforest than the DRC.[19] Loss of a vast area of moist tropical rainforest can also affect the temperature and climate of the DRC and, by extension, the precipitation regime. Studies in the Colombian portion of the Amazon rainforests reveal significant decreases in annual rainfall, ranging between 21 and 24 percent when compared with past records.[20]

In view of the fact that the DRC has (as of this writing) become a country that fits the definition of a failed state, people there are desperately resorting to personal coping strategies. The process of mass pauperization did, of course, begin under the kleptocratic order of Mobutu Sese Seko, who amassed fortunes for himself by renting out the country's natural resources to multinational firms. In 1988, the Mobutu regime set aside 21 million ha for timber production, most of which was slated for export to the European market. At the time of Mobutu's ouster, 45 million ha of forest areas were being worked by logging firms under dubious arrangements. Indeed, European logging firms have been freely operating in the country's forests since independence from Belgium in 1960 without a regulatory regime. The giant logging firm Siforco, a subsidiary of the German company Danzer, has a series of concessions covering 2.9 million ha of forests in the DRC.[21]

The scandalous expropriations of the DRC's rainforests have been facilitated by an interlocking class alliance between the neocolonial companies and the internal kleptocrats. The concessions granted to the logging firms have been extraordinarily generous: $286 per 200,000 ha.[22] There is a built-in incentive in the concessions granted to the firms: because of the vast sizes of the concessions, the firms would focus only on the most prized timber. It is not surprising that the average yield per ha is less than one tree. This incentive encourages exponential rummaging of rainforests. Although there has been a legal fig leaf in the book, requiring concessionaires to return to the allotted sites to make a second cut and plant new trees, none comply. The firms simply proceed to new sites and selectively fell high-value luxuriant trees. In return for the generous concessions, the multinational firms distribute 10 percent of their profits among kleptocratic generals, government bureaucrats, and local chiefs.[23]

The commercial firms are increasingly aided by international financial institutions. The World Bank, for instance, exerted sustained pressure on the Mobutu regime to permit the felling of more trees in order to pay off its outstanding debt. To widen the scope of concessions and accelerate the felling of trees, the World Bank extended $12 million in loans to the Mobutu regime in 1990. Even when the Cabila regime made a modest attempt in April 1999 to distinguish itself from the Mobutu regime by imposing a ban on forest extraction to protect the moist rainforests, the logging multinational firms and their international supporters put pressure on the regime. In consequence, the regime lifted the ban and the logging firms returned to business as usual.[24]

The post-conflict environment in the DRC appears to provide a context for accentuating (rather than mitigating) the prospects for further forest destruction. Under pressure from nongovernmental organizations, in 2002, the regime in Kinshasa formulated a forest code to provide regulatory mechanisms for the protection and "sustainable" exploitation of the country's forest resources. As a demonstration of commitment to the new forest legislation, the regime rescinded (after discovering the fraudulent nature of many of the contracts) 25 million of the 45 million ha of forest areas that were under logging contracts.[25] The World Bank was involved in the preparation of the new forest code in that it introduced the concept of zoning into the forest code; the country's forest resources would now be divided into different zones for industrial logging, community-based development, and biodiversity conservation. A review of the World Bank's documents by the Rainforest Foundation indicates that 60 million ha of the DRC's forests fall under the industrial logging zone. This is likely to increase commercial timber production by 60- to 100-fold. The World Bank couches this new wave of vandalization in such sugarcoated terms as transparency, accountability, and social responsibility by which commercial logging corporations are supposedly governed. The banality of the forest code, embedded in the notion of "sustainable" exploitation of forest resources, was exposed just one year after the code was enacted when the government succumbed to corporate pressure and restored to logging firms 6 million of the 25 million ha rescinded in 2002, and granted fresh concessions to a Portuguese logging company, amounting to 2.4 million ha in contravention of the moratorium that the regime had imposed.[26]

Ironically, commercial logging has also become instrumental in the lives of destitute communities. Following the network of roads prepared by logging firms, poor farmers (pushed off of their land holdings by powerful chiefs) have simply moved into the forest land already partially cleared by the firms' first cut. They engage in shifting cultivation to make ends meet; the cycle is vicious. The ongoing civil war and the expanding context of destitution accentuate this sad reality. More than 80 percent of the people in the DRC are said to languish under absolute poverty and chronic malnutrition. The per capita GDP at $98 in 2003 was the lowest in Africa.[27] It is not surprising that a multitude of destitute people are descending on the rainforests to eke out a living. In proportion to the disintegration of the formal sector, subsistence occupation and informal activities must pick up the slack. In the 1980s, agriculture contributed just 25 percent to GDP; by 1994 it accounted for 50 percent, which rose to 56.3 percent by 2003. In 1998, subsistence farming and informal activity together accounted for 78 percent of GDP.[28]

Rwanda and Burundi are the other key players in the upper reaches of the Nile system. Together, they dominate the Kagera basin, which drains 60,000 sq km, and accounts for 20 percent of the total water flow into Lake Victoria (Sutcliffe and Parks: 20). The Kagera basin is particularly vulnerable to degradation in the context of growing demand from Rwanda and Burundi for ecological resources. Extensive cultivation in the basin has resulted in high levels of erosion and sedimentation. Further enchroachment by humans into the basin poses grave threat to the 1,400-sq-km lakes and swamps straddling the basin (Sutcliffe and Parks: 22). Thus, the long-term ecological integrity of the Kagera basin cannot be understood in isolation from the internal particulars of Rwanda and Burundi.

Both Rwanda and Burundi are textbook cases wherein overpopulation, shrinking cultivable land, collapsing ecology, socially constructed ethnic markers of identity, and elite class manipulation of external markers have produced recurrent tragedies of biblical proportions. The two countries are mirror images in terms of ethnic composition, social differentiation, ecological determinants, and political uncertainties. best described these parallels: "Their common histories, their comparable social structures, (and) their constant amount of obsessive mutual scrutiny favor them to be natural mirrors of each other's hopes, woes, and transformations."[29] While in Rwanda, the Hutu make up 84 percent of the total population and Tutsi constitute 15 percent, in Burundi the proportions are 87 percent and 13 percent, respectively. Because both countries share similar topographies, altitudes (ranging between 2,000 m and 4,500 m), and precipitation over 2,000 mm annually, they grow more or less the same subsistence and cash crops and engage in livestock production with equal passions.[30]

Although it is often exaggerated, colonialism has played some role in reconfiguring the ethnic maps of the two countries. In the first instance, the Belgian colonizers resorted to the familiar method of divide-and-rule to ensure internal stability and the docility of the populace. The seeming differences in the external markers between the Hutu majority and the Tutsi minority perfectly fit into the colonial machination. Only by reinforcing preexisting differences, or by creating new ones, could colonial domination perpetuate itself. By according the Tutsi higher order in the construction of the social map, the Belgians fostered the apparent differences between competing interests. The fact that 95 percent of the chiefs and 88 percent of the civil servants in the colonial administration were drawn from among the Tutsi gave concrete expression to the external markers of difference between the competing ethnic groups in Rwanda.[31]

The arrested development of the two countries was the second factor that offered material context to the political relevance of apparent ethnic differences. Lacking opportunities for incomes in nonagricultural sectors, Rwandans and Burundians competed among themselves for

shrinking ecological resources. Their colonial condemnation to specialize in the production of subsistence crops for themselves and a limited
number of cash crops for export may have, in the long run, contributed
to the sharpening of social antagonisms and class contradictions in both
countries, masked beneath the garb of ethnicity.

Traditionally, Rwanda was generally regarded as secure in terms of
food production. However, overpopulation and overcultivation during
the second half of the twentieth century combined to erode food security.
The problem is that the country, just over 26,000 sq km in area, has little space for horizontal agrarian expansion. The country's potentially irrigable 9,000 ha in the Congo river basin are few considering its rapidly
growing population.[32] A full 90 percent of Rwandans eke out their living from the land. During the last forty years, 60 percent of Rwandans
saw their farm holdings slashed to less than a half ha per farmer on average, as the population density on cropland rose from 85 persons per sq
km in 1934 to 380 people per sq km in 1989. In some parts of the country, population densities reached 668 persons per sq km prior to the 1994
genocide.[33] With an annual birthrate of 3.7 percent, Rwanda's population has doubled every decade since the 1930s. At this rate, the projection
is that the country's population will reach the 50 million mark by 2040
from 8.2 million in 1994. By the 1980s, population growth had already
outstripped food production, transforming the country into a "Malthusian" basket case.

Total dependence on subsistence economy, equally vulnerable to the
vagaries of nature and global price fluctuations, exacerbated the country's problems. The subsistence crops are sweet potatoes, cassava, plan-
tains, beans, maize, sorghum, and bananas. Dwindling acreage, drought,
and heavy rain strongly affect the country's food security. In 1998, for
example, the country food deficit stood at around 100,000 tonnes due to
crop damage from heavy rain.[34] Rwandans supplement their diet with a
modest fish catch from Lake Kivu. The annual catch has been rising from
1,198 tonnes in 1975 to over 3,550 tonnes in 1993. According to the
1998 estimates, the fishing sector could still accommodate 5,000 additional fish harvesters.[35]

Rwanda's main cash crops have been affected by the vagaries of
weather and global price fluctuations. Before the 1994 genocide, Rwanda
used to produce 40,000 tonnes of coffee annually. However, the 1984–1986
price collapse practically killed coffee as a major source of surplus extraction
for the ruling elite. According to James Gasana, Rwanda's former minister
of agriculture and later of defense, the value of coffee on a per head basis fell
from $60 in the 1970s to $13 in 1991.[36] In the 1996–1997 season, the country could produce only 15,400 tonnes of coffee.[37]

The gross mismatch between Rwanda's land area and its population
size (compounded by poor land use, declining soil fertility, and insufficient

investment in farm inputs) had long created objective antecedent conditions for unforeseen tragedy in the context of class domination. Beginning in the early twentieth century, large numbers of Rwandans left for neighboring countries as economic migrants. Through agreements with Great Britain and Belgium, the Rwandan migrants were allowed to benefit from naturalization and permanent settlement. As a result, some 1.3 million Rwandans became integral to the demographic makeup of Belgian Congo; another 700,000 Rwandans integrated into Uganda's population.[38] The 1959–1964 and the 1972–1973 anti-Tutsi pogroms created a new wave of Rwandan exodus, this time political in character. By 1991, there were 775,000 Rwandan political refugees in the DRC, Uganda, Tanzania, and Burundi.[39]

In search of domestic legitimation, the Hutu regime simultaneously pursued a dangerous discriminatory ethnic policy and an ill-conceived and poorly implemented agrarian one. According to the official policy, the presence of Tutsi in schools, civil service employment, academia, and similar professions would not exceed 9 percent, regardless of merit or the country's need for trained professionals. The regime also encouraged the conversion of Tutsi-owned grazing pastures into farmlands for intensive cultivation in the hope of increasing food production. In the midst of agrarian confusion, some 80,000 Hutu farmers were dislocated; they subsequently pioneered on their own into previously untouched virgin forests and hill slopes to settle.[40] Apart from creating the permissive context for elite manipulation of interethnic tensions, along with rural mobilization to mask internal class contradictions, Rwanda's total dependence on fuel wood for energy, subsistence farming, and limited cash crops to generate foreign exchange earnings weighed heavily on the environment. Since 90 percent of Rwanda's energy is from fuel wood, the country annually consumed 2.3 mcm of firewood more than it produced before the 1994 genocide.[41] In fact, although the government projected 1.9 mcm of wood extraction for 1991, the actual consumption rose to 4.5 mcm.[42] Today, only 5 percent of the country's 26,338 sq km surface area is under forest cover, down from 30 percent a century ago.[43]

Rwanda's remaining forest parks, known for rare species like the golden chimpanzees, mountain gorillas, monkeys, and so on, are under a serious threat. The Nyungwe National Park, once covering 250,000 ha, now covers a mere 87,000 ha with further loss in prospect. Moreover, Akagera and Gishwati parks have lost 75 percent of their original forest cover.[44] Reports note discernible climatic changes in Rwanda, including an unusual rise in temperature and prolonged dry seasons. Historically, Rwanda's high altitude, temperate climate, and relatively abundant rainfall of over 2,000 mm per annum kept the country free from malarial mosquitoes and sleeping-sickness tsetse flies. The disease vectors are, however, steadily climbing Rwanda's highlands.

In the midst of growing population, land scarcity has thus forced the natives to convert wetlands and grazing pastures into farms, and to cultivate the slopes and hillsides to grow subsistence crops, in the process creating favorable conditions for deforestation, habitat destruction, soil erosion, and flooding. By 1989, 50 percent of Rwanda's farms were on steep slopes with marginal soil, ideal for erosion to occur. By then, erosion was said to claim the equivalent of 8,000 ha of precious soil per annum, or enough to grow food crops for 40,000 people annually.[45] Gradual conversion of grazing pastures meant substantial reduction in the number of cattle and therefore loss of manure, which led to underfertilization of cropland.[46]

Lest land scarcity and overpopulation be seen as causal variables, a caveat is in order here. Both land scarcity and overpopulation are social in character and have a strong political context. The process of underdevelopment, which began during the colonial era, has been at work to keep the country as a producer of primary commodities, namely, coffee, tea, and tin. The absence of industrial progress meant that the rural subsistence economy continued to self-reproduce endlessly. To make matters worse, the class competition for rural resources gradually acquired ethnic dimensions, which the colonizers and later the national ruling elites exploited in order to perpetuate class domination. The Hutu elite cleverly blamed land scarcity on Tutsi domination, and promised the Hutu peasantry more land by restricting Tutsi access to rural resources. The net result was intensification of competition both within the Hutu and between the Hutu and Tutsi. In the context in which ethnic ideology had sufficiently dwarfed class cleavages, it was natural for external markers to assume a preponderant role in the competition for ecological resources. Landlessness, mass unemployment, lack of alternative access to nonagrarian source of income, and continuous land grabbing by the ruling elite and their local allies were conveniently cast in ethnic terms.[47]

The problem for the Hutu elite was that, even if every Tutsi were evicted from his or her birthplace, there are still insufficient agrarian resources to satisfy every Hutu peasant. After all, the collapse of the global commodity market had already begun to affect the internal class cohesion of the Hutu elites. After the global recession following the second oil shock in 1979, Rwanda's earnings from commodity export had begun to sharply fall. In fact, a price slump for tin forced the country to close ten tin mines in 1984–1986.[48] Since coffee, tea, and tin (the three pillars of Rwanda's economy) collapsed, the country was hanging by the thread on foreign aid, with which the Hutu elite subsidized their parasitic lifestyle. By the late 1980s, foreign aid accounted for 22 percent of GDP.[49] In the midst of shrinking national resources, the Hutu elite increasingly resorted to playing the ethnicity card to ensure regime survival.

External developments in Rwandan refugee camps and in their host countries also began to influence Rwanda's internal turmoil. Rwandan refugees were increasingly seen as burdens on the economies, politics, and cultures of their host countries. Sustained harassments made the refugees feel unwelcome. This objective reality created yearnings among Rwandan refugees to go home. The puzzle they had to resolve was, of course, how and by what means. The Tutsi elite found the answer to the various armed struggles taking place within the Nile system itself, especially in Uganda and Eritrea. Not only did they see how Yoweri Museveni seized power by the barrel of the gun, but they also participated in the armed struggle that finally brought him to power. In fact, the Rwandans who participated in Museveni's movement eventually determined to follow the path of armed struggle in order to return home. In 1990, the Rwandan elites in exile formed the Rwandan Patriotic Front (RPF) to begin their journey homeward. The die was cast. The formation of the RPF simultaneously sharpened the class contradictions and interethnic tensions inside Rwanda itself. The culmination of these contradictions and tensions (in the end) expressed itself in the genocide of 800,000 Rwandans followed by the internal displacement of two million, and the exodus to neighboring countries of another two million.[50]

In the wake of the 1994 genocide, the Rwandan government has been developing a national land policy whereby the country's fragmented land holdings can be consolidated, registered, and democratically allocated among Rwandans. One aspect of the national land law is to require landowners to bear the cost of registering their holdings. This may favor rich farmers at the expense of poor cultivators and women.

As in Rwanda, Burundi's agriculture is poorly developed, even though the country fares better than Rwanda in terms of potential irrigation. Burundi has 105,000 ha in the Congo river basin that can be irrigated, given water availability and investible funds.[51] The majority (93.6 percent) of Burundi's population is engaged in subsistence farming, producing such crops as potatoes, sorghum, bananas, pulses, cassava, maize, sweet potatoes, and beans, and women take full credit for 70 percent of agrarian production. Like Rwanda, Burundi depends on cash crops that include coffee, tea, sugar, tobacco, palm oil, and cotton. Until the 1980s, Burundi managed to maintain an acceptable level of food self-sufficiency by putting more acreage under cultivation. Since the 1990s, however, the country has run out of farming land. By the mid-1990s, the per capita food production had fallen by 20 percent. In the context of growing population, political violence, deteriorating ecology, underfertilization of cropland (due to the lack of manure), and recurrent drought, the country has become increasingly dependent on foreign food aid. According to FAO numbers, the country's food deficit rose from 40,000 tonnes in 1998 to 70,000 tonnes in 1999.[52] The country's food security is further weakened by decline in fish catches. The fish industry, which shares Lake Tanganika with other fish harvesters from neighboring countries, claimed a mere 3,000 tonnes of catch in 1997 compared with the 22,000 tonnes of annual catch before 1993.[53]

As in Rwanda, Burundi's coffee and tea are the major foreign exchange earners. In 1995, these crops accounted for 87 percent of total export earnings.[54] The two cash crops are equally affected by similar forces: poor rains, underfertilized fields, plant diseases, and falling international prices. For example, Burundi barely managed to harvest 16,566 tonnes of coffee in the 2001–2002 season, of which only 20 percent passed as premium, compared with the 35,000 tonnes it annually produced in the 1980s, 70 percent of which was considered premium. Likewise, in 1999, the country barely managed to harvest 2,400 tonnes of raw cotton compared with the annual production of 9,000 tonnes before 1993. In fact, since 1993, Burundi lost half of its cotton fields and, consequently, 5,000 cultivators lost their source of livelihoods.[55]

Burundi's growing population (in the context of a weak food regime and the nation's total dependence on a limited basket of exportable commodities) means that the country's forest cover will continue to be the casualty. In 1993, the proportion of the country's surface area under forest cover was 5 percent; since then deforestation has actually accelerated. In 1999–2000 alone, 2 percent of the forest cover was destroyed by human-induced fire.[56]

Burundi's food deficit, poverty, overpopulation, ecological deterioration, and absence of a meaningful development trajectory have served to supply the conditions for social antagonism and interethnic competition. As in Rwanda, the Hutu represent some 87 percent of the population, a demographic condition that has created a siege mentality among the Tutsi minority. Burundi's Tutsi intellectuals and army officers have long internalized the lesson that, if they would thwart possible anti-Tutsi pogroms, the solution was to construct a Tutsi-dominated political order. They have become convinced that this is the only sure way of ethnic survival. Such antidemocratic impulses have been major obstacles to the democratization project in Burundi for a long time. It is instructive to recall that in the 1972 massacres, between 150,000 and 250,000 Hutu were murdered compared with 2,000 Tutsi deaths. Following the 1972 massacres, 300,000 Hutu became refugees in neighboring countries.[57]

What took place in June and October 1993 is equally instructive. Under a fair and free election, the Hutu-dominated political party controlled the national assembly by capturing over 71 percent of the vote. For the first time in Burundi's history, a Hutu president, Melchior Ndadaye, democratically assumed power. In October, barely three months into office, however, Tutsi army officers kidnapped and murdered Ndadaye. The event set the stage for Hutu unrest, encouraged by Hutu officials. In the ensuing anti-Tutsi pogroms and anti-Hutu assaults, an estimated 100,000 to 150,000 Tutsi lost their lives, 150,000 Tutsi sought protection in army barracks, and another 700,000 Hutu are estimated to have sought refuge in Hutu-controlled Rwanda and other neighboring states.[58]

In summary, two crucial conclusions emerge from the present discussion. First, in the context of gross governance deficits, growing ecological degradation, runaway population growth, and stark poverty, the peoples in the uppermost reaches of the Nile basin will have no option in the future other than to vandalize the remaining ecological resources. The resulting degradation of ecosystem services and the potential modification in climate and precipitation regimes can be detrimental to all riparian societies in the Nile basin. Second, ecological resource depletion is likely to accentuate the social contradictions and interethnic cleavages in each society of the uppermost reaches of the Nile. In the effort to cope with the internal legitimation crisis, and to mitigate the social effects of resource depletion and mass pauperization, the national elites in each state are likely to access the water resources of the Kagera and Semleki rivers (and their feeder streams) to promote irrigation-based farming and hydropower-based industrialization. When, and if, such moves become reality, both Lakes Victoria and Albert may experience substantial diminution of flows from the Kagera and Semleki rivers. Given these real possibilities, it will be in the best interest of all Nile states to proactively seek collaborative accommodation on the basis of integrative dialogue.

The Puzzle

Even though the amounts of water resources that the DRC, Rwanda, and Burundi together contribute to the Nile system are by no means negligible, the most crucial role that the three uppermost riparian states can play is in the preservation and protection of the watershed ecology in their portions of the Nile and the Congo river basins. Politically, too, they can make an immense contribution to the Nile system by removing the conditions that give rise to refugee formation in neighboring countries. The greatest question for enlightened leaders, public intellectuals, and civic organizations in the uppermost riparian states is how to create permissive conditions to simultaneously thwart interethnic competition and forge solidaristic cooperation and social integration on both national and regional bases. It seems that the geographic and social proximity of the peoples in the three countries, along with their shared hydrological and ecological determinants, would favor a vigorous thinking in terms of a regional union of peoples. In addition to sharing the upper reaches of the Nile order, the three countries occupy crucial portions of the Congo river basin.

The amalgamation of the peoples in the three countries in a broader political context can possibly dilute the negative attributions often attached to ethnicity. The hydrologic, land, and mineral resources of the DRC, if properly harnessed, can accommodate all peoples in the three countries. The Nile and the Congo River serve as the unifying factors. Perhaps it is instructive to remember that the annual discharge of the Congo River, as measured at around Kinshasa and Brazaville, is 1.269 trillion cu m, or 32 percent of the total renewable freshwater of the African continent.[59] The drainage area of the Congo River covers 3.7 sq km, making it second to the Amazon in drainage area, and the Congo River is 4,586 km long. It is also second only to the Amazon basin in the size of its moist tropical rainforests. The Congo River has 700 species of fish, most of them endemic and, like the Amazon River, yields about 210,000 tonnes of fish annually.[60]

The Democratic Republic of Congo is thus the epicenter of a regional order in the uppermost basin of the Nile system, given its size in terms of population, geography, and natural resources. The terrible conundrum is whether the Congo will put its house in order and tie its destiny to that of Rwanda and Burundi on a trajectory of hope and progress. Paul Salopek is perhaps right when he raises the fundamental question:

> Africa is the most unpredictable continent in the world. Yet no African nation confronts the future so unscripted, so fraught with disaster and sheer possibility as the misnamed Democratic Republic of the Congo. Will war resume and Congo shatter into smaller squabbling states? Possibly. Can a frail but hopeful peace last, allowing Congo finally to put its fabulous riches to work? Conceivably.[61]

Chapter Seven

Thinking about the Future

Since the advent of modern colonialism, the scramble in the Nile basin has primarily been over water resources. European colonial powers and Egypt all had thought that they were entitled to the waters of the Nile. To effectuate this presumed entitlement to the Nile, they all tried to use military power. But then it was the age of what Lipschutz calls imperialism and social Darwinism, embedded in the dictum: "What is mine is mine and what is yours is open to a fair game," one that would include open competition and the exercise of force.[1] Buffered by the Westphalian notion of state sovereignty and the presumed sanctity of territorial boundedness, the legacy of imperial proclivity and Darwinian mentality still persists today. So long as the mode of unfettered capitalism remains the prevailing social order in human civilization, a meaningful and substantive change will be difficult to imagine. The puzzle that must be investigated and resolved now is how the Nile riparian states can overcome old habits and usher in a new era of solidaristic relationships, based on the notion of equal regional citizenship, shared destiny, and impartial entitlement of all to the resources of the Nile basin. This requires new thinking and looking forward.

Hydrological resources must be understood in their broader contexts and contours. The members of the World Commission on Dams are right when they note that:

> The issues surrounding dams are the issues surrounding water, and how water-related decisions are made. . . . The issues all relate to what the dam will do to river flow, to rights of access to water and river resources, to whether it will uproot existing human settlements, disrupt the culture and sources of livelihood of local communities and deplete and degrade environmental resources. Conflicts over dams are more than conflicts over water.[2]

In this concluding chapter, I will attempt to offer some thoughts that will, I hope, provoke constructive discussion about what ought to be done to thwart potential ecological collapse, social disintegration and political turmoil in the Nile basin at both national and regional levels.

Toward an Integrative Epistemology and Regional Authenticity

The humanist British historian Basil Davidson observes that knowledge is power.[3] Indeed, knowledge is power, whether used by oppressors or liberators. As Andrew Linklater aptly puts it, in order for knowledge to be critically useful, its possessors must have awareness, reflexivity, mutual recognition of shared knowledge, and greater sense of empowerment.[4] These elements should enable the users of knowledge not only to resist the structures of oppression and domination but also to develop strategies of emancipation. Knowledge thus presupposes the simultaneity of its many-sidedness and social character. In its many-sidedness, knowledge rejects totalization. An authentic, interactive, and dynamic knowledge should claim humanism, holism, rationalism, and realism as integrative expressions of its definition. The first and foremost aim of an authentic knowledge ought to be the emancipation of all humans. Regional human self-realization and self-fulfillment in the Nile basin can be achieved only under solidaristic conditions, where every person in Egypt sees every person in Ethiopia as his partner, jointly engaged in the common cause of prosperity and happiness, where individuals in Rwanda and the Sudan see each other as bound by a common fate, sharing a single ecology and entertaining the same hopes, aspirations, and future.

Humanism and human emancipation should also be conceived in the context of a holistic understanding of the organic relationship between humanity and nature. Human emancipation should not deny the legitimate existence of the ecology. Human liberation and ecological protection must be seen as two sides of a single organic whole. Although the precise locus of humanity in this relationship is still a matter of debate even among ecologists themselves, public intellectuals and civic organizations in the Nile basin should join the debate to begin the process of reconciling humanity to the regional ecology. The competing orientations, respectively based on human-centered disquisitions that tend to privilege humanity over nature, on the one hand, and ecology-focused arguments that defend the equality of nature with humanity, on the other, should move forward in tandem to present new opportunities to search for a holistic alternative.

Today, our epistemological orientation is in a state of confusion as the defenders of anthropocentrism continue to argue in favor of an alternative in which human emancipation can be attained within the context of ecologically sustainable socialist modes of production, while ecocentrists advance the notion of human emancipation within a radical framework that recognizes and defends the equal moral standing of nature.[5] To illustrate the difference between the two camps of the emancipatory movement, Robyn Eckersley uses the debate over the population controversy as an entry point. Those who are in favor of the human-centered arguments like to direct attention to the social causes of the demographic problem and the unequal distribution of national wealth. Their arguments seem to rest on the presupposition that, once an equitable distribution of wealth is achieved and the social sources of the problem are addressed, overpopulation need not be a problem. Ecosocialists, like David Pepper, argue that without altering the prevailing capitalist mode of production, the realization of sustainable development is unimaginable. Pepper in particular highlights four essential points. The first, resource conservation, or doing with less under capitalism, runs counter to the logic of capital accumulation. The second involves the externalization of the costs of production. Installing clean technologies or pollution control devices means reduction of profit. Thus, destroying the virgin environment and externalizing the harmful effects of production are not only inherent to capitalism but also crucial sources of profit. Third, the inherent tendency of capitalism toward the centralization of production and the concentration of capital by definition excludes the majority of society from access to the wealth created. As a result, mass unemployment and poverty are also externalized to the rest of society by the minority who own and control the means of production. Finally, Pepper takes a strong exception with those who peddle with "deep ecology" as an alternative. He rejects the eco-anarchist view that small is beautiful, as well as the notion that sustainable development can occur within an egalitarian framework at the local level without a central machinery of coordination and accountability.[6] For Pepper, problems of ecology, ignorance, poverty, spread of diseases, and political turmoil cut across communities, nations, and regions, and thus require a sufficient degree of democratic centralization of politics and economics.

In contrast to the anthropocentric position within the emancipatory movement, ecocentrists argue that a mere regulation of population growth rate is insufficient to restore the holistic relationship between humanity and nature; such a policy should be followed by radical measures to reduce the human numbers, who have already overwhelmed nature's carrying capacity. Moreover, ecocentrists contend that according priority to nature and decentralizing the political machinery are critical to emancipatory politics.

These contrasting arguments offer invaluable insights for those with deep concern for the Nile ecology. As indicated in chapter one, presently the Nile states have proven totally unable to provide the basic necessities of life to their collective populations of 358 million. The question then becomes: what are they going to do when their combined populations reach 850 million forty years hence? Admittedly, the attainment of the ideal ecocentric position is not in prospect presently, given the enormity of the problems prevailing in the Nile basin. But the debate must begin without losing sight of the practical necessity of addressing the priorities of the workless and working poor. It is here where the third aspect of knowledge—namely, realism—finds its relevance. Those who are championing emancipatory politics need to go beyond theory building and strategy determination to offer concrete and practical steps that can serve as building blocks. A sense of realism is crucial in differentiating the possible from the impossible and the probable from the improbable, given the subjective social limitations of the target audience and the entrenched class position of the target adversary. It is through a healthy sense of realism about what is achievable within the objective reality that the way forward can be discovered and sustained. One thing is clear, though: trying to imitate the Western lifestyle is not only improbable to achieve but also dangerous.

The dream to raise the living standards of the broad masses in the Nile basin along capitalist lines would involve not only the deployment of huge investment, but also massive consumption of ecological and hydrological resources, the construction of megadams, the building of megacities, the development of internal markets as well as the deep penetration of foreign markets. The veritable consequences of these human activities are likely to result in resource depletion and the generation of huge quantities of pollutants and contaminants if the Nile actors continue to cling to the anachronistic mode of production. Thus, the principal task for public intellectuals is how to provide a complete picture of reality by offering a vigorous social analysis and undertaking goal-oriented research. This is the first crucial step toward the decolonization of reality and theory in search of regional authenticity.

Finally, the synergistic values of humanism and holism can be realized only in the context of modern rationalism. Rational thought, informed by science and technology and when properly understood, provides the means of harnessing intellectual resources for the betterment of the lives of the peoples of the region. Although rationalism is often understood in instrumental and utilitarian terms, it need not be so. Rationality, often regarded as the justifying reason for the objectification of nature, can and should be reinterpreted from a class angle in order to judge its mode of application. In civilizational terms, the Nile countries are in transition; their cultures are still permeated through and through by premodern conceptions of their relationships with nature as well as with each other, and by religious mythology, superstition, fatalism, differentiation of gender roles, and other ascriptive factors. These factors cannot be conducive to formulating proper responses to the problems posed by overpopulation, for example. Adequate protection of nature, equitable allocation of resources, proper utilization of ecological resources, and good population governance all require secular knowledge, encapsulated in the term "rationality."

Insofar as the social content of knowledge is concerned, it should be evaluated on the basis of the social purpose it serves. This distinction is a key to understanding the class character of ideas, policies, plans, and strategies, especially in the present context in which the debate over the appropriate mode of resource conservation and human emancipation has become one over language. Since the cooptation of seemingly progressive terminology by even ecology-vandalizing corporations has become almost total, unmasking the social relations of production and the social character of transactions in the era of late capitalism is essential. Ecological degradation and human poverty are not causes of each other but rather consequences of something larger and deeper that appears to unite them as mutually reinforcing identities. In truth, the underlying structural cause for both resource depletion and mass immiseration is the growth paradigm itself, which has continued to provide the crystal waters to unfettered capitalist accumulation. The drive-by capital for the extraction of an ever-larger surplus value under the Schumpeterian logic of "creative destruction" is inherently inimical to resource conservation and ecological protection.[7] Likewise, the circular character of the concentration of capital in ever-fewer hands imposes structural impediments on an equitable distribution of nationally created wealth, therefore becoming a structural cause of rural poverty and urban impoverishment.

Given this built-in social character of production and distribution under the growth regime, neither ecological equity nor human emancipation could ever be achieved, no matter how hard the phraseology of "sustainable development" is pushed to the fore in mainstream literature to obscure the social character of both knowledge and capital. Lele's sardonic observation splendidly captures the obscurantist aspect of the debate:

> Sustainable development is a "metafix" that will unite everybody from the profit-minded industrialist and risk minimizing subsistence farmer to the equity-seeking social worker, the pollution-concerned or wildlife-loving first worlder, the growth-maximizing policy maker, the goal-oriented bureaucrat, and therefore, the vote-counting politician.[8]

The point here is that, behind every idea, every policy, and every plan or strategy, there is a social purpose to which knowledge is deployed. For example, when Western governments and international financial institutions trivialize public ownership of water resources and extol the virtue of privatizing ownership of those resources under the guise of promoting efficiency and accountability, they are actually advancing the interest of a definite social class: that of the owners of capital. For example, when Vivendi Environment ran into the problem of corporate overstretch and sought to sell part of its assets in late 2002 to reduce its financial exposure, the suggestion created an uproar in France lest French water resources fell into foreign hands. This fear was echoed by none other than President Jacques Chirac himself who cautioned: "Water supply is very much a public service and we should pay attention that Vivendi doesn't fall into bad hands."[9] By "bad hands," of course, Chirac meant foreign ownership of this vital resource. In fact, the French government rushed to assemble an array of public institutions to buy Vivendi's shares in order to preempt foreign investment in French water facilities. This French double standard, calling—as it were—for domestic water protection and foreign water penetration simultaneously, reveals the complex social character of international relations and the means (knowledge) used to justify such Janus-like strategies.

Shielded behind the idea of market efficiency, Western governments and global capitalist agencies have been thus calling for demolishing the last frontiers of human social existence: that of water. Johan Bastin, an official of the European Bank for Reconstruction and Development (EBRD), illustrates this point when he observes: "Water is the last infrastructure frontier for private investors."[10] During the November 2001 WTO conference in Qatar, the E.U. trade commissioner Pascal Lamy (who happened to be French) hastened to insert a clause in the text of the resolution for the "reduction, or, as appropriate, elimination of tariff and nontariff barriers to environmental goods and services," including water services.[11] Subsequently, the E.U. Commission opened its doors to water companies and invited them to closely work with the commission to negotiate market access to water resources; the conditionality rule would be liberally used when negotiating trade relations with countries receiving European aid. Using the conditionality rule, the European Bank for Reconstruction and Development, for example, enabled Vivendi and Suez to obtain water contracts in twenty-three cities in nine east European countries without open bidding.[12]

From epistemological considerations, the view I am expressing in this section amounts to a call for the decolonization of social thought and theory from the reigning neoclassical growth regime, not only rejecting totalization of knowledge but also rebelling against the hegemonic domination of the neoclassical theory of economics and politics. By offering math-centered prescriptions of growth, neoclassical economic theory has hitherto misdirected our social research and policy. Because the growth theory and the prescription supplied by international institutions that impose this theory on Nile countries have had noxious effects on the development trajectory of the basin countries, it is critical that we understand the full dimensions of the reigning hegemony of neoclassical economics.

The primary assumption of this theory is that markets are composed of rational households and firms, operating under perfect competition with complete information mediated by the malleability of labor and the flexibility of prices, which seek and inevitably achieve equilibrium. Because what defines markets is objective rationality and spontaneity, the natural tendency of markets is always toward equilibrium with respect to optimal production and efficient allocation of resources, including water resources. The corollary assumption of the theory is that, by virtue of their naturalness or givenness, market forces are objective whose properties are amenable to quantification and whose behaviors are predictable through mathematical modeling. The notion of gross national product or gross domestic product is central to the presumed objective measurement of how markets optimally produce and efficiently allocate resources. The third assumption is that, if markets fail to demonstrate the expected optimality and efficiency in the production and allocation of resources, it must be owing to some exogenous forces, namely, politics. To neoclassical theorists, nonmarket human rationality is subjective and therefore susceptible to ideological contamination and political manipulation, whereas economics (unless corrupted by politics) is objective, amenable to empirical investigation and scientific conclusion. If the state (which controls the sphere of politics) interferes in the market, its actions readily lend themselves to the rise of labor rigidity, distortion of price signals, and asymmetric distribution of information, leading to all kinds of disequilibriums.

These three assumptions together inform the neoclassical theory of growth. If this line of analysis holds, the Nile states will be well advised to build a "Chinese wall" between economics and politics, keeping noneconomic scholarship at bay and the state at arm's length, allowing market forces to do their job and find their natural equilibrium. Unless confronted by a vigorous intellectual counterinsurgency, the socialization in the neoclassical outlook can only serve to stifle imagination and reflective thought. Precisely because the institutions of higher learning and policy research agencies in the Nile countries simply duplicate the curricula in social sciences of the advanced countries, understanding the full range of being socialized in the growth theory is all the more critical for redirecting the social research endeavor. As Edward Fullbrook puts it:

> The neoclassical monopoly in the classroom and its prohibition on critical thinking has meant that it has brainwashed successive generations of students into viewing economic reality exclusively through its concepts, which more often than not misrepresent or veil the world, especially today's world. Nearly all of these neoclassical notions have a bearing on judgments about social, cultural and economic policy. Consequently, if society were to learn to think about economic matters outside the neoclassical conceptual system, it would almost certainly choose different policies.[13]

A number of downsides are associated with the neoclassical positivist epistemology. First, by presenting economics as a natural science, reliant on mathematical axioms and self-quantifiability, neoclassical theorists deny the constructive role that intersubjectivity plays in discursive transdisciplinary communication and pedagogy. This makes growth theory above and beyond scrutiny, because what is natural and objective cannot be questioned and scrutinized by methods other than mathematical science. Curves, graphs, and diagrams are plentifully generated to show the presumed scientificness of the theory. Alternative perspectives on and approaches to growth cannot capture the science of the growth theory because they are subjective, full of distorted predilections and cognitive limitations.

The second pitfall of neoclassical economics involves presenting the notion of GDP as a scientific tool of measurement of progress. As a scientific tool of measuring growth, GDP has to be discriminate with regard to the variables it purportedly measures or quantifies. By definition, non-market goods and services that are not amenable to quantification are ignored or excluded from the quantifying enterprise. Only those variables whose costs and benefits are readily amenable to mathematical manipulations are accounted for. For example, if Kenya draws down its forests for timber, lumber, or charcoal, the costs incurred in cutting the trees and the benefits accruing from felling them are measured. Because wage-earners are hired to do the felling of trees, and the job of hauling the trees is subcontracted to some trucking firms, and export firms bring in foreign exchange revenue, the costs and profits involved in these transactions are measured. This will definitely show expansion of the economy, hence growth. In fact, reproduction of the same activities in the second round of extraction will show even more growth. The logging firms engaged in the timber extraction activity are likely to reinvest part of the gains they made during the first round in new tree-cutting machines and new hauling trucks. With this come important experience curve and scale economy. This would allow the loggers to accelerate the cutting of trees and the transporting of the timber. When a given forest area is logged to the ground, new forest areas will be auctioned off to loggers at minimal price.

In the language of neoclassical theorists, the continuous growth of the economy, resulting from the more efficient and faster harvesting of the forests, becomes a "virtuous" cycle. However, the "virtuous" harvesting of forest properties cannot take place apart from the vicious cycle of forest destruction. Because internalizing the present and future costs of destroying the forest ruins the entire architecture of neoclassical economics, the simultaneity of the presumed "virtuous" cycle of growth and the inevitable vicious cycle of destroying the forests is conveniently ignored or denied. Forest resources, so long as no factors of production are applied to them, have no exchange value. Hence, the extent to which raw forest resources contain no inherent monetary value would justify the preclusion of the negative consequences of timber extraction for the future health of the forests from the costs of producing the timber.[14]

In other words, GDP by design does not measure the negative externalities associated with drawing down the natural resources unsustainably. The delivery of essential services from the complex structures and functions of ecosystems does not figure in the computation of GDP because internalization of the costs to nonmarket goods and services would undermine the logical foundation of efficiency. As we saw in chapter one, the structures and functions of ecosystems are critically responsible for capturing, cycling, processing, and storing nutrients within the biosphere; for converting solar energy fluxes into biomass and plant growth; for moving and retaining water in the biosphere via the evapotranspiration regime; for the production of oxygen, biotic sequestration of carbon dioxide, decomposition of dead matter, and the absorption of organic compounds; for regulating humidity, temperature, wind, precipitation, and climate; for modulating dry and wet cycles, purifying water, preventing soil erosion, and retaining sediment; for providing chemical and biotic substances critical in manufacturing medicinal drugs; and for removing and detoxifying nonnutrients and pollution.[15] These complex services are hard to quantify and therefore do not factor in the calculation of GDP. Since we don't buy and sell these services in open markets using dollars and cents, ecosystem valuation equals zero. In 1997, a group of ecological economists and natural scientists calculated that the worth of the global ecosystem services was $33 trillion a year, more than twice the combined GNP of all countries in the world.[16] This ecosystem valuation does not actually include the value of natural capital, which produces the services.

Finally, the metaphysical certitude supplied by neoclassical theory with regard to the presumed infiniteness of market fundamentalism is both illusory and dangerous. Nature is taken for granted as something that will always be there to supply infinite quantities of raw resources and waste sinks; the only limiting factors are technology and investible capital. This sharply contradicts the principles of evolution, which is full of uncertainties and surprises. Even the World Bank has recently acknowledged the growing salience of natural surprises, something that prompted the bank to set up the Independent Evaluation Group (IEG) as an autonomous body within the bank itself to study the phenomena of natural disasters and develop coping or mitigating strategies. According to the report of the IEG, the number of natural disasters, such as tsunamis, earthquakes, tropical storms, floods, and fires, has sharply risen to an average of four hundred a year today from one hundred a year in the 1970s. In the last two decades alone, four billion people have been directly affected by these disasters. In the 1990s, natural disasters destroyed property worldwide worth $652 billion; this amount is fifteen times greater than the economic losses caused by natural disasters in the 1950s. The temporal and spatial dimensions of the consequences of natural disasters are important here. Although 1.6 billion people were directly affected by natural disasters between 1985 and 1995, the number affected by the same natural forces rose to 2.6 billion in the past ten years; 95 percent of the casualties occurred in underdeveloped countries and the harmful effects of the disasters are one hundred times higher in underdeveloped countries than in developed countries.[17] This reality indicates that nature is not only finite in its ability to furnish raw resources and waste sinks but also that its evolutionary trajectories are full of uncertainties and surprises. These uncertainties and surprises happen to result from the complex interplay of anthropogenic factors and naturally occurring phenomena. The growing problem of desertification and the accompanying loss of agricultural lands and water resources illustrate the point.

In the estimation of the UN Environment Program, desertification currently affects 3.6 billion ha in one hundred countries, which is 70 percent of the total dry lands used for cultivation or grazing. The world as a whole loses $42 billion annually owing to the growing problem of desertification.[18] Africa in general and the countries on the southern margins of the Sahara Desert (including most of the Nile countries) in particular are vulnerable to the gathering crisis of desertification. In 1968, for example, unprecedented drought struck the Sahel region on the southern margins of the Sahara desert. The drought continued for six years, destroying natural resources and livelihoods. Over a quarter of a million people perished along with millions of domestic animals; as the Niger and Senegal rivers failed to flood, Lake Chad lost two-thirds of its size and the shallow wells in the Sahelian region dried up. This was largely due to the creeping push of the Sahara Desert southward. Human overpopulation, the removal of vegetation cover to make way for cultivation, overgrazing, and deforestation supplied permissive conditions to worsen the situation. Today, the influence of the Sahara is rapidly moving to the Nile basin. It is in this context that the current drought and famine in the African Horn and the gathering hydrographic competition among the ten Nile states for vital water resources must be understood. The main point here is that ecological factors are determinative in how a healthy economy is constructed and maintained. Since the reigning growth regime treats the ecology as exterior to the economy, it cannot account for ecological uncertainties and surprises. And because neoclassical theorists advise nations to entrust their chances of survival to the objective and spontaneous will of market forces, the prescription is dangerous. Thus, a new theory of political economy is required to better prepare the Nile countries coping with the impending ecological crisis. The first order of priority in such a theory must be to make a realistic determination of an optimal scale in which the biological requirements and the societal needs throughout the region are brought into congruity. This entails not only internalizing the costs of ecological externalities and vigorous population control throughout the region but also framing a new social order within which issues of redistribution of national incomes are addressed. Without confronting the burning issues of urban unemployment, rural poverty, ecological degradation, and the lack of universal education and public health, I don't believe that the impending crisis in the Nile basin can be averted. Ultimately, though, the effort to establish an optimal scale relating to the economy and ecology in each Nile state depends on the supply of a vigorous intellectual infrastructure and a new political architecture. The primary purpose of progressive pedagogy is not to offer mere explanations of social realities but rather to use social explanations of realities to suggest ways of overcoming the limitations of the present order and envisioning future possibilities.

My critical arguments directed against neoclassical theory of growth are strengthened by the sort of epistemological revolution that has been taking place in Europe in recent years among students of economics. It is very heartening to know that economics students in the advanced countries have now woken up to the oppressively stifling obscurantism of neoclassical economics. In June 2000, fifteen French students of economics at the country's elite university gathered in a room to share their disillusionment with the math-centered theory of economics, utterly detached from history, social reality, and the ecology. During the discussion, one of the students called the neoclassical economic dogma "autistic," and the label stuck. What emerged from the informal discussion among the students was the Post-Autistic Economics movement. The students then followed up their discussion by circulating a petition (signed by hundreds of students) among their professors and university authorities as well as government officials demanding the total revision of the economics curriculum to take full account of the complexities and uncertainties surrounding modern societies. The enlightened rebellion of French students quickly spread to Spain, Britain, and other European countries. In 2001, 750 economics students at the Cambridge School of Economics issued their own manifesto demanding a change in direction in the way economics courses were being taught. Like autism, the students argued, the growth theory of neoclassical economics is rooted in "abnormal subjectivity" and fanciful expectations that markets solve everything.[19] The net outcome of the canonization of the neoclassical scientism is the exclusion of critical discourse on alternative perspectives and approaches from consideration in the economics curriculum.

The point that I am trying to advance here is that what the Nile countries desperately need at this critical juncture is a new theory of political economy, one that simultaneously rejects the social pathologies of neoclassical economic theory and understands ecological protection and intragenerational and intergenerational equity as the necessary preconditions of economic development. The debate over the allocation of water resources in the Nile basin can only serve to segue into the dynamic issues of progress, advanced internally or regionally. Ecological economists tell us that a genuine development depends on three fundamental goals: sustainable scale, just distribution, and efficient allocation.[20] The essential glue that holds these three goals together is the idea of sustainable scale, which is the size of the economy relative to the ecosystem on which it depends for inflow of resources and outflow of waste.

The notion of sustainable scale entails prior determination of the interactive relationship between the proper size of the economy and its regenerative and waste absorption capacity. Economic development does not occur in a vacuum; it requires continuous flows of raw resources from the ecology and continuous export of wastes to the ecology. As population grows and the economy expands, more raw resources are needed and more wastes in the form of pollution, contamination, and hazardous chemicals are dumped on the ecology, simultaneously short-circuiting its regenerative capacity and overwhelming its waste absorption capacity. We have seen in chapter five how "rational" fish harvesters have compromised the sustainable scale principle in Lake Victoria when they introduced the giant Nile perch into the lake and modernized their fishing gears in search of growth. We have also seen how crowding of people around the lake has begun to degrade its entire basin. The introduction into the lake's basin of such disturbance regimes as invasive species, fire, logging, clear-cutting, cultivation, and settlements, along with the removal of riparian vegetation, have created permissive conditions for the rapid eutrophication of the lake. This indicates that, if the goal of sustainable scale is not attained, the other goals cannot be realized. A healthy economy cannot be created and maintained without a healthy ecology. It is here where the idea of sustainable scale runs into collision with the reigning neoclassical theory of growth. By definition, prior determination of sustainable scale presupposes the necessity to put a brake on growth in order to ensure that there is a balance between the optimal size of the economy and the sustainable capacity of the ecology so that finite ecosystems can continuously lend us their raw resources and absorb our wastes. Putting a brake on growth is what neoclassical economists abhor most since it runs counter to the logic of accumulation. Without limitless expansion of the economy and overexploitation of ecological resources, on the one hand, and without externalizing the negative costs of production and poverty to the ecology and society, on the other, continuous growth cannot occur and consequently accumulation of capital cannot take place. The daunting challenge facing the Nile countries today is how to make the hard choice between holding on to the growth theory and then risk ecological collapse and pauperization on a massive scale and changing course in order to make development sustainable. To bring the point to a sharper focus, one has only to consider the dilemma associated with the size of the region's burgeoning populations and its per capita water resource availability. Nine of the ten Nile countries are already either in the water stress or water scarce category with just 360 million combined populations, the majority of them with no access to clean drinking water and safe sanitation services. In a generation or so, the combined populations of the region are projected to reach 850 million. Given this fact, how realistic is it that the Nile countries can satisfy the competing demands for water resources from the growing populations and expanding economies?

Sustainable scale is intrinsically connected with the notion of social justice both in its intragenerational and intergenerational dimensions. The relationship between the concentration of wealth and income in the hands of the few (which is the veritable result of growth) and the pauperization of the masses have a direct bearing on the integrity of the ecology. To survive, the poor must clear-cut the forests for firewood, building material, or to make and sell charcoal, and to make way for farms. In the words of Daly and Farley: "people who are too poor will not care about sustainability. Why should they worry about the welfare of the future when they are not even able to provide for their own basic needs?"[21] Thus, our concern about the welfare of our fellow human beings has both utilitarian and ethical dimensions. In the utilitarian sense, when poor people destroy their ecological neighborhood in search of land to grow their food, to collect firewood and building material, or to make charcoal, their collective action has a direct bearing on our personal lives. The climate can be modified, soil erosion and sediment flows can choke our lakes and dams, and negative conditions can be created to foster the spread of vector diseases; the intense competition among rural people for ever-shrinking ecological resources can lead to conflicts of all sorts, thereby undermining social cohesion or threatening political instability, which will directly affect us all personally. The ethical dimension of our obligation to humanity and nature must be understood as the necessary precondition for human civilization as an evolving partnership.[22] From humanistic considerations, there is something unethical about condemning future generations to live in poverty and degraded ecology because the present generation desires to satiate an ever-increasing set of wants.[23] If the current generation in the Nile countries claims entitlement to the resources and services of the natural system, the entitlement of future generations to the same resources and services from the ecology must be presumed also. To the extent that current and future generations are part of the ecology, by virtue of which they are equally entitled to enjoy the benefits of nature, every generation has an obligation to transmit the natural system to the next generation (at a minimum) in the condition it was found. Simply put, future generations in the Nile basin should not be worse off than the present generation because of what we have done to the environment. Therefore, our collective action to conserve, protect, and restore ecosystem resources and services is the moral foundation of our obligation to future generations. In the final analysis, considerations of self-interest and ethical values are inseparable because the ethics of ecological resource conservation and ecosystem service protection enhances our own intellectual growth and material well-being here and now while, at the same time, it allows us to meet our moral obligations to posterity.

The views expressed in the foregoing paragraphs do not suggest total abrogation of market principles at this juncture; nor should they be interpreted as implying an endorsement of state capitalism. The ideas I have expressed should rather stimulate the generation of alternative choices. The crucial point here is that, without foundational examination and contestation of the prevailing social order, no constructive alternative can be imagined. Rationalism requires open-mindedness to learn from the experiences of other countries—not to repeat their mistakes while striving to incorporate their positive insights and practices into the alternative choice. For example, the idea of accounting for the full cost of water services cannot and should not be dismissed out of hand. Under a legitimated political system and accountable government, citizens should be made to pay the full price of the water resources they use, although a legitimate exception can be made for the poor. Under corrupt regimes, ownership wouldn't matter anyway, since private water companies can be equally corrupt, inefficient, and wasteful, wholly bent on maximizing the bottom line on the cheap by bribing officials, by not investing in water infrastructure and maintenance, or by providing unclean water to the public. In fact, according to the French Institute for the Environment, public water companies offer not only superior services when compared to private corporations but also lower rates than private firms.[24] It is instructive to note that of the 55,000 water companies in the United States in 2000, only 6,000 were private holdings.[25] The 49,000 public companies continued to remain as public entities because they delivered services competently to the satisfaction of customers. When municipalities choose to offer lower rates to users, in part it is to lower the cost of production to corporations, an incentive to induce their relocation or to discourage their out-migration. The problem facing water service providers in the United States is that manufacturing plants and chemical, pharmaceutical, and other companies pollute and contaminate the water sources, requiring municipalities to spend huge sums of money to purify the water supplies. The point here is that there is no reason why full-cost accounting is not and cannot be incorporated into the public water systems. What is required of public water companies is that they have genuine independence, transparency, accountability, regulation, and monitoring. Sheila Olmstead put it best:

Because of the cost structure of water supply, the most efficient way to supply water to a community is to have a single treatment and distribution system—a monopoly. So the choice is really between regulated public monopolies and regulated private monopolies, not between upstanding public service institutions and profiteering capitalists. The key lies in the word "regulated." In practice, provided a strong and effective regulatory system is in place, a well-managed and well-regulated public water supplier should look very much like a well-managed and well-regulated private water supplier.[26]

Another useful idea that can be borrowed from the growing corpus of water literature is that of importing "virtual water" to optimize domestic water resources use. Within this context, water resources utilization can be enhanced by constructing a rational division of labor. This should involve both production levels and trading networks. If one country, say, Egypt, specializes in finished goods, the other co-riparian states must be bound to buy these goods from Egypt under a preferential trading regime. In turn, Egypt should buy the agricultural goods it needs from upstream riparian states. In this way, the complementarity of regional production systems can be achieved and sustained. The details of the sort of division of labor and the trading system appropriate to the region will have to be negotiated. Of course, it is up to public intellectuals, countervailing civic institutions, and indigenous social movements to discover and popularize the alternative.

By virtue of their position and experience, public intellectuals in particular must provide the requisite leadership in the search for an alternative. They can achieve this in two steps. First, public intellectuals must struggle to create and/or capture part of the public space monopolized by the corrupt state bourgeoisie. The effort to do so should provide an important demonstration effect for other countervailing civic and indigenous social movements to learn from. The methodology and experience of the Moslem Brothers in Egypt offer an invaluable model of the sorts of things that public intellectuals can do to develop positive visions of the future and connect with the broad masses as well. Even though the aim of the Moslem Brothers to ultimately establish a theocratic Islamic state is dangerously exclusionary and illusory, the nonviolent way in which they have thus far played in Egyptian politics is something worth emulating. By transforming the mosque into a parallel institution, or the center for everything—education, legal service, health care, and welfare services—they have been able to make their vision and program genuinely appealing to the dispossessed, the alienated, and the frustrated. This is why the Moslem Brotherhood has been effectively successful in penetrating Egypt's professional syndicates so much so that the Moslem Brothers are whom the government fears most today. The Kenyan Nobel laureate Professor Wangara Maathai also exemplifies the sort of secular leadership that public intellectuals can provide to a counterhegemonic movement. She single-handedly spearheaded the formation of a network of over 600 women's groups tending to over 6,000 multipurpose tree nurseries across Kenya. The result was the planting of 30 million trees, which have begun providing food, fruits, fuel wood, and construction materials to the pioneering women, while, at the same time, promoting ecological conservation and restoration.

The second step involves the task of linking all domestic opposition movements and civic organizations in a highly coordinated and united regional front. This effort should begin with public intellectuals. An authentic alternative to the Westphalian compartmentalization of Nile societies into incoherent congeries of historical accidents requires new orientation and new thinking. If we accept the fundamental premise that the Nile system is unitary, for which there appears to be a conceptual consensus, then the territorial compartmentalization of the region ought to be reconceptualized and the emergent political order will have to be reconfigured in order to realistically come to terms with the crises.

As the Jewish philosopher Emmanuel Levinas notes, human emancipation can occur only within the context of deterritorialized political relationships, where the responsibility of every person is toward others. Because responsibility, in its deterritorialized dimension, presupposes an interdependent condition, it is the central pillar of human emancipation.[27] Our training in Western modes of thinking and doing things, including our voluntary or involuntary acceptance of capitalism as a system without alternative, hasn't served the peoples of the Nile basin well. Interpreting Levinas, David Campbell is correct when he notes,

> The dominant traditions of international relations are strategically disenabling when it comes to thinking about possible resolutions. Addressing these political problems in a practical manner must begin, therefore, with thinking through an approach to responsibility, which is cognizant of the way in which reterritorialization of states necessitates deterritorialization of theory.[28]

Toward a Nile Family of Nations

"Capacity building" has of late become buzz phraseology in the language of global organizations and donor nations. Client recipients of donations have appropriated the same terminology and more. In October 1998, over 150 so-called experts gathered in Cairo to consider alternative ways of conserving and managing water resources. On the rhetorical level, the specialists said all the good things, including the need to develop realistic water management strategies, institution building, comprehensive treatments of economic, political, and environmental issues at all levels, and the participation of local communities in the formulation and implementation of decisions regarding water management. The World Commission on Dams is even more comprehensive in its assessment of the long-range implications of the contemporary hydrographic race for the control of water resources for inter-riparian relations. In its sobering evaluation, the commission concludes that the core values of "equity, sustainability, efficiency, participatory decision-making, and accountability" have increasingly become eroded by the proliferation of dams. To restore these core values to their wholesomeness, the Commission promotes seven strategic priorities, including: "gaining public acceptance, comprehensive options assessment, addressing existing dams, sustaining rivers and livelihoods, recognizing entitlements and sharing benefits, insuring compliance, and sharing rivers for peace, development, and security."[29] No one would quarrel with the enunciation of these strategic priorities to restore or protect the enumerated core values against further erosion. The fundamental question is whether these core values can be attained within the present structural framework such as that existing in the Nile basin. Indeed, expecting these good things to happen within existing political structures is like giving a patient a new liver after the cancer has spread all over his other vital organs and then expecting him to recover. Under miraculous circumstances, he may recover. Reality would dictate otherwise.

The analogy may sound outrageous, but it is hardly far-fetched. All human societies and their ecological determinants in the Nile basin today languish under outright dictatorships or quasi-authoritarian political systems. So all this talk about sustainable development, transparency, institutional capacity building, equity, and so on is nonsensical. If anything, such talk reveals that the ruling national elites and their international patrons have come to realize that they can no longer maintain the status quo without appropriating the language of progress and pretending to be doing something to address the needs and demands of the broad masses. The truth is that the problems of poverty, underdevelopment, ecological degradation, misrule, and domination are such that they can no longer be resolved by window dressing. The resolutions of these problems can be attained by thinking anew about radical structural configurations. The political boundaries of the Westphalian Nile states must be renegotiated in order to achieve coherence, compatibility, and sustainable interdependence. Territorial reconfiguration of the Nile states can help to reduce redundant institutions that work at cross-purposes, promote regulatory and legal coherence, dampen interethnic tensions, promote sustainable water resources utilization, and avoid duplications, like the perceived need to build separate hydropower plants.

For the moment, I can envision four political formations. The first with great potential for faster political integration are the three east African states: Kenya, Uganda, and Tanzania. In addition to being similar in many ways, such as hydrological interdependence, shared historical experiences under the same colonial rule, and relatively higher levels of economic relationships, the east African states are sufficiently conditioned to the idea of an east African community. What this idea lacks is a progressive leadership to give the momentum a tangible expression toward reality.

The uppermost riparian states of Rwanda, Burundi, and the DRC can possibly form an integrated political whole. Together, they can reap several advantages. The creation of a union among the three states can possibly provide permissive conditions for intercommunal solidarity. The fault lines along Hutu and Tutsi cleavages in Rwanda and Burundi can be contained and ultimately resolved within the context of a larger reterritorialized state. Likewise, the flow of refugees across boundaries would possibly stop. Under a democratic order, the minerals and waters of the DRC can be harnessed to provide the necessary means to begin a process of sustainable development. This way, interethnic solidarity and watershed protection could be achieved.

A constellation of new political entities under a genuine federal system can also be constructed in the African Horn. There are a number of important aspects that Eritrea, Ethiopia, Somalia, and Djibouti share, including cultural, historical, economic, and ecological ones. Here again, unnecessary duplications of projects, plants, and institutions can be avoided, border disputes can be rendered superfluous, and focused attention can be devoted to the real and burning issues of progress.

Finally, the Sudan and Egypt should form the fourth quadrant of the new Nile order. Until the "free officers" under Nasser came to power in 1952, the idea of "unity of the Nile Valley" had been the battle cry of Egyptians. There is no reason why this idea cannot and should not be resurrected. Egypt and the Sudan can pool their water resources together in ways that optimize resource utilization. Rather than squandering precious water resources to create desert blooms in Egypt's desert, the water resources can effectively be used to irrigate the Sudan's arable land to realize the old vision of an Arab breadbasket. The Sudan can also handsomely benefit from Egypt's advances in hydrological and irrigation sciences. In turn, the efforts toward reterritorializing the state must be embedded in a dense cluster of mutually reinforcing regional institutions capable of tackling collective action problems. The efforts to stabilize population growth, to conserve and protect ecological resources and ecosystem services, to cope with the spread of diseases, to share scientific and technological resources, and to deal with general forces of destabilization can only be effective within the framework of regional institutions of coordination and collaboration. Although political arrangements like those outlined earlier may not presently appear possible, an intellectual vision of this sort and the effort needed to sustain the vision can represent a significant milestone in the evolution of an integrative riverine order in the Nile basin.

Toward Holistic Economies

William Finnegan, writing in *The New Yorker*, made the point that national water security is not a matter of abundant rainfalls, but how the water is used and nurtured. He cites Poland's situation as instructive in this regard. Its rich water endowment notwithstanding, Polish lakes, rivers, and sources of groundwater are so contaminated that the country's utilizable water resources are as little as those of Bahrain.[30] It is here where the demand side management of water resources becomes determinative of the extent to which water is protected and properly used. To focus on supply augmentation alone by each Nile state is a faulty strategy. The Nile states, separately as independent entities and collectively as belonging to an integrated hydrological and ecological system, can enhance the supply and quality of their water resources only by focusing their attention, energy, and resources on the demand side of water resources management. As the chapters in this volume show, each Nile riparian state is presently scrambling to achieve national food security through supply augmentation strategy—that is, by increasing their shares of Nile waters. To realize this national mission, all co-basin states are simultaneously looking to the Nile River, its tributaries, and the lakes throughout the region for precious water resources. If all the states do whatever they choose with their shares of Nile waters and other ecological resources in the basin without a regional machinery put in place, they may all share the burden of environmental exhaustion and the degradation of essential ecosystem services in equal proportions.

Demand-side management has natural and anthropogenic aspects. The natural aspect involves knowledge of the region's meteorology, hydrology, and ecology. This knowledge allows policy makers, planners, and project managers not only to predict the supply of water but also to develop adaptive responses and innovative strategies to cope with the scenarios that present themselves. For purposes of efficacy, dependability, burden sharing, collective action, and optimization of resource use, knowledge of the region's hydrological patterns and ecological demands must be centralized at the regional level to which all national agencies can have prompt access. Since knowledge is a function of data collection, data analysis, and data synthesis, as well as timely dissemination of valuable data, such tasks are better handled by a resource-rich and well-staffed regional center, one that is capable of forecasting weather patterns and the future availability of water. By determining precipitation and evaporation rates at different points of the Nile in particular time frames, such a regional center can be in a position to develop probabilistic scenarios of floods, droughts, and so on from which all co-basin states can benefit. In light of such regional distribution of information, the Nile states can simultaneously trigger their emergency responses when needed and adjust their policies and programs accordingly with minimal economic disruptions and social miseries to the peoples of the region. Centralization of information with equal access to all would also allow the states to pool resources so as to introduce next-generation technologies, such as remote data sensing and geostationary and polar orbiting satellites.[31] The additional benefit of a move to the next-generation technologies is that it would increase the reliability of data as well as the timely dissemination of high-quality data to all users.

Another area of urgency for regional cooperation involves energy appropriation and use. The major cause of forest depletion in the Nile basin is the overdependence by the broad masses on virgin forests for wood fuel. This problem can be solved (or at least substantially mitigated) by a combination of integrating energy sources and increased resort to solar energy. In theoretical terms, Ethiopia and the DRC have huge untapped hydropower potential. On the basis of a regionally integrated grid, the majority of the peoples in the basin can be hooked to a reliable energy source. A sustained move toward regional electrification can enormously ameliorate the living conditions of the region's people, conserve and protect the forests, and, by extension, strengthen the regional climate and precipitation regimes. Such effort toward regional electrification can be augmented by taking advantage of the new solar technologies. Since the incoming solar radiation and the outgoing terrestrial radiation are relatively predictable in the region, solar technologies can be an excellent source of energy.

Another area in need of integration is that of food production. As a normative goal, the search for national food security is laudable. But for such a goal to be sustainably realized, the search ought to be in the context of holistic economies and regional food security. There should be a clearly defined regional division of labor in the production and supply of agricultural goods and services. Within the context of a regional water budget, the co-basin states ought to determine what crops can be efficiently grown and in which countries. To give a realistic scope and sustainability to such a division of labor, horizontalized trading structures in both agriculture and industry must be put in place.

These considerations certainly would call for a radical restructuring of the agricultural sector in each co-basin country with allocation of water resources in mind. Although not the ultimate solution, conserving water resources through better demand-side management and better technology is a key, if used in conjunction with other steps, such as control of rural population growth. Since agriculture uses up to 80 percent of water resources even in highly developed countries, efficient alternatives to present irrigation methods must be explored. Egypt, for example, uses a full 86 percent of its water resources for irrigated agriculture. Key to developing holistic agriculture is to learn from the past mistakes of other countries in order not to repeat them.

Indeed, the Nile states can benefit enormously from the experience of California's San Joaquin Valley; with 4.7 million acres under irrigation, the agriculture in the valley is one of the most productive agricultural developments in the world. In the early 1980s, scientists were confounded by the rapid population decline and reproductive problems among aquatic species and waterfowl in the Casterson National Wildlife Refuge in the San Joaquin Valley. They made a tedious discovery that the problems were due to unprecedented concentrations of selenium, salts, chemical contaminants, and other trace elements in the ponds of the refuge. This discovery led further to another startling discovery of the root source of the problems, which was associated with irrigation-induced water-quality degradation.[32] The radical alteration or modification of the native ecology, by removing native flora and fauna and introducing alien species into the ecology, together with modern methods of farming, complicated the problems.

For example, prior to the pioneer capitalists making a daring move to the west, California's central valley had had up to 5 million acres of wetlands, which provided natural protective and filtering mechanisms to the region's ponds, lakes, and streams. By 1985, these wetlands were reduced by human action to between 300,000 and 400,000 acres.[33] The water quality in the San Joaquin Valley was of such major concern that the U.S. federal government set up an eighteen-person panel of experts in 1985 to investigate the problems and make recommendations on how to solve them. The early discovery was that there was a vicious cycle at work, having to do with excessive applications of water, and salt accumulation, worsened by a poor drainage system. As the water on the cropland dried through evaporation, salt was left on the surface. To mitigate the effects of primary salinization or to flush out the accumulated salt, farmers had to apply more irrigation water. In the absence of an adequate drainage system, they simply worsened the situation by creating the permissive condition for secondary salinization. Salt accumulation was accompanied by the concentrations of other chemical residues from fertilizers.

The problems were not entirely caused by human actions but also by the interaction between irrigation works and natural processes. In fact, the panel's key recommendation was that the resolution of the problems responsible for the irrigation-induced water-quality degradation required the promotion of a comprehensive understanding among policy makers and policy users of the complex interaction between biophysical processes and human activities. In the view of the panelists, the obstacles to resolving the problems involved the competing goals of stakeholders and other cost factors. "In many ways, the solutions to irrigation-induced water quality problems are hindered less by scientific and technical uncertainties than they are by conflicts in the social and legal realms."[34] Presently, most irrigation fields worldwide rely on a gravity system to carry water whose average efficiency rate is only 45 percent while sprinklers, surge, and level basin systems have efficiency rates of about 70 percent. With efficiency rates of 90 percent, drip irrigation, where water is slowly applied to the root zones of crops as needed, is superior to all other known systems.[35] For example, growing tomatoes in Egypt under a drip irrigation system is said to consume 40 percent less water than under traditional irrigation methods.[36]

Crop selection is another important strategy for conserving water. Rice and sugarcane, for example, are generally regarded as water-intensive crops. However, these steps associated with demand-side management and technology must be seen in a broader context of doing things radically differently. What is needed is to move away from the capitalist notion of agricultural accumulation to a holistic conception of food security, one that makes social justice and ecological integrity the center of any agrarian production system. For starters, the essential steps that must be taken toward the attainment of this holistic agriculture are found in what Horne and McDermott (2001) call *The Next Green Revolution*. The authors of this holistic prescription identify eight foundational steps to an agrarian system that is ecology-friendly, healthy, sustainable, just, and profitable. I will build my modest concluding remarks around these eight guidelines. Because their cautionary recommendations are so comprehensive and sensible, I extensively rely on their contribution to a holistic agrarian system. The caveat here is that these guidelines can attain self-sufficient coherence only in the context in which the hegemony of unfettered capitalist agriculture is vigorously contested and an alternative is negotiated.

Horne and McDermott are correct in forwarding the proposition that a holistic economics of agriculture cannot be seen in isolation from a healthy ecology and a sound social foundation. Therefore, the first crucial step to the holistic agrarian system that they put forth requires the maintenance of healthy soil as an organism full of living creatures, energy, air, and water. The authors of *The Next Green Revolution* correctly note that natural soil is by far superior to chemical-dependent soil in the long run in terms of texture, mineral particles, water-retention capacity, composition of biologically active organisms, and organic nutrients. Chemical-dependent soil masks a lot of things in terms of hydrological, ecological, social, and human costs. In 1989, one-third of U.S. corn fields were wholly dependent on insecticides. This was in addition to the 219 million pounds of herbicides used on those fields. Dependence on chemical fertilizers, even though it does boost production in the short run, is equally costly both ecologically and socially by producing harmful pollutants and contaminants. Even the generally pro-business U.S. Environmental Protection Agency acknowledges that agriculture is the principal source of water pollution and contamination. The problem gets worse as farmers increase their chemical uses to boost production. In 1995, for example, American farmers used 23 billion pounds of nitrogen fertilizer (a major source of nitrate contamination), representing a twenty-five-fold increase since 1945.[37]

The second essential lesson involves the conservation and protection of water quality. Protecting the sources of water resources from pollution, contamination, and sedimentation is akin to a supply augmentation strategy by other means. The third step requires the repudiation of the industrial model of agrarian production as a way of thwarting pollution and contamination associated with standardized processes of agrarian production. As we all know, the first principle of capitalist agriculture is size. But we also know that "big" is not always necessarily good. The search for bigger scale economy does not only lead to the depletion of natural resources and overexploitation of water resources but also to the degradation of water quality and ecosystem services as a result of heavy chemical use. After a decade-long study of fifty-one river basins and aquifer systems, for example, the U.S. Geological Survey found the presence of forty of the one hundred pesticides in use at detectable levels in almost all streams and wells across the United States. A significant amount of the one billion pounds of pesticides that Americans use every year ends up in streams and groundwater, contributing to outbursts of neurological disorders, birth defects, and cancers. The study found that more than 50 percent of agricultural streams and more than 80 percent of urban streams have pesticide concentrations that exceeded the water quality benchmark for aquatic ecosystems. What is particularly disturbing is that organochlorine pesticides (like DDT, dieldrin, and chlordane that were eliminated long time ago) are still frequently present in sediment and fish in many streams throughout the United States at levels greater than the benchmark for aquatic ecosystems. Because some of the chemicals resist biodegradation, they tend to bioaccumulate in the environment over time, posing long-term health problems to humans and animals. Even more distressing is the discovery that the pesticides occur in complex compounds, something that magnifies their toxic potency.[38]

The fourth step requires the selection and use of animal and plant species that are in organic harmony with the native ecology. The introduction of invasive species into the local ecology, as we saw with the Nile perch in Lake Victoria, can undermine the sustainability principle in substantial ways. Agricultural modernization along the Western model (based on the fetishism of diversification or convenient crop selection) can grossly undercut the integrity of local ecosystems.

The fifth cautionary advice requires the preservation and promotion of biological diversity as an essential integral part of a sustainable agriculture within a healthy native ecology. The dominant paradigm of accumulation has hitherto taken ecological resources and nonhuman species for granted. This must change. The search for national food security, without appropriate attention given to ecological demands, is shortsighted and self-defeating. Forests, riparian vegetation, wetlands, aquatic species, and the necessity to dilute pollutants and contaminants all demand that sufficient water be left to flow in natural channels. Sustainable agriculture is one that values biodiversity as the first principle of holistic economics. Such an approach must be embedded in what Richard Fern refers to as "a holistic ethics of nature."[39] This understanding of the relationship of the economy to nature has practical and moral considerations. Fern grounds these considerations in the principles of "decency," "necessity," and "deference." By virtue of their entitlements and subjection to the laws of evolution and/or creation, nonhuman living things must be seen as having a valid moral standing under the "decency" principle and therefore humans have the moral obligations to treat them ethically. Nature is not something to be abused, exploited, and degraded, since doing so would disrupt the natural processes and violate the "deference" principle. Of course, if we absolutely adhere to these two principles, then we run into an irresolvable moral paradox that involves the moral worth of nonhumans in their relations to humans. Fern resolves this moral paradox by introducing the principle of "necessity," which gives humans a privileged position in the ordering of nature. In other words, humans can use ecological resources by necessity so long as they use them ethically and respectfully. Although this theology-focused argument is useful as far as it goes, it glosses over the deep dilemma as to whether nature can be treated "ethically" and "respectfully" under the prevailing mode of production, something that calls for a vigorous contestation of the dominant capitalist agriculture.

The crucial point to remember here is the fact that agriculture thrives only in the context of its natural environment, which provides critical nutrients and blue-collar working animals that assiduously serve as pollinators and pest eaters. Noting the importance of forests to farming, one scholar made the point that one-third of the food consumed in the United States comes from plants that are pollinated by birds, bats, bees, and wasps, all of which make their natural habitats in forests or patches of woods.[40] In fact, birds, bats, wasps, bees, insects, and other animals worldwide contribute $534 billion worth of services by pollinating food crops and controlling pests.[41] The role forests play in this complex relationship between agriculture and the natural environment illustrates this point. For example, a group of researchers recently made a spectacular discovery with respect to the role bees play in the pollination of flowering coffee trees. By focusing on one coffee plantation in Costa Rica, the researchers measured the contribution of pollination of coffee crops by bees to the overall productivity of the plantation. The bees from the rainforests made twice as many visits to the flowering coffee trees near the forests and twice as much pollen deposition as they made to the coffee trees far from the forests. As a result, the yields from the coffee trees near the forests were 20 percent higher than from the trees far from the forests; a full 7 percent of the plantation's annual coffee production was directly attributed to pollination by bees from the forests. In addition, the coffee plants near the forests were found to be much less susceptible to producing deformed beans than those far from the forests.[42] Since seven of the ten Nile countries are major coffee producers, this finding must be of immense importance; more important, though, the study of this single ecosystem service indicates how much worth the total ecosystem services can be. In fact, natural scientists tell us that forests produce ecosystem services worth $5 trillion per annum.[43] This figure does not actually include the value of the capital component of the forests.

The sixth cautionary advice draws attention to the danger that such chemicals as pesticides, insecticides, and fertilizers pose to both human health and ecological integrity. These anthropogenic sources of pollution and contamination are harmful to all riparian interests because of the substantial reduction of vital water resources available to them as a result of water-quality degradation. The seventh step to a holistic agriculture calls for the conservation of hydrocarbon sources of energy and the increasing resort to regenerative sources of power. This entails widespread application of solar technology in which the Nile states can establish a comparative advantage in light of the abundant solar radiation with which the region is endowed.

The final step, which Horne and McDermott advocate, calls for finding new ways by which we can reduce risk and enhance agrarian profitability. This requires harnessing modern science to make sustainable agriculture a reality and a rewarding enterprise. This, in turn, requires an open renunciation of corporate agriculture, solely driven by growth and profit motives. Here I go beyond what Horne and McDermott have proposed. Profitable agricultural undertakings need not be individual farms. One of the factors underlying rural poverty in the Nile basin is the increasing fragmentation of land under the private landholding regime. Rectification of this structural problem would consequently necessitate the reaggregation of farms under cooperative arrangement. This would permit not only the rationalization of production and the reaping of the advantages of scale economy under conditions of social production, but also efficient use of resources and distribution channels.

Toward a Politics of Self-Reliance

Over the decades, many analysts have debated the causes and consequences of underdevelopment in Africa. In the main, the debate has been
between internalizers and externalizers. For internalizers, African poverty
is essentially due to bad government.[44] This dominant view finds full expression in the growing corpus of corruption literature and in various
World Bank and IMF reports. As internalizers would present the case,
corruption nurtures red tape, substandard accounting, distortion of priorities, and entrenches patronage. As a result, it discourages foreign investment and undercuts donor-funded development programs; it
undermines economic growth; it diminishes the delivery of public services
to the poor; it weakens poverty reduction efforts.[45] Insofar as the de-
scription goes, the position of internalizers sounds right. But the problem
with this view is that we already know that Africa is plagued with bad
governments. The issue is why bad governments have become the hall-
mark of the continent. There must be some unexplained structural causes
or cultural factors that can be discovered and understood. Until we do so,
we may not be able to make a proper diagnosis of the problem and offer
the right prescription for a cure.

Externalizers trace the origins (rampancy and entrenchment) of corruption in Africa to colonialism and the contemporary international environment.[46] The danger inherent in this view is the tendency to exonerate oneself
from the problem and avoid critical self-reflection by presenting internal
forces simply as passive agents of history and victims of exterior forces.

Taken separately, the internal versus external arguments are reductionist. Even taken together, they offer neither an adequate explanation
for, nor a satisfactory solution to the problem of underdevelopment and
poverty in Africa. In the hope of bridging this gulf between internalizers
and externalizers, Jeffrey Sachs, Columbia University professor and director of the UN Millennium Development Goals, has lately become the standard bearer of an updated version of the "modernization" theory. To
Sachs, African poverty is not necessarily the result of corruption or bad
government, but rather a function of the acute shortage of development
funds. Accordingly, the solution lies in increasing development aid to
Africa by the advanced countries.[47] In Sachs's view, the "corruption" argument is overplayed by those who seek to deflect the debate away from
the call for more aid for the continent. He may have a point here. After all,
the history of capitalism is a history of corruption. Whether expressed in
the form of resource vandalization and exploitation of labor under colonialism, or in its modern form of hyperconcentration of capital in fewer
hands by maintaining corrupt practices such as double bookkeeping and
hidden offshore accounts (as global corporations always do), influencing
electoral politics, and controlling legislative processes, corruption has been

integral to accumulation. In fact, according to the World Bank's own estimates, public officials globally receive over $1 trillion in bribes every year. This amount does not include public embezzlement. In Russia alone, corrupt officials siphon off $300 billion in bribes each year from manifold transactions.[48] The UN Commission, set up to investigate the Iraqi Oil for Food program, recently discovered that 2,392 giant international corporations, including DaimlerChrysler, Siemens, and Volvo, had been implicated in giving $1.8 billion to Saddam Hussein in kickbacks.[49] In recent years, revelations of a series of corporate scandals in the United States triggered a bust of the stock market, causing pension funds, institutional investors, and employees to lose $6 trillion. In mid-May 2006, Boeing Corporation chose to settle for $615 million with the U.S. federal government for fraud and corruption to preempt prosecution on felonious charges and hefty financial penalties.[50] Indeed, Western transnational corporations and financial institutions have been the principal enablers and the chief harvesters of the fruits of corruption in Africa.

Although Sachs's prescription leaves a lot to be desired, his contention that singling out "corruption" as the monocausal factor to explain African poverty is in part correct. From my perspective, corruption under capitalism is virtually unavoidable. The problem in Africa is not corruption, but rather its inefficient and wasteful use. In fact, the gross inefficiency and wastefulness of African corruption are what distinguish it from other forms of corruption in the advanced countries. In the first instance, wealth obtained through corruption or bad practices in the advanced countries does not leave the circulatory arteries of capitalist accumulation. As such, it has no impact on macroeconomic processes and performances. In Africa, by contrast, ill-gotten wealth (and there is lots of it) leaves the continent and enters the circulatory processes in the advanced countries, in effect subsidizing capitalist development in the advanced countries. The World Bank estimates that over 40 percent of privately held wealth in Africa is either stashed away offshore or invested in the global north.[51] Nigeria has reportedly exported over $300 billion worth of oil since the 1970s, which has presumably entered the circulation process in the global north without any evidence of benefit for the home country. In fact, the per capita income of Nigerians plummeted from $1,000 in the 1970s to $390 in early 2006; two-thirds of the country's population live on less than a dollar a day.[52] In the second instance, a significant proportion of African wealth obtained through kickbacks and illicit payments is squandered on conspicuous consumption of imports. Here again, rather than reinforcing domestic production activities, the wealthy class in Africa subsidizes capitalist growth in the advanced countries by demanding greater volumes of imports.

Contrary to conventional wisdom, the primary reason why the Nile states are poor and underdeveloped is not because of a shortage of external capital inflows to the region, but because too many resources are leaving the region. Sachs and others wrongly assume that the Nile states, like all African states, are maintaining their existence by receiving critical nourishments via feeding tubes from the advanced countries; thus, increasing the supply of vital nourishments can solve their ills. In truth, though, it is the other way around. They are integrated into global capitalism in order to nurture the reproduction of capitalism in the core capitalist countries in its present form. Like all states in the global south, the Nile states do this in three ways. The first is by specializing in the production and supply of ever-depreciating primary commodities—raw cotton, coffee, tea, sesame, groundnuts, and an assortment of minerals. The crucial anomaly inherent in the present global division of labor is the fact that the relationship between the values of primary commodities and those of finished goods is radically inverse. Whereas finished goods have a built-in indexation, allowing them to quickly adjust to inflation by pushing prices upward to reflect the change in values, the prices of primary commodities move in the opposite direction. In effect, efficiency gains made in the production of primary commodities are passed on to manufacturers in the global north, which transform the raw materials into finished goods for sale on domestic and international markets, thereby reaping superprofit by controlling the upper end of the value chain of economic activity. Moreover, efficiency gains in the production of primary commodities veritably lead to structural oversupply and low input prices, which allow transnational corporations to dramatically increase the value-added components of economic transactions. For instance, world market prices for coffee beans fell from $1.20 a pound in the 1980s to $.55 in the early years of this decade while the value-added component of processed coffee went up. In the early 1990s, coffee-exporting countries used to capture $10–12 billion of the value of the retail sales of $30 billion. In year 2003, however, of the annual retail sales of $70 billion, coffee-exporting countries could claim a mere $5.5 billion; this is principally due to structural oversupply of coffee beans, the modernization of production processes, and too many countries supplying coffee beans. In 2001, for example, sixty countries produced 132 million bags of coffee beans while the global demand for coffee beans was only 108 million bags.[53] Nothing illustrates this anomaly more than the experience of sub-Saharan Africa. Although sub-Saharan African states increased the export of primary commodities by 30 percent between 1986 and 1989, they lost $56 billion because of structural oversupply as well as the secular and cyclical decline of commodity prices.[54] Moreover, between 1997 and 1999, prices for African primary commodities, on average, fell by 25 percent, while the prices of goods from the advanced countries soared.[55] According to UNCTAD, twelve of the fourteen primary commodities critical to African foreign exchange earnings suffered from wild gyration in real prices between 1960 and 2000, and nine showed significant secular decline.

In fact, the price index of primary commodities from sub-Saharan Africa declined by over 50 percent between 1997 and 2001.[56] Small wonder that world market share for primary commodities from sub-Saharan Africa dropped from 6 percent in 1980 to 4 percent in 2000 while total merchandise exports from the region plummeted from 6.3 percent to 2.5 percent over the same period.[57] This unequal exchange between the African countries and the advanced countries is reflected in the decline of the relative incomes of the former. Between 1989 and 1999, for example, the real per capita income as measured by GDP in fifteen of the poorest countries in the world, including Burundi, the DRC, Ethiopia, Tanzania, and Uganda, fell by an average of 5.5 percent a year while the real income of the fifteen richest countries in the global north increased by 15.5 percent per annum.[58] This structural impediment to generating sufficient foreign exchange earnings (critical to capital formation) is exacerbated by the fact that sub-Saharan African states are overdependent not only on primary commodities but also on a narrow range of primary commodities. In 1987, for example, eleven sub-Saharan African countries depended on a single primary commodity for 75 percent of their foreign exchange earnings; in fact, exports of primary commodities accounted for a full 92 percent of all African exports between 1970 and 1991.[59]

The global tariff regime now in place (contrary to the neoliberal rhetoric of "free trade") also disadvantages primary commodity producers in Africa. The culprits here are import restrictions and subsidies. Even the World Bank acknowledges that, if the rich countries were to remove the barriers to trade with Africa, exports from sub-Saharan African countries would rise by 14 percent per annum. If the rich countries were to cut off the U.S. $360 billion given to their farmers in subsidies in the year 2000, which actually rose to $400 billion in 2004, exports by African producers of primary goods and farm products would rise even higher; they would be in a favorable position to compete and benefit from an authentic free trade regime.[60] In 2002, for example, the cotton-producing countries in Africa south of the Sahara saw a revenue loss of $300 million because of subsidies in advanced countries; this was more than the $230 million that the World Bank and the IMF approved in debt "relief" in that year for nine cotton-exporting states in west and central Africa.[61] There is a cruel irony involved here in that the advanced countries use their huge financial resources to shield the 3–4 percent of their populations engaged in agriculture against the vagaries of price volatility by subsidies and sophisticated forms of trade restrictions while simultaneously demanding underdeveloped African countries to demolish all forms of barriers to trade, thereby exacerbating the pauperization of the 70–80 percent of the rural populations who depend on the production of primary commodities (UNCTAD 2004).

Sub-Saharan African underdevelopment or poverty trap is thus a function of the commodity trap, which not only determines the macro-economic performances of African states but also defines their net barter terms of trade vis-à-vis the global north.[62] On the one hand, the values of African exports of nonfuel primary commodities continually diminish; on the other hand, however, African imports of food, petroleum, capital, and consumer goods progressively rise. The result is unequal exchange between the two baskets of exports and imports. It is this structural inequity, giving rise to price volatility and secular losses in net barter terms of trade, that explains the poverty trap in the Nile basin and beyond.[63]

The so-called Singapore paradigm is even more ominous from the African perspective. When meeting in Singapore in 1996, trade negotiators from the advanced countries introduced into the negotiation regime a new set of issues involving the liberalization of trade in services, public procurement and investment, and transparency in competition. This new penetration strategy has been designed to control those areas in which northern corporations have had difficulty making a foray. Penetrating and controlling services industries, such as banking operations and insurance companies, would certainly contribute to the cyclical reproduction of capitalism. It is instructive to note that the service industries in the United States employ 80 percent of the workforce and account for 63 percent of GDP. The value of service exports from the United States soared from $199 billion in 1994 to $340 billion in 2004; this is a 70 percent increase over a decade.[64]

The second way by which the Nile countries contribute to the sustenance of global capitalism at their own expense is via the importation of consumer goods, capital goods, military weapons, and the awarding of contracts to northern corporations. Integration of Africans into the cosmopolitan pattern of consumption is critical to the cyclical reproduction of capitalism. One of the latest mechanisms for this purpose is the introduction of plastic credit cards. The salience of this methodology is nowhere more apparent than in Kenya. By the end of 2004, there were 100,000 plastic cards in circulation in Kenya. Impressed by the experiment, credit card bureaus in Nairobi were poised to issue more than half a million new cards during 2005.[65] The World Bank is among the chief promoters of credit card issuance, under the rubric of achieving transparency and stimulating growth. To state the obvious, subjecting Africans to the addiction of credit card use will only intensify resource transfer from the continent to the global north through the intensification of imports of consumer goods and the crippling interest charges.

The final way for resource transfer from the Nile region to the north is through so-called foreign aid. Over a period of three decades, Africa as a whole made repayments of more than $550 billion to northern creditors on the $540 billion the continent received in loans during the same period. Not only did Africa's payout in interests plus amortization exceed what the continent borrowed, but also the continent's debt stood at $295 billion at the end of 2004, still costing the continent $15 billion each year to service the outstanding debt.[66] In fact, Africa's debt became so obscene that even ordinary citizens in the global north felt the need to do something to get rid of the odious debts. The response by the rich countries to the grassroots mobilization against the global debt has been the launching of the so-called heavily indebted poor countries (HIPC) initiative. The initiative camouflaged in "debt forgiveness" would reduce (not eliminate) the debt owed by poor third world nations on condition that they adhere to free market principles—in effect, driving the state out of the regulatory business. If a country demonstrates its worthiness in this area within three years, then its debt would be reduced to a "sustainable" level.

Uganda under Museveni became among the early graduates from the HIPC school of neoliberalism. Its debt was reduced to a "sustainable" level. The problem was that its debt went up again, dangerously crossing the "sustainability" threshold. Uganda had to go back to school a second time. As of this writing, Uganda was applying for admission into the school for its third time. The problem for Uganda is that not all the money it borrowed came from multilateral institutions. It had borrowed from commercial banks, which sued the country in early 2005 to collect their money; the underlying reason why Uganda's debt continued to climb, despite debt relief, is because the HIPC initiative was window dressing. In the 1990s, Uganda was paying out $17 on servicing its debt for every $3 it spent on health care.[67]

The way out of the historical morass of underdevelopment, poverty, and ecological degradation for the Nile states points to the imperative of self-reliance. This involves regional demilitarization, the promotion of horizontal trade, the championing of producer cooperatives in all sectors of their economies, and making a transition from natural resource-dependence to nonfarm sources of income. A proper understanding of the impact of militarization on internal security and economy as well as on interstate relations is crucial here.

It is helpful to bear in mind that the armament industry is central to the continuous reproduction of capitalism in the advanced countries, made possible in no small part by large markets for arms readily available in the third world. To put it into perspective, between 1969 and 1988, the Soviet Union by itself exported $236 billion worth of arms while the United States, France, and Great Britain together exported $215 billion worth of weapons during the same period. By some estimates, between 15 and 33 percent of third world debts was accounted for by arms imports, forcing developing countries to surrender up to 85 percent of their foreign earnings to global arms exporters and money lenders.[68] This global arms bonanza has not shown any sign of abating even in the post–cold war era as military expenditures and arms purchasing by developing countries have been on the rise since 1993, reaching a historic record of $232 billion in 1997, accounting for 28 percent of the total global arms purchases of $842 billion. Between 2001 and 2004, countries of the global south accounted for 57.3 percent of all global arms purchases; in 2004, developing countries accounted for 58.4 percent of the $956 billion global military expenditures.[69]

As members of the global south, the Nile states are loyal consumers of weapons from the global north. The role of Egypt and Ethiopia (the two biggest arms purchasers in the Nile basin) in the global arms transfers will suffice to illustrate the significance of arms purchases. Over a three-year period, between 1995 and 1997, Egypt received arms shipments worth $5.3 billion from foreign sources; between 1997 and 2004, Egypt signed a series of new arms deals worth $12.8 billion. In fact, in 2004, Egypt was the fourth largest arms importer in the world; of the $2.1 billion annual U.S. aid for Egypt, $1.3 billion actually goes to subsidize Egypt's military parasitism.[70] Ever since the end of the cold war, Egypt has feverishly been modernizing its armed forces. The country's air fleet is said to have 550 jet fighters, including 190 F-16s, all imported.[71] Although the official defense budget runs between $2.1 and $2.7 billion a year, observers believe that the actual defense outlay is between $15 and $17 billion a year if one includes "off-the-shelf" expenditures in the general military budget.[72] One wonders why Egypt has seen the urgency to accumulate such military power by diverting precious resources from projects essential to human necessities. Is Egypt preparing for war against Ethiopia, which controls much of the "blue gold"? If this is the case, Egypt may be gravely disappointed in trying to find hope in military solutions to the problem of water resources.

Like Egypt, Ethiopia has long been parasitically dependent on arms imports to battle the Eritreans and suppress rebel nationalists inside the country. In the 1980s, Ethiopia imported $1 billion worth of Soviet arms a year, during which time 50 percent of the country's foreign exchange earnings went to the military sector.[73] The amount of resources the country spent each year in the 1980s on arms purchases was two times the amount spent on education and eight times the amount spent on health care.[74] This was at a time when over one million Ethiopians perished from starvation and another eleven million were saved by feeding tubes from the West. In 1999, when Ethiopia reengaged the Eritreans in a bloody war, the country's arms imports accounted for 20.5 percent of total imports for that year.[75]

Apart from the obvious contribution that militarization of Nile societies makes to the reproduction of capitalism in the advanced countries, the phenomenon has a harmful impact on internal and regional relationships. The imported arms are used to repress domestic opposition or foment interethnic violence as well as to sponsor regional proxies or spark costly interstate wars. This allows the ruling elites to perpetuate themselves in power by presenting internal stability and external security as the justifications for postponing democratic reforms. In sum, the armed forces in each Nile state are an ever-present threat to society; they can neither offer internal safety nor guarantee external security.

Establishing and nurturing horizontal networks of economic relationships at the regional level constitute the second mode of promoting collective self-reliance. By historical circumstances, the Nile states are vertically integrated into the Western economic order as suppliers of primary commodities. In the 1970s, the DRC derived two-thirds of its foreign receipts from exporting copper to the West while half of Egypt's foreign exchange earnings came from cotton.[76] The pattern, in this unequal exchange between the Nile countries and the West, has changed little today. Virtually all Nile states depend on a handful of primary commodities (mainly cotton, coffee, tea, and minerals) to generate external revenue. The prices for these commodities are set by the industrial establishments in the advanced countries. Furthermore, primary commodities are generally vulnerable both to the vagaries of nature and the tempestuous and volatile demand conditions in the advanced countries. Discoveries of substitutes and the growing dematerialization of production processes in the advanced countries have the tendency of exacerbating the problem by putting downward pressure on the value of primary commodities from the Nile basin. Modernization of production processes and the increased supply of primary goods simply serve to further depress prices. Ethiopian coffee growers, for example, have increasingly resorted to growing khaat, the bushy leaf with psychotropic effects, because they could no longer subsist by growing coffee. The only solution to this vertical dependence on the global north is for the Nile countries to wean themselves from total reliance on primary commodities for export to the global north and, instead, to cultivate horizontal economic interactions among themselves.

Horizontal regional economic networks offer two advantages. First, because the Nile states are more or less on the same development trajectory, the terms of trade are likely to be roughly even due to relative symmetry in overall cost of production. This can overcome or reduce the vulnerability of the region to unequal exchange of trade with the advanced countries. Second, incomes from trade among the Nile states can remain within the region, even if some trading partners within that region may gain more than others from horizontal trade relations.

However, regional collective self-reliance is an outward expression of a prior transformation of internal forces of production within each Nile country. It thus goes without saying that the promotion of internal self-reliance ought to be the first priority of each Nile state. If properly nurtured, producer cooperatives can be the pioneers in redirecting economic growth toward genuine development, which will not only increase the overall output of the economy but also substantially improve the quality

of life for the majority of the producers. Today, even some nongovernmental organizations are championing the value of cooperatives as an alternative to the prevailing mode of production. For example, Care
International, a consortium of twelve humanitarian aid organizations, by-
passed official channels and began providing enabling facilities to poor
Kenyans to establish thirty independent farming cooperatives. In the
Makueni District of Kenya's eastern province, these small farmers received very modest loans to purchase irrigation pipes, tools, seeds, and
fertilizers to begin work on their newly leased landed properties along the
Athi River. Each cooperative accommodates thirty participating farmers
who pay small membership fees. Until the cooperatives were able to stand
on their feet, Care International would continue to provide them with
technical assistance in such matters as budgeting, accounting, and han-
dling of fertilizers and pesticides. In no time, the cooperatives were able
to demonstrate what could be achieved under conditions of full ownership of labor and the means of production. They began growing a variety of vegetables, including chili peppers, okra, baby corn, cabbage, and
bitter gourd, all of which found hospitable markets in Europe and Asia.
In early 2004, the average monthly income of the farmers in the cooperatives was $100. This was a marked improvement in income in a coun-
try in which 56 percent of the population lives on less than a dollar a day.
Once the cooperatives become fully operational, the average monthly
income of the farmers is expected to rise to $1,000.[77]

Making a transition from overdependence on primary commodity
production to higher forms of economic activity is the final step that the
Nile states must take. In December 2005, an interesting study (sponsored
by the World Bank) was released, comparing the per capita wealth of
120 countries. The study identifies natural capital (resources found in
nature like minerals, forests, cropland, pasture, etc.), produced capital
(machinery, building, infrastructure), and intangible capital (raw labor,
human skills, rule of law) as the key components constituting national
wealth. The study reveals that the greater the proportion of the intangible
capital of wealth, the wealthier the nation. Conversely, the greater the
proportion of the natural capital of wealth, the poorer a nation becomes.
What is even more revealing is the fact that $353,339 of the $439,063 of
the per capita wealth of high-income countries consists of intangible capital, measured in years of schooling spent by their populations and the
quality of their institutions or rule of law. By comparison, in sub-Saharan
African countries, the intangible capital represents a mere $6,746 of their
total per capital wealth of $10,730. Not surprisingly, while the top ten
richest nations (with $439,063 per capita wealth) are in the global north,
the bottom ten countries (with $7,532 per capita wealth) are in the global
south, nine of them in sub-Saharan Africa; two Nile states (Ethiopia and
Burundi with $1,965 and $2,859 per capita wealth, respectively) share

the dubious distinction of being last and next to last. To put this in perspective, the per capita wealth in Switzerland is $648,241.[78]

Here is the relevance of the study to the Nile countries. Approximately 80 percent of sub-Saharan Africa's combined populations of 700 million depend on natural capital. Such overdependence involves distressing depletion of resources and degradation of critical ecosystem services, something that points to the urgency of moving a large number of people from rural production to the manufacturing and service sectors. To meet this challenge, however, African countries must create eight million jobs each year, an enormous task to accomplish.[79] But here is the rub: with $13 trillion in GDP, the United States averages two million new jobs a year; sub-Saharan African combined GDP is less than $1 trillion. So, the hope of generating eight million new jobs each year is a pipe dream. After all, the number of African workers, subsisting on less than a dollar a day, rose by a staggering twenty-eight million between 1994 and 2004 and the number of Africans who go hungry every day rose from 160 million in 1960 to 315 million by 2004.[80] Thus, the natural resource dependence of the Nile states simultaneously suggests a vulnerability of the basin's watershed ecology to widespread degradation and the urgency to make a transition to higher forms of economic activity. Of course, this begs the question: how can the Nile countries (individually and collectively) make the transition to a sort of social order that is optimally sustainable and socially just without compromising the integrity of their shared ecology?

Although ecosocialists offer a plausible alternative to the present order, I don't believe that the subjective conditions for realizing an ecosocialist vision are presently ripe. So, a halfway house between the prevailing order, aided by the notion of destructive creation, and the long-term vision of ecosocialism must be found. I believe that the burgeoning corpus of ecological economics now offers a very useful direction to countries seeking to achieve sustainable development. This involves the deliberate determination of an optimal scale of the economy relative to the regenerative and waste-absorption capacity of the ecology. The fundamental organizing principle of this objective is "sufficiency." This in turn requires a realistic understanding of the fact that the Nile countries can no longer depend on the infinite bounty of the ecology to furnish infinite quantities of water resources, virgin material resources, nutrient-rich soil, and other essential ecosystem services. In general, I believe that each Nile country must take a number of critical steps to achieve a genuine social progress.

1. *Political self-determination.* Throughout, I have reiterated the point that democratic governance, social justice, and ecological integrity are inseparable. However, political self-determination is the fundamental cornerstone in this tangle of relationships; remove political self-determination from the equation and you will have neither social justice nor ecological equity. The painful reality must be acknowledged that the regular gatherings

of self-proclaimed experts and their government bosses in luxurious hotels, the seminars they organize, and the voluminous materials they produce to establish their self-worth are all an exercise in futility. Any move that pays sheer lip service to popular participation in considerations of water resources and other issues of development is doomed to failure. Therefore, the crucial task facing each Nile country is how to get citizens actively involved in the current debate over the future direction of social progress. Without citizens consciously owning the issues of development and without their active engagement to frontally tackle these issues, there is no way forward. However, citizen activism does not occur in a void; it requires secular vision and intellectual leadership to educate, enlighten, mobilize, and organize local communities everywhere for sustained mass actions. The Kenyan women's groups, who planted and own over thirty million multipurpose trees under the intellectual leadership of Professor Maathai, showed us how much progress could be achieved under an authentic partnership between the broad masses of the people and the learned professions.

2. *Population control.* The present size of the combined populations of the Nile states is already above the ecological sustainability threshold. Since 80 percent of these populations live in the rural areas, the broader ecological implications for constructing and maintaining a sustainable scale of the economy are particularly apparent. Therefore, a substantial reduction of population growth is essential not only for poverty alleviation but also for replenishing and conserving the region's natural capital as well as for protecting the critical ecosystem services that the natural capital generates. Hence, the step toward determining the optimal scale of the rural economy requires the simultaneous control of rural population growth and finding alternative opportunities for the "surplus" rural people to generate incomes in nonagrarian sectors.

3. *Rejecting the growth theory and globalization.* The social progress of a nation is measured not by the mere accumulation of wealth but by how natural resources are used and how national incomes are distributed so that everyone in society can lead a healthy and productive life. However, this overriding objective requires constructing an economy that values a greater degree of ecological integrity by consuming virgin resources sustainably and generating fewer negative externalities. National self-sufficiency and regional self-reliance are the operative concepts here, which value better over bigger.

4. *Creating new national patterns of consumption.* One of the major problems in the Nile countries (as in the rest of Africa) is the fact that the middle and upper classes are integrated into the global patterns of consumption. Most imports into the region do not contribute to development; they merely satisfy the vanity of the consumers—depleting national wealth, undermining national capital formation, and socializing the young generations into social parasitism.

5. *Redesigning cities.* The construction sector in the Nile countries is modeled after what prevails in the advanced countries. Highrises, fortress mansions, and villas in enclaves are characteristically on display throughout the region while, at the same time, slums and shanty sections are sprawling in all urban centers. Such modern buildings are both resource and energy depleting. The way forward in urban development is to abandon the imported notion of "big" in favor of homegrown "small." There are ways in which simpler homes can be built with fewer virgin materials and still be energy-efficient.

6. *Developing a dependable public transportation system.* Almost all Nile countries are oil importers; the exceptions are Egypt and the Sudan and the energy independence even of these two countries is hardly long term. The development of a national transport system can reduce the need to import private vehicles and, by extension, reduce the oil import bill, pollution, and smog.

Conclusion

Explicitly or implicitly, I have argued in this and other chapters that a discourse on water resources is about shared concerns with respect to development issues. I have also reiterated throughout that development requires a shared understanding of the intrinsic and complex relationship among various ecological factors, hydrological determinants, demographic aspects, the politics of governance, and the economics of social justice. The hydrographic competition among the Nile countries is a surrogate response to the collective internal incapacity to address in full the population dilemma, the gross social injustice, the widespread political repression, the devastation of natural capital, and the growing deterioration in ecosystem services.

In the final analysis, though, the fundamentals of the position taken in this work boil down to two essential conclusions. The first is that the Nile states must grapple with the kind of economic order that they have to put in place. Any progress along the lines of a neoliberal model is not in prospect. To think that the Nile countries will achieve Western-style capitalist civilization by adhering to externally supplied economic prescriptions represents a fatal failure of imagination wrapped in illusion. Under the neoliberal growth regime, no Nile country can ensure the adequate supply of water resources to its citizens nor can it make a useful contribution to the protection of the Nile River and its watershed ecology.

The second essential imperative points to the necessity of having a counterhegemonic movement. To turn the tide against ecological devastation, mass poverty, and the regional scramble for vital water resources will require radical political leadership and new intellectual infrastructure. Seen in this light, the discourse on Nile water resource allocation cannot be considered apart from the general struggle to liberate both the social researcher and the policy maker from the tyranny of mathematical modeling and quantification of the growth axioms of neoclassical economics. The national elites, already entrenched in power, are constrained by their class interests to chart an alternative to the prevailing social order. Given this reality, the historic responsibility to offer a counterhegemonic vision and leadership rests on public intellectuals. The task requires the initiation of a comprehensive process of decolonization of social thought. The neoliberal project is not a divinely sanctioned universal model. It is a historical product of social innovation, subject to contestation, modification, and even repudiation. There is no predestination in history; humans determine their present status and shape the direction of their future in relationship with one another and in interaction with their natural environment. The biggest piece of the jigsaw puzzle is if the Nile states can produce enlightened public intellectuals who understand the burden of history, and who are also willing (and able) to bear that burden.

Notes

Chapter One

1. Collins, 2002, 178.
2. Starr, 17–36.
3. Ashraf, 1915.
4. Renner et al., 19.
5. Thurow, 6.
6. Berner and Berner, 229–234; Nathanson, 12–13; George Cox, 148–156.
7. Abdel Mageed, 157–183.
8. Villiers, 228.
9. Gleick, 179–212.
10. Waterbury, 2002, 8.
11. M. J., 34–40.
12. M. J., 34–40.
13. Daly and Farley, 62–63.
14. Erlich and Erlich, chapters 3–4.
15. Brown and Kane, 1995.
16. Daly and Farley, 34.
17. Hinrichsen, 34–35.
18. Postel, 1988, 103–109.
19. U.S. Council on Environmental Quality, 1980.
20. Nathanson, 45.
21. Barlow and Clark, 16.
22. Barlow and Clark, 60.
23. UNEP, 1988, 97–102.
24. World Commission on Dams, 2000; Seckler, 45–46; Kitissou.
25. Horne and McDermott, 14–21.
26. Kitissou.

27. Kitissou.

28. Barlow and Clark, 24.

29. Millennium Ecosystem Assessment, 2005.

30. International Food Policy Research Institute, August 2005.

31. World Bank, September 2004; CIA: the *World Fact Book*, July 2004.

32. Athanasiou, 36.

33. Ashraf, 1915.

34. Abdel Mageed, 157–183.

35. Abdel Mageed, 157–183.

36. Ashraf, 1915.

37. Athanasiou, 76.

38. Athanasiou, 89; Ehrlich and Ehrlich, 181–205.

39. Abu Zeid, 67.

40. Poincelot, 35; Battelle, 4–7.

41. Poincelot, 28–29; Battelle, 4.

42. Poincelot, 45–47; Dodds, 80.

43. Poincelot, 26.

44. Poincelot, 32–33.

45. Barlow and Clark, 16.

46. Dodds, 5.

47. Dodds, 8; Barlow and Clark, 44.

48. Poincelot, 2.

49. Barlow and Clark, 49.

50. Barlow and Clark, 9.

51. Dodds, 8–9; Horne and McDermott, 98.

52. Horne and McDermott, 24.

53. Odum, 78.

54. Barlow and Clark, 24–32, 51; Dodds, 288–292.

55. George Cox, 233–238; Dodds, 286–287.

56. George Cox, 238.

57. George Cox, 236; Dodds, 281–282.

58. George Cox, 238–239.

59. Dawoud, 30–31.

60. Hinrichsen, 34–35; World Commission on Dams, 2000.

61. Falkenmark and Widstrand, 1992; Renner et al., 150–152.

62. Berner and Berner, 12–13.

63. Berner and Berner, 14–15, 37–39.

64. Postel, 1988, 103–109.

65. Berner and Berner, 24.

66. Burroughs, 5–11, 18–19, 50–55.

67. Burroughs, 37–38.

68. Rickleff, 2–3.

69. Rickleff, 13–14.

70. Millennium Ecosystem Assessment, 2005.

71. Millennium Ecosystem Assessment, 2005.

72. Ayres et al., 41.

73. Ayres et al., 158.

74. Hinrichsen, 34–35; Daily et al., 123–132.

75. Hinrichsen, 34–35.

76. Ayres et al., 159.

77. Horne and McDermott, 77–78.

78. Odum, 17–18, 37–43 and 274; Barnes et al., 8–11.

79. El-Taweel and Shaban, 258–290.

80. May, 8.

81. World Health Organization, 1988, 81–83. Nathanson, 5–7.

82. Barlow and Clark, 51.

83. World Health Organization, 1988, 81–83.

84. May, 8.

85. Sternberg, 469–476.

86. Barlow and Clark, 53.

87. Ayres et al., 189.

88. Barlow and Clark, 32.

89. May, 8.

90. Nathanson, 247–252.

91. Kjekshus, 127–130.

92. Kjekshus, 165–166.

93. Kjekshus, 166.

94. Associated Press World Stream, 20 September 2005.

95. Gramsci, 1971; Robert Cox, 162–175.

96. Ward, 81–82.

97. Lipschutz, 118–119.

98. World Commission on Dams, 2000; Postel, 1999, 63–65.

99. World Commission on Dams, 2000; Postell, 1999, 61, 69, 86–88, 210; Barlow and Clark, 48.

100. World Commission on Dams 2000; Leslie, 3–10; Waterbury, 2002, 10; Barlow and Clark, 164–165.

101. Postel and Wolf, 60–67.

102. Barlow and Clark, 161–163.

103. Barlow and Clark, 130.

Chapter Two

1. Moncrieff, 425–428.

2. McFarlane, 372–382.

3. Gemill, 295–312.

4. Gemill, 295–312.

5. Gemill, 295–312.
6. Gemill, 295–312.
7. Postell, 1999, 72.
8. Villiers, 223.
9. Sutcliffe and Parks, 155.
10. Sutcliffe and Parks, 155; Collins, 2002, 151–156.
11. Soffer, 35.
12. Abdel-Shafy et al.; Postell, 1999, 71–72.
13. Hvidt, 90–100; Abdel-Shafy et al., 3–21.
14. Collins, 2002, 110–111, 123–124, 201.
15. *Engineering News Record*, 18 November 2003; Ford, January 2003, 40–45; Alexander, 21–25; Wahby, 86–91; Postel, 1999, 72.
16. Alexander, 21–25.
17. Ford, January 2003, 40–45.
18. Alexander, 21–25.
19. Alexander, 21–25.
20. Postel, 1999, 32–44.
21. Alexander, 21–25.
22. Postel, 1999, 71–72.
23. Alexander, 21–25.
24. George,15.
25. *Africa Analysis*, 13 July 2001.
26. Ford, January 2003, 40–45; George,15.
27. Mostafa, 2003; Hvidt, 90–100.
28. Hvidt, 90–100
29. Alexander, 21–25.
30. Alexander, 21–25.
31. Renner et al., 88.
32. Hulme, 140–147.
33. Conway and Hulme, 127–151.
34. Murakami, 1995.
35. Hvidt, 90–100.
36. Elarabawy et al., 310–319.
37. Elarabawy et al., 310–319.
38. Villiers, 220.
39. Villiers, 220.
40. EIU Country Report Online, Egypt, 1 August 2004.
41. Elarabawy et al., 310–319.
42. Elarabawy et al., 310–319.
43. Commonwealth Knowledge, 2005.
44. The Saudi Arabia Information Resource, 2005.
45. Ford, May 2005; Villiers, 286.
46. Villiers, 287.
47. Stanhill, 261–269.

48. Postel, 1988, 103–109.
49. Elarabawy et al., 310–319.
50. Hoke, December 1990; Khalil, May 2004.
51. Barlow and Clark, 21–22.
52. Stanhill, 261–269.
53. Stanhill, 261–269.
54. Dethier and Funk, 20–27; Weimbaum, 119–126; Stewart, 459–480.
55. Dethier and Funk, 20–27.
56. Dethier and Funk, 20–27.
57. EIU Country Report Online, Egypt, 1 August 2004.
58. EIU Country Report Online, Egypt, 1 August 2004.
59. Collins, 2002, 191.
60. Collins, 2002, 187–189.
61. World Commission on Dams, 2000.
62. Roudi, November 2001.
63. Stewart, 459–480.
64. Abdel Mageed, 157–183.
65. Abdel-Shafy et al., 3–21.
66. Abdel-Shafy et al., 3–21.
67. Hvidt, 90–100.
68. El-Awady, 54.
69. Miller et al., 1980.
70. Miller et al., 1980.
71. Hvidt, 90–100.
72. Hvidt, 90–100.
73. Hvidt, 90–100.
74. Mostafa, 2003.
75. McFarlane, 372–382.
76. Sutcliffe and Parks, 156; El-Manadely et al., 81–86; Collins, 2002, 123–124, 185.
77. Postel, 1999, 144–146.
78. Collins, 2002, 123–124; Postel, 1999, 53–54.
79. Postel, 1999, 71–72; Ayres et al., 32.
80. Hashimoto, 222–239.
81. Abdel Mageed, 157–183.
82. Hinrichsen, 34–35; Postel, 1999, 131–138.
83. Murakami, 1995.
84. El-Manadely et al., 81–86.
85. Collins, 2002, 190.
86. Villiers, 228.
87. Tafesse, 104.
88. Arab Republic of Egypt, 2005.
89. Murphy, 1.

90. Murphy, 1.
91. Owen, 202.
92. Yohannes, 2001, 207–210.
93. Murphy, 1.
94. Yohannes, 2001, 290–296; Owen, 180–181.

Chapter Three

1. FAO, February 2006; Hamad and Battahani, 28–41.
2. Collins, 2002, 80–83; Sutcliffe and Parks, 105–106.
3. Daly, 214–218.
4. Daly, 217–218.
5. Daly, 220–222.
6. Hance, 253–270, 253–270.
7. Hance, 253–270; Fruzzetti and Ostor, 154–160; Daly, 222.
8. Gemill; Collins, 1990, 252–257.
9. FAO, February 2006.
10. Collins, 1990, 274; Yohannes, 1997, 295–299.
11. Roden, 498–516.
12. Collins, 1990, 271–272.
13. FAO, February 2006; Hamad and Battahani, 28–41.
14. FAO, February 2006; O'Brien, 20–26.
15. Kaikati, 99–123.
16. Library of Congress Country Studies, 2005.
17. FAO, February 2006; Hamad and Battahani, 28–41.
18. Hamad and Battahani, 28–41.
19. FAO, February 2006.
20. Embassy of the Sudan, 2005; FAO, February 2006.
21. Hamad and Battahani, 28–41; FAO, February 2006.
22. Embassy of the Sudan, 2005.
23. Embassy of the Sudan, 2005.
24. Kaikati, 99–123.
25. O'Brien, 20–26; Kaikati, 99–123.
26. Waterbury, 2002, 3.
27. O'Brien, 20–26.
28. Niblock, 15–18.
29. Dewal, 2005, 17.
30. Embassy of the Sudan, 2005.
31. FAO, February 2005.
32. Wallach, 417–434; FAO, February 2006; Embassy of the Sudan, 2005; Waterbury, 2002, 135–136.
33. Collins, 2002, 86.
34. Wallach, 417–434.

35. EIU Country Report Online, Sudan, 18 February 1997.
36. FAO, February 2006.
37. Waterbury, 2002, 108 and 136.
38. Reina, 2004.
39. Reina, 2004; International Rivers Network, March 2006.
40. Wallach, 417–434.
41. Fruzzetti and Ostor, 162.
42. Fruzzetti and Ostor, 164–165.
43. Bernal, 447–479; Barnett, 45–73.
44. Bernal, 454.
45. Barnett, 89–100; O'Brien, 20–26; Bernal, 447–479.
46. El-Farouk, 167–182.
47. Coates, 81–96; Madsen, 853–866.
48. El-Farouk, 167–182.
49. El-Farouk, 167–182.
50. FAO, February 2006.
51. Dewal, 2005, 17.
52. *Al Bawaba*, 19 September 2005.
53. Barbour, 243–263.
54. O'Brien, 20–26.
55. O'Brien, 20–26.
56. O'Brien, 20–26.
57. Wallach, 417–434.
58. International Rivers Network, November 2005.
59. International Rivers Network, March 2006.
60 . Roden, 498–516.
61. House, 201–231.
62. Roden, 498–516.
63. O'Brien, 20–26.
64. Sutcliffe and Parks, 105–113.
65. Sutcliffe and Parks, 77–78, 100; Howell and Lock, 276.
66. Sutcliffe and Parks, 64–72; Howell and Lock, 258–260; Collins, 2002, 64–68, 80–83.
67. Collins, 2002, 58–62; Daly, 220.
68. Collins, 2002, 64.
69. Waterbury, 2002, 59, 140–145; Collins, 2002, 143, 154–155.
70. Collins, 2002, 161; Waterbury, 2002, 140–144.
71. Sutcliffe and Parks, 116; Howell and Lock, 243, 275; Tafesse, 44.
72. Howell and Lock, 276; Collins, 2002, 64.
73. Waterbury, 1979, 91.
74. Hulme, 139–162; Sutcliffe and Parks, 9–15, 165; Howell and Lock, 248–249.
75. Dodds, 7.
76. Waterbury, 1979, 90.

77. Roden, 498–516,

78. World Commission on Dams, 2000; Barlow and Clark, 61; Renner et al., 92.

79. *New Internationalist*, December 1992; El-Farouk, 167–182.

80. Embassy of the Sudan; El-Farouk, 167–182.

81. Walsh et al., 181–197.

82. Hulme, 139–162; Hamad and Battahani, 28–41.

83. Walsh et al., 181–197.

84. Hamad and Battahani, 28–41.

85. Conway and Hulme, 127–151.

86. Burroughs, 5–11.

87. Lange, 60–67.

88. Lange, 60–67.

89. Dewal, 2004, 20.

90. Reeves, 21–25.

91. UNICEF, 3 October 2005.

Chapter Four

1. FAO, 2005; M. J.; Arsano and Tamrat, 15–27; Waterbury, 2002, 106.

2. FAO, 2005; Dejene, 2003; Amer et al., 3–14; Arsano and Tamrat, 15–27.

3. Collins, 2002, 89–90, 98–99.

4. Arsano and Tamrat, 15–27.

5. Arsano and Tamrat, 15–27; Tafesse, 85, 97, 114.

6. Collins, 2002, 80–83; Tafesse, 103.

7. Arsano and Tamrat, 15–27; Tafesse, 85.

8. Tafesse, 95.

9. Collins, 2002, 169–171; Tafesse, 49; Waterbury, 2002, 116.

10. Whittington and McClelland, 144–154; Postel, 1999, 136, 158–161.

11. Waterbury, 2002, 113–114.

12. FAO, 2005; Thurow, 2003, A1.

13. EIU Country Report, Ethiopia, 18 February 1997.

14. Dejene, 2003.

15. World Resources Institute, Earth Trends, 2003.

16. UN Population Fund, 24 October 2005.

17. Abdel Mageed, 157–183; Waterbury, 2002, 94.

18. Calder, 9–10.

19. UN/FAO Mission to Ethiopia, 2001; Dejene, 2003; Waterbury, 2002, 95–96.

20. Dejene, 2003.

21. Postel, 1999, 143–149; Collins, 2002, 169–171; Tafesse, 49; Waterbury, 2002, 69–70.

22. Postel, 1999, 158–161; Waterbury, 2002, 119.

23. FAO/WFP Mission to Ethiopia, 2001.

24. World Food Program, 2005.

25. FAO/WFP Mission to Ethiopia, 2001; FAO, 2005.

26. Waterbury, 2002, 92.

27. Ford, 2003.

28. Arsano and Tamrat, 15–27.

29. McGrath and Inbaraj, 2004

30. Arsano and Tamrat, 15–27.

31. *Africa Analysis*, 2 April 2004.

32. Arsano and Tamrat, 15–27.

33. Thurow, 2003, A1.

34. Thurow, 2003, A1.

35. McGrath and Inbaraj, 2004.

36. Postel, 1999, 158–161; FAO, 2005.

37. Postel, 1999, 143–149.

38. Ford, 2003.

39. EIU Country Report Online, Ethiopia, 1 April 2005.

40. EIU Country Report Online, Ethiopia, 1 February 2005; World Bank, Country Briefing, September 2005.

41. EIU Views Wire, 15 March 2005.

42. UN/FAO Mission to Ethiopia, 2001; FAO, 2005.

43. Keller, 1989; Yohannes, 1997, 67–77.

44. *The Observer*, 3 December 2005.

45. FAO, 2000.

46. U.S. Department of State, Ethiopia: Background Notes, May 2003; FAO, September 2004.

47. UNDP, Human Development Indicators 2002; FAO, 2005.

48. Rajan et al., 138–150.

49. Reuters, 20 October 2005.

50. Moncrief, 425–428.

51. Beaumont, 475–495.

52. FAO, 2005.

53. Postel, 1999, 160.

54. USAID, July 2005.

55. *US Fed News*, 1 April 2005.

56. FAO, 2005.

57. USAID, July 2005.

58. *US Fed News*, 1 April 2005.

59. EIU Views Wire, 29 June 2005.

60. EIU Views Wire, 29 June 2005.
61. *The Observer*, 3 December 2005.
62. World Bank, Country Briefing, September 2005.
63. Doyle, 24–26.
64. FAO, October 2000.
65. Dixon, chapter 4.
66. Associated Press Worldstream, 20 September 2005.
67. Adams, chapter 3.

Chapter Five

1. Collins, 2002, 198.
2. Mulama, 2004.
3. Mulama, 2004.
4. Tafesse, 29–30.
5. FAO, 10 July 2000.
6. Mulama, 2004.
7. IRIN, 28 March 2006.
8. *The Nation* [Nairobi], 5 June 2005.
9. *The Nation* [Nairobi], 13 January 2006.
10. Agence France Presse, 17 January 2006.
11. Waithaka et al., October 2003.
12. Amer et al., 3–14.
13. EIU Country Report Online, Kenya, 19 July 2004.
14. Anderson, 48–61.
15. Ojany and Ogendo. 130–136.
16. Ojany and Ogendo. 137–138.
17. Ojany and Ogendo, 139–144.
18. Anderson, 233–245.
19. Quoted in Anderson, 242.
20. Declan Walsh, A4
21. Ololdapash, 1–4.
22. Ngotho, 2005.
23. Ololdapash, 1–4.
24. Oluoch, 22.
25. Oluoch, 22.
26. BBC News Online, 14 July 2005.
27. Astill, 8.
28. Oluoch, 22.
29. Matheson, 2005.
30. Phombeah, 2005; Pflanz, 2005.
31. Phombeah, 2005.
32. BBC News Online, 14 May 2004.

33. Webster, 2005.
34. Pflanz, 2005.
35. Ngotho, 2005.
36. Kellett, 2003.
37. IRIN, 5 September 2005.
38. Kellett, 2003.
39. Radford, 7.
40. Myangito et al., 191–194.
41. Myangito et al., 194–198.
42. Global Trade Negotiations, 2005.
43. Global Trade Negotiations, 2005; *The Independent* [London], 1 February 2006.
44. Global Trade Negotiations, 2005.
45. Myangito et al., 198–202.
46. Myangito et al., 201–202; *Africa News*, 26 September 2006.
47. Odek et al., 2003; Myangito et al., 202.
48. Odek et al., 2003.
49. Myangito et al., 206–207; Innocenti, 2004.
50. Innocenti, 2004.
51. FAO, 2005; Innocenti, 2004; Myangito et al., 205 and 208.
52. Myangito et al., 209.
53. Kilbride et al; Wainaina, 37–50.
54. Kilbride et al., 2000.
55. Wainaina, 37–50; Kilbride et al., 2000.
56. Mageria, 11.
57. BBC International Monitoring, 16 March 2005.
58. Ohito, 2006.
59. *Africa News*, 31 January 2006.
60. *Africa News*, 31 January 2006.
61. England, 5.
62. England, 5.
63. Lore, 2001.
64. White, 2006, 2; Cann, 2006.
65. Waterbury, 2002, 154.
66. Nkrumah, 11 June 2004.
67. Nkrumah, 11 June 2004.
68. Mulama, 2004; England, 5.
69. EIU Country Report Online, Tanzania, 1 May 1997.
70. Skarstein, 334–362; EIU Country Report Online, Tanzania, 1 August 2004; Goldman.
71. Skarstein, 334–362.
72. Skarstein, 334–362.
73. Skarstein, 334–362.
74. Baffes, 2004.

75. Skarstein, 334–362.
76. IRIN, 16 February 1999.
77. Maganga, 2001.
78. Maganga, 2001.
79. Maganga, 2001; Kashimbiri et al., 451–467.
80. Maganga, 2001.
81. *Africa News*, 7 February 2006.
82. Reina, 2002.
83. EIU Country Report Online, Uganda, 1 January 2005.
84. Place and Otsuka, 105–128.
85. *Africa News*, 23 August 2005, and 31 January 2006.
86. *The Nation* [Nairobi], 19 January 2006.
87. Xinhua General News Service, 20 January 2006.
88. Amer et al., 3–14; Waterbury, 2002, 154.
89. Ellis and Freeman, 1–30.
90. EIU ViewsWire, 12 April 2005.
91. Otieno, 2003.
92. Allen, 2006.
93. EIU ViewsWire, 10 June 2005.
94. Mulama, 2005.
95. *The Economist*, 2 July 2005.
96. *The Economist*, 16 April 2005.
97. EIU Country Report Online, 1 January 2005.
98. EIU Country Report Online, 15 January 2002.
99. EIU Country Report Online, 15 January 2002.
100. George Cox, 1993, 158; Dodds, 101; Stiassony and Meyer, 64–69.
101. Springle, 510–528.
102. O'Reilly et al., 766-768.
103. EIU Country Report Online, 15 January 2002.
104. World Bank, 1996; GEF, March 2005.
105. Stiassony and Meyer, 64–69; Ntiba, 211–216.
106. Balirwa et al., 703–715; George Cox, 1993; Stiassony and Meyer, 64–69.
107. Deweerdt et al., 40–43.
108. Dweerdt et al., 40–43.
109. Lowe-McConnell, 570–574; World Bank, 1996.
110. GEF, March 2005.
111. Opio, 9 January 2007.
112. Ntiba, 211–216.; Schindler et al., 56-64.
113. Schindler et al., 56-64
114. Lowe-McConnell, 570–574.
115. Balirwa et al., 703–715.
116. Ntiba, 211–216.

117. Xinhua News Agency, 18 January 2005.

118. Opio, 9 January 2007.

119. Ntiba, 211–216.

120. Campbell, 455–484

121. World Bank, 1996.

122. The following discussion on lake stratification extensively draws on the following sources: Nathanson, 9–13, 80–92; Rickleff, 29–33, 59, 86–87, 179–185; Berner and Berner, 230–234, 252–264; George Cox, 1993, 148–156; Dodds, 103–107, 287–292, 337–350, 461–462.

123. Kaufman, 601–666.

124. World Bank, 1996.

125. Kaufman, 601–666.

126. Kaufman, 601–666.

127. Kaufman, 601–666; Lowe-McConnell, 570–574; Balirwa et al., 703–715.

128. Berner and Berner, 229–230, 268–269.

129. Berner and Berner, 229–234; Nathanson, 70, 101, 357–358.

130. *Africa News*, 20 November 2006.

131. *Water and Environment International*, September 1999.

132. *Africa News*, 31 December 2006.

133. Xinhua General News Service, 4 February 2007; *Africa News*, 20 November 2006.

134. Zimmerman, 1996; Harman, 8.

135. Zimmerman, 1996.

136. Johnson et al., 439–447.

137. Johnson et al., 439–447.

138. Lwanga et al., 85–92.

139. United Republic of Tanzania, 2004; UNDP, 2004.

140. United Republic of Tanzania; UNDP, 2004.

141. World Bank, 1996; GEF, March 2005.

142. World Bank, 1996; GEF, March 2005.

143. GEF, March 2005.

144. GEF, March 2005.

145. GEF, March 2005.

146. GEF, March 2005.

147. ReadNews, 1 January 2005.

148. ReadNews, 1 January 2005; BBC Monitoring Africa, 19 January 2005.

149. ReadNews, 1 January 2005.

150. BBC Monitoring Africa, 19 January 2005.

151. ReadNews, 1 January 2005.

152. Green Belt Movement, 2005.

153. Women's International Network News, 1991.

Notes to Chapter 6

Chapter Six

1. Barnes et al., 161–162; George Cox, 60.
2. George Cox, 58–64; Barnes et al., 154–162, 255–275.
3. Daly and Farley, 96.
4. Tangley, 60–61; Prugh et al., 15–16.
5. FAO, Global Forests Assessment 2005.
6. FAO, Global Forests Assessment 2005.
7. Tafesse, 74.
8. Sarnowski, 2005.
9. Forests Monitor LTD, 2001.
10. FAO, 2005; *US Fed News*, 1 June 2005.
11. FAO, 2005.
12. FAO, 2005.
13. Burroughs, 5–50.
14. Emmel, 124.
15. UNESCO Courier, April 1995.
16. African Wildlife Foundation, 2005.
17. M2 Press Wire, 12 September 2005.
18. Emmel, 131.
19. Forests Monitor LTD, 2001.
20. Emmel, 124.
21. Forests Monitor LTD, 2001; Rainforest Foundation, 2004; World Bank, February 2006.
22. World Bank, February 2006.
23. Forests Monitor LTD, 2001.
24. Forests Monitor LTD, 2001.
25. Rainforest Foundation, 2004; World Bank, February 2006.
26. Rainforest Foundation, 2004.
27. *US Fed News*, 1 June 2005.
28. EIU Country Report Online, DRC, 12 November 1998; *US Fed News*, 1 June 2005.
29. Prunier, 199.
30. David Newbury, 255–314.
31. Moghalu, chapter 2; Gasana, 24–33; Catharine Newbury, 1988.
32. FAO, 2005.
33. Prunier, 75–78; Clay et al., 1995.
34. EIU Country Report Online, Rwanda, 31 July 1998.
35. EIU Country Report Online, Rwanda, 31 July 1998.
36. Gasana, 24–33.
37. EIU Country Report, Rwanda, July 31, 1998.
38. Prunier, 86–89.
39. Prunier, 90.
40. Mitchell, 1997.

41. Mitchell, 1997.
42. Gasana, 24–33.
43. Mitchell, 1997.
44. Pan-African News Agency, 16 October 2000.
45. Gasana, 24–33.
46. Mitchell, 1997.
47. Andre and Platteau, 1–47.
48. Prunier, 111–112.
49. Prunier, 113.
50. Power, chapter 10; Moghalu, chapter 2.
51. FAO, 2005.
52. EIU Country Report, Burundi, 17 March 2000, and 1 July 2004.
53. EIU Country Report, Burundi, 28 March 2001.
54. EIU Country Report, Burundi, 1 June 1996.
55. EIU Country Report, Burundi, 28 March 2001, and 1 July 2004.
56. EIU Country Report, Burundi, 28 March 2001.
57. Watson, 26–31.
58. Watson, 26–31; FAO, 2006.
59. FAO, 2005.
60. George Cox, 162, 164.
61. Salopek, 93.

Chapter Seven

1. Lipschutz, 118–119.
2. World Commission on Dams, 2002, 2.
3. Davidson, 11.
4. Linklater, 1992.
5. Eckersley, 25–28.
6. Pepper, chapter 3.
7. Korten, chapters 1–2.
8. Lele, 613.
9. Center for Public Integrity, 2005.
10. Finnegan, 43–53.
11. Center for Public Integrity, 2005.
12. Center for Public Integrity, 2005.
13. Fullbrook, 2005.
14. Daly and Farley, chapter 1; Princen, chapter 3; Prugh et al., chapter 1; Costanza and Folke, 49–68; Goulder and Kennedy, 23–47.
15. Tilman, 93–112; Myers, 215–235, 366–386.
16. Prugh et al., 16.
17. Independent Evaluation Group, April 2006.
18. UN Convention to Combat Desertification, June 2006.

19. Daly and Farley, xxi; Fullbrook, 2004.
20. Cobb and Daly, 1994; Daly and Farley, 2004; Prugh et al., 2000; Princen, 2005.
21. Daly and Farley, 359.
22. Smith; Daly and Farley, 48–50, 389–402.
23. Smith; Daly and Farley, 390–392; Princen, 15–21.
24. Center for Public Integrity, 2005.
25. Tully, 342–349.
26. Olmstead, 31.
27. Levinas, 55–59.
28. Campbell, 457.
29. World Commission on Dams, 2002, 3–4.
30. Finnegan, 43–53.
31. Barrett, 46–50.
32. National Research Council, 1–4.
33. National Research Council, 17.
34. National Research Council, 6.
35. Seckler, 45–46.
36. Mostafa, 2003.
37. Horne and McDermott, 19, 60–69, 77.
38. US Geological Survey, 2006.
39. Fern, 2–7.
40. Tangley, 60–61.
41. Tangley, 60–61.
42. Withgott, 1100–1101.
43. Tangley, 60–61; Prugh et al., 15–17.
44. *The Economist*, 17 January 2004; Guest, 2004; Ayittey, 1998.
45. World Bank, 1998.
46. Mulinge and Lesetedi, 51–67; Magbadela, 89–101.
47. Sachs, chapters 14 and 16.
48. Heineman and Heimann, 75–86.
49. Gordon, 2006.
50. Associated Press Online, 15 May 2006.
51. *The Economist*, 17 January 2004.
52. Taylor, 2006.
53. UNCTAD, 2004; Frank, 4 January 2004.
54. Jones, 179–182, 206–208; Khorr, 2002.
55. *The Economist*, 24 February 2001.
56. UNCTAD, 2004.
57. UNCTAD, 2004.
58. Daly and Farley, 334–335.
59. McGowan and Nel, 316.
60. *The Economist*, 24 February 2001; McLymont, 2005.
61. UNCTAD, 2004.

62. UNCTAD, 2004.

63. UNCTAD, 2004.

64. McLymont, 2005.

65. Vesley, 2005.

66. *The Nation* [New York], 18 July 2005.

67. *Canada and the World Backgrounder*, March 2005.

68. Adams, chapter 12.

69. US Department of State, Bureau of Verification and Compliance, 21 August 1998; Lobe, 2005; Global Issues, 2006.

70. US Department of State, Bureau of Verification and Compliance, 21 August, 1998; Lobe, 2005.

71. Pine, 2003.

72. Pine, 2003.

73. *New Internationalist*, December 1992.

74. Adams, chapter 12.

75. World Bank, 2002.

76. Russett et al., 2006.

77. Melvin, 2004, 1F.

78. World Bank, "Where Is the Wealth of Nations," 2006.

79. UN News Service, 19 December 2005.

80. UNCTAD, 2004; UN News Service, 19 December 2005.

Bibliography

"A Long-Standing Leader's Mixed Legacy." *The Economist* (16 April 2005): 12–13.

"A Tough Act for Kenya's World Bank Boss." *World Bank Intranet: Trade Research; Internal News* (February 2006). http://econ.worldbank. org/WBSITE/EXTERNAL/EXTDEC/EXTRESEARCH/EXTPRO GRAMS/EXTTRADERESEARCH/0,,contentMDK:20828848~ menuPK:215762~pagePK:210083~piPK:152538~theSitePK: 544849,00.html.

Abdel Mageed, Yahia. "The Nile Basin: Lessons from the Past." In *International Waters of the Middle East: From Euphratis/Tigris to Nile*, edited by A. K. Biswas, 157–183. London: Oxford University Press, 1994.

Abdel-Shafy, Hussein I., et al. "Water Issue in Egypt: Resources, Pollution, and Protection Endeavors." *Central European Journal of Occupational and Environmental Medicine* 8, 1 (2002): 3–21.

Abu Zeid, Mahmoud. "River of Hope and Problems." *UN Chronicle* (September–November 2001): 67.

Adams, Patricia. *Odious Debts: Lose Lending, Corruption, and the Third World's Environmental Legacy*. London: Earthscan, 1991.

"Africa's Elusive Dawn." *The Economist* 358, 8210 (24 February 2001): 17–18.

African Wildlife Foundation. *Virunga: Mountain Gorillas at Risk*. Available at http://www.awf.org.

Ahmad, Samir. "Principles and Precedents in International Law Governing the Sharing of Nile Waters." In *The Nile: Sharing a Scarce Resource: A Historical and Technical Review of Water Management and of Economic and Legal Issues*, edited by P. P. Howell and J. A. Allan, 351–364. Cambridge: Cambridge University Press, 1994.

Alexander, Doug. "Just Add Water." *Geographical Journal* (February 2002): 21–25.

Allen, Karen. "Drought Threat to Kenya's Parks." BBC News Online (17 February 2006).

Amer, Salah et al. "Sustainable Development and International Cooperation in the Eastern Nile Basin." *Aquatic Sciences* 37, 1 (March 2005): 3–14.

Anderson, David M. *Eroding the Commons: The Politics of Ecology in Baringo, Kenya 1890s–1963.* Athens: Ohio University Press, 2002.

Andre, Catherine and Jean-Philippe Platteau. "Land Relations Under Unbearable Stress: Rwanda Caught in the Malthusian Trap." *Journal of Economic Behavior and Organization*, 34, 1 (January 1998): 1–47.

"Another African Land Grab." *The Economist* (6 April 2002): 41.

Arab Republic of Egypt. *Poverty Reduction in Egypt: Diagnosis and Strategies*, Vol 1 (29 June 2002). http://www-wds.worldbank.org/servlet/ WDSContentServer/WDSP /IB/2002/08/23/000094946_0208090 4030162/Rendered/PDF/multi0page.pdf.

Arsano, Yacob, and Imeru Tamrat. "Ethiopia and the Eastern Nile Basin." *Aquatic Sciences* 67, 1 (March 2005): 15–27.

Ashraf, Harmon. "Poverty Linked to Accessed Water." *Lancet* (14 December 2002): 1915.

Associated Press Worldstream. "Lions Eat 20 Ethiopian Villagers in a Single Week" (20 September 2005).

Astill, James. "Tribal Trials: The Ogiek Face Eviction from their Ancestral Forest Home." *The Guardian* (13 March 2002): 8.

Athanasiou, Tom. *Divided Planet: The Ecology of Rich and Poor.* New York: Little, Brown, 1996.

Ayittey, George B. N. *Africa in Chaos.* New York: St. Martin's, 1998.

Ayres, Ed. "Desalination Getting Serious." *World Watch* 16, 5 (September–October 2003): 7.

Ayres, Ed. et al. (Eds.). *The World Watch Reader on Global Environmental Issues.* New York: W.W. Norton, 1998.

Baffes, John. *Tanzania's Tea Sector: Constraints and Challenges in a Global Environment.* 2004. Available at http://www.world bank.org/afr/wps.

Balirwa, John S. et al. "Biodiversity and Fishery Sustainability in the Lake Victoria Basin: An Unexpected Marriage." *Bio-Science* 53, 8 (August 2003): 703–715.

Barbour, K. M. "Irrigation in the Sudan: Its Gross Distribution and Its Potential Extension." *Transactions and Papers* 26 (1959): 243–263.

Barlow, Maude, and Tony Clark. *Blue Gold: The Fight to Stop the Corporate Theft of the World's Water.* New York: New Press, 2002.

Barnes, Burton et al. *Forest Ecology*, 4th ed. New York: Wiley, 1998.

Barnett, Tony. *The Gezira Scheme: An Illusion of Development.* London: F. Cass, 1977.

Barrett, Curtis B. "Development of Global Integrated Water Management Systems." *Journal of Management and Engineering* 15, 4 (July/August 1999): 46–50.

Battelle Memorial Institute. *Agriculture 2000: A Look at the Future.* Edited by Mary Bucher. Columbus, Ohio: Battelle Press, 1983.

Beaumont, Peter. "The 1997 U.N. Convention on the Law of Non-Navigational Uses of International Water Courses: Its Strengths and Weaknesses from a Water-Management Perspective and the Need for New Workable Guidelines." *Water Resources Development* 16, 4 (2000): 475–495.

Benvenisti, Byal. "Collective Action in the Utilization of Shared Fresh Water: The Challenge of International Water Resources Law." *American Journal of International Law* 90, 3 (July 1996): 388–415.

Bernal, Victoria. "Colonial Moral Economy and the Discipline of Development: The Gezira Scheme in Modern Sudan." *Cultural Anthropology* 12, 4 (November 1997): 447–479.

Berner, Elizabeth K., and Berner, Robert A. *The Global Water Cycle: Geochemistry and Environment.* Englewood Cliffs: Prentice-Hall, 1987.

Bieler, Andreas, and Morton, Adam David. "Globalization, the State and Class Struggle: A Critical Economy, Engagement with Open Marxism." *British Journal of Politics and International Relations* 5, 4 (2003): 467–499.

"Boeing Reportedly to Settle with Federal Prosecutors for $615 million." Associated Press Online (15 May 2006).

Brown, Lester R., and H. Kane. *Reassessing the Earth's Population Carrying Capacity.* London: Earthscan, 1995.

Burroughs, William James. *Climate Change: A Multi-Disciplinary Approach.* Cambridge: Cambridge University Press, 2001.

Calder, Ian R. *The Blue Revolution: Land Use and Integrated Resources Management.* London: Earthscan, 1999.

"Call to Step Off African Hunger." BBC News Online (12 August 2005).

Campbell, David. "The Deterritorialization of Responsibility: Levinas, Derrida, and Ethics After the End of Philosophy." *Alternatives* 19 (1994): 455–484.

Cann, Vicky. "Water Privatization in Dar es Salaam, Tanzania: No Water for the Poor" (2006). Available at http://www.wdm.org.uk/campaigns/aid/casestudies/waterprivtanzan.pdf.

Center for Public Integrity. *The Water Barons* (2003). Available at http://www.icij.org/water/report.

"Cholera Outbreak Kills 18 in Niger, U.N. Says." Associated Press World Stream (22 September 2006).

Clay, Daniel et al. *Promoting Food Security in Rwanda through Sustainable Agricultural Productivity: Meeting the Challenges of Population Pressure, Land Degradation, and Poverty.* Department of

Agricultural Economics, Michigan State University: International Development Papers 17 (1995). Available at http://www.ec.msu.edu/agecon/fs2/polsyn/no6.htm.

Coates, D. "A Survey of the Fish Fauna of Sudanese Irrigation System with Reference tothe Use of Fishes in the Management of Ecological Problems." *Fisheries Management* 15, 3 (July 1984): 81–96.

Cobb, John, and Herman E. Daly. *For the Common Good: Redirecting the Economy Toward Community, the Environment, and a Sustainable Future,* 2nd ed. Boston: Beacon Press, 1994.

Collins, Robert O. *The Nile.* New Haven: Yale University Press, 2002.

———. *Waters of the Nile: Hydropolitics and the Jonglei Canal.* New York: Oxford University Press, 1990.

Conway, D., and M. Hulme. "Recent Fluctuations in Precipitation and Runoff over the Nile Sub-basins and Their Impact on Main Nile Discharge." *Climatic Change* 25, 2 (October 1993): 127–151.

Costanza, Robert, and Carl Folke. "Valuing Ecosystem Services with Efficiency, Fairness and Sustainability as Goals." In *Nature's Services: Societal Dependence on Natural Ecosystems,* edited by Gretchen C Daily, 49–68. Washington, D.C.: Island Press, 1997.

Cox, George W. *Conservation Ecology: Biosphere and Bio-Survival.* Dubuque: William C. Brown, 1993.

Cox, Robert W. "Gramsci, Hegemony and International Relations." *Millennium: Journal of International Studies* 12 (1983): 162–175.

Daily, Gretchen C. et al. "Ecosystem Services Supplied by Soil." In *Nature's Services: Societal Dependence on Natural Ecosystems,* edited by Gretchen C Daily, 113–132. Washington D.C.: Island Press, 1997.

Daly, Herman E., and Joshua Farley. *Ecological Economics: Principles and Applications.* Washington D.C.: Island Press, 2004.

Daly, M. W. *Empire on the Nile: The Anglo-Egyptian Sudan, 1898–1904.* New York: Cambridge University Press, 1986.

Davidson, Basil. *The Blackman's Burden: Africa and the Curse of the Nationstate.* New York: Times Books, 1992.

Dawoud, Khaled. "Taming the Nile's Serpents." *UNESCO Courier* (October 2001): 30–31.

Dejene, Alemneh. *Integrated Natural Resources Management to Enhance Food Security: The Case for Community-Based Approaches in Ethiopia.* Environment and Natural Resources Working Paper 16. Rome: United Nations Food and Agricultural Organization, 2003.

"Democratic Dawn in Ethiopia Fades as Abuses Come to Light." *The Observer* (3 December 2005).

Dethier, Jean-Jacques, and Kathy Funk. "The Language of Food: PL 480 in Egypt." *Middle East Research and Information Project* 145 (March/April 1997): 20–27.

Dewal, Alex. "Sudan's Historic Peace Deal Is Only the Start." *Financial Times* [London]. (13 January 2005):17.

———. "The Real Story of a Genocidal War that Rages Thru Darfur."
    The Observer (25 July 2004): 20.
Deweerdt, Sara. "Dark Secret of the Lake." *New Scientist* (28 February
    2004): 40–43.
Dixon, Alan B. *Indigenous Management of Wetlands: Experiences in
    Ethiopia.* Aldershot: Ashgate, 2003.
Dodds, Walter K. *Fresh Water Ecology: Concepts and Environmental
    Applications.* New York: Academic Press, 2002.
"Down, Down, Up, and Maybe Down." *The Economist* (2 July 2005).
Doyle, Jeremy. "A Question of Choice: Access to Energy Solutions in
    Ethiopia, Kenya, and Uganda." *Refocus* (May 2002): 24–26.
"E.A. Sugar Players Seek Ways to Improve, Counter Competition."
    Africa News (26 September 2006). Available at http://www.
    lexisnexis.com/academic/.
"East African Budgets Diverge." EIU ViewsWire (10 June 2005). Avail-
    able at http://www.proquest.umi.com/pqdweb?RQT=302&cfc=1.
Eckersley, Robyn. *Environmentalism and Political Theory: Toward an Eco-
    centric Approach.* Albany: State University of New York Press, 1992.
Editorial. Page 4. The *Nation* [New York] (18 July 2005).
EIU Online. "Country Profile: Burundi." *The The Economist* (1 July 2004).
———. "Country Profile: Burundi." *The Economist* (28 March 2001).
———. "Country Profile: Burundi." *The Economist* (17 March 2000).
———. "Country Profile: Burundi." *The Economist* (1 June 1996).
———. "Country Profile: Congo (Democratic Republic)." *The Econo-
    mist* (12 November 1998).
———. "Country Profile: DRC." *The Economist* (12 November 1998).
———. "Country Profile: Egypt." *The Economist* (1 August 2004).
———. "Country Report: Ethiopia." *The Economist* (1 April 2005).
———. "Country Profile: Ethiopia." *The Economist* (1 February 2005).
———. "Country Profile: Ethiopia." *The Economist* (5 February 2005).
———. "Country Profile: Ethiopia." *The Economist* (10 December 1997).
———. "Country Profile: Kenya." *The Economist* (19 July 2004).
———. "Country Profile: Rwanda." *The Economist* (31 July 1998).
———. "Country Profile: Sudan." *The Economist* (28 February 2005).
———. "Country Profile: Sudan." *The Economist* (1 September 2001).
———. "Country Report: Sudan." *The Economist* (19 February 1997).
———. "Country Profile: Tanzania." *The Economist* (1 August 2004).
———. "Country Profile: Tanzania." *The Economist* (1 November 2003).
———. "Country Profile: Tanzania." *The Economist* (15 January 2002).
———. "Country Profile: Tanzania." *The Economist* (1 May 1997).
———. "Country Profile: Uganda." *The Economist* (11 April 2005).
———. "Country Profile: Uganda." *The Economist* (1 January 2005).
Elarabawy, Mohsen et al. "Water Resources in Egypt: Strategies for the
    Next Century." *Journal of Water Resources, Planning and Man-
    agement* 124, 6 (November/December 1998): 310–319.

El-Awady, Nadia. "Reporting from the Nation of the Nile." *Nieman Report 59*, 1 (Spring 2005): 53–55.

El-Farouk, Abdel Helim El-Bashir. "Economic and Social Impact of Environmental Degradation in Sudanese Forestry and Agriculture." *British Journal of Middle Eastern Studies 23*, 2 (November 1996): 167–182.

El-Manadely, S. M. et al. "Characteristics of the Delta Formation Resulting from Silt Deposition in Lake Nasser, Egypt: Approach to Tracing Lake Delta Formation." *Lakes and Reservoirs, Research and Management 7*, 2 (June 2001): 81–86.

El-Taweel, Gamila E., and Ahmad M. Shaban. "Microbiological Quality of Drinking Water at Eight Water Treatment Plants." *International Journal of Environmental Health Research*, 11, 4 (November 2001): 285–290.

Ellis, Frank, and H. A. Freeman. "Rural Livelihoods and Poverty Reduction Strategies in Four African Countries." *Journal of Development Studies 40*, 4 (April 2004): 1–30.

Embassy of Sudan. "Water Resources in Sudan." Available at http://www.sudani.co.za/Economy/Water%20Resources.htm.

Emmel, Thomas C. *An Introduction to Ecology and Population Biology.* New York: W. W. Norton, 1973.

"Empty Promises, Aid and Corruption, Kenya." *The Independent* [London] (1 February 2006): 26.

England, Andrew. "Tanzania: Infrastructure Failings Put More Pressure on Access to a Vital Resource, Water." *Financial Times* [London] (3 August 2005): 5.

"Eritrea: Economic Background." EIU ViewsWire (29 June 2005).

"Eritrea: Widespread Food Shortages." *IRIN* (24 May 2005). Available at http://www.irinnews.org/Report.aspx?ReportId=54596.

Erlich, Paul R., and Anne H. Erlich. *One with Ninevah: Politics, Consumption, and the Human Future.* Washington D.C.: Island Press, 2004.

"Ethiopia: Land Tenure Tackled." EIU ViewsWire (15 March 2005).

"Ethiopia: UN Humanitarian Partners Appeal for Assistance for 2005." M2 Press Wire (24 December 2004).

Falkenmark, Malin, and Widstrand, Carl. "Population and Water Resources." *Population Bulletin 47*, 3. Washington, D.C.: Population Reference Bureau, 1992.

Farrands, Christopher, and Owen Worth. "Critical Theory in Global Political Economy: Critique? Knowledge? Emancipation?" *Capital and Class 85* (Spring 2005): 43–61.

Fern, Richard L. *Nature, God, and Humanity: Envisioning and Ethics of Nature.* New York: Cambridge University Press, 2002.

Finnegan, William. "Leasing the Rain." *The New Yorker* (8 April 2002): 43–53.

"First Get the Basics Right." *The Economist* (17 January 2004): 3–4.

"Fishermen to Protest over Lake Victoria Lease." *The East African Standard* [Nirobi]. (14 January 2005).

"Fixing the Sugar Sector." *The East African Standard Online* (9 August 2005).

Food and Agricultural Organization. "Global Forest Resources Assessment 2005." FAO Forestry Paper 147 (2006). Available at http://www.fao.org/forestry/site/fra/en/.

———. "Aquastat-FAO's Information System on Water and Agriculture" (2005). Available at http://www.fao.org/ag/agl/aglw/aquastat/countries/sudan/index.stm.

———. "Safeguarding Africa's Water Jewel: Rescuing Lake Tanginika." In *Protecting International Waters, Sustaining Livelihoods* (August 2002): 7. Available at http://www.undp.org/gef/undp-gef_publications/publications/iw_brochure_complete.pdf.

———. "Strategy to End Hunger in the Horn of Africa" (31 October 2000). Available at http://www.fao.org/News/2000/001004-e.htm.

———. "Crop and Food Supply Situation in Kenya: FAO Special Report" (July 2000). Available at http:// www.fao.org.

———. "Water Resources Development and Management in Eritrea, Proceedings of IWRA's XV World Water Congress" (March 2000). Presented by Geraghty P. and G. Temnewo. Available at http://www.fao.org/ag/agl/aglw/aquastat/countries/Eritrea/index.stm.

———. "Irrigation Potential in Africa: A Basin Approach, the Congo-Zaire Basin." *FAO Land and Water Bulletins* 4 (1997). Available at http://www.fao.org/drcrep/W4347E/4347.e0n.stm.

———. "Reducing Poverty and Hunger: The Critical Role of Financing for Food, Agriculture." FAO Economic and Social Development Paper 147 (1993). Available at http://www.fao.org/docrep/003/Y6265e/y6265e04.htm.

Ford, Neil. " Egypt: Striking a Balance." *Middle East* (May 2005): 50–51.

———. "Controlling the Nile." *International Water Power and Dam Construction* (July 2003): 18–20.

———. "Ethiopia: The Economy Moves Forward." *African Business* (March 2003): 54–59.

———. "Greening Egypt's Desert." *Middle East* (January 2003): 40–45.

———. "Gulf Water: A Multibillion dollar Business." *Middle East* (November 2002): 46–50.

Forests Monitor LTD. "Sold Down the River; Democratic Republic of Congo" (2001). Available at http://www.forestsmonitor.org/reports/solddownriver/drc.htm.

Frank, Josh. "Coffee and State of Authority in Colombia" (4 January 2004). Available at http://www.zmag.org/content/showarticle.cfm?ItemID=4789.

Fruzzetti, Lino, and Akos Ostor. *Culture and Change Along the Blue Nile: Courts, Markets, and Strategies for Development.* Boulder: Westview Press, 1990.

Fullbrook, Edward. "The Rand Portcullis and PAE." *Post-Autistic Economics Review* 32 (5 July 2005).

Fullbrook, Edward, ed. *A Guide to What Is Wrong with Economics.* London: Anthem Press, 2004.

Gasana, James. " Remember Rwanda?" *World Watch* 15, 5 (September–October 2002): 24–33.

Gasse, Francois. "Hydrological Changes in Africa." *Science* (22 June 2001).

Gauch, Sarah. "US Tries To Clean the Air in a Mega-City Spewing Lead Fumes to Millions." *Christian Science Monitor* (29 March 1995): 17.

Gemmill, Paul F. "Egypt Is the Nile." *Economic Geography* 4, 3 (July 1928): 295–312.

George, Alan. "Friction Flows over Nile Waters." *Middle East* (May 1998): 15.

Giordano, Meredith A., and Aaron T. Wolf. "Incorporating Equity into International Water Agreements." *Social Justice Research* 14, 4 (December 2001): 349–366.

"Giving Africa a Hand." *The Nation* (18 July 2005): 3. Available at http://www.lexis-nexis.com/universe.

Gleick, Peter H. "Water and Conflict: Fresh Water Resources and International Security." *International Security* 18, 1 (Summer 1993): 179–212.

Global Environmental Fund. "Lake Victoria Environmental Management Project" (March 2005). Available at http://www.gef.web.org.

Global Issues. "Arms Trade: A Major Cause of Suffering" (9 November 2006). Available at http://www.globalissues.org/Geopolitics/Arms Trade.asp.

Global Trade Negotiations Home Page. "Kenya: Summary" (April 2004). Available at http://www.cid.harvard.edu/cidtrade/gov/kenyagov.html.

Goldman, Anthony. "Tanzania: Survey 2000, Sewing Seeds for the Revival of Agriculture." *Financial Times* [London] (24 July 2000).

Gordon, Joy. "Accountability and Global Governance: The Case of Iraq." *Ethics and International Affairs* 20, 1 (2006): 79–98.

Goulder, Lawrence H., and Donald Kennedy. "Valuing Ecosystem Services: Philosophical Bases and Empirical Methods." In *Nature's Services: Societal Dependence on Natural Ecosystems*, edited by Gretchen C Daily, 23–47. Washington, D.C.: Island Press, 1997.

Graedel, Thomas E., and Paul J. Crutzen. *Atmospheric Climate and Change.* New York: Scientific American Library Services, 1997.

Gramsci, Antonio. *Selections from the Prison Notebook.* London: Lawrence and Wishart, 1971.

Green Belt Movement. "Achievements." Available at http://www.greenbeltmovement.org/achievements.php.

Guest, Robert. *The Shackled Continent: Power, Corruption, and African Lives*. Washington, D.C.: Smithsonian Books, 2004.

"Gulf States Treat Ethiopian Workers as Slaves." Reuters (20 October 2005).

Hamad, Osman, and Atta El-Battahani. "Sudan and the Nile Basin." *Aquatic Sciences* 67, 1 (March 2005): 28–41.

Hammer, Mark J., and Mark K. Hammer Jr. *Water and Waste Water Technology*, 5th Edition. Upper Sattle River, NJ: Prentice-Hall, 2004.

Hance, William A. "The Gezira: An Example in Development." *Geographical Review* 44, 2 (April 1954): 253–270.

Harman, Danna. "Chemical Culprit Suspected in Deaths of Kenya's Flamingos." *Christian Science Monitor* (27 June 2001): 8.

Hashimoto, Ryutaro. "The Current Status and Future Trends in Fresh Water Management." *International Review for Environmental Strategies* 3, 2 (2002): 222–239.

Heineman, Ben W. Jr., and Fritz Heimann. "The Long War Against Corruption." *Foreign Affairs* (May–June 2006): 75–86.

Hinrichsen, Don. "Down to the Last Drop." *International Wildlife* 31, 6 (November–December 2001): 34–35.

Hoke, Franklin. "Satellite Divination." *Environment* 32, 10 (December 1990): 22–25.

"The Horn of Africa: The Facts." *New Internationalist* 235 (December 1992).

Horne, James E., and M. McDermott. *The Next Green Revolution: Essential Steps to a Healthy, Sustainable Agriculture*. Oklahoma City: Food Products Press, 2001.

House, William J. "Population, Poverty, and Underdevelopment in the Southern Sudan." *Journal of Modern African Studies* 27, 2 (June 1989): 201–231.

Howell, Paul. "East Africa's Water Requirements: The Equatorial Nile Project and the Nile Waters Agreement of 1929." In *The Nile: Sharing a Scarce Resource: A Historical and Technical Review of Water Management and of Economic and Legal Issues*, edited by P. P. Howell and J. A. Allan, 81–108. Cambridge: Cambridge University Press, 1994.

Howell, Paul, and Michael Lock. "The Control of the Swamps of the Southern Sudan: Drainage Schemes, Local Effects, and Environmental Constraints on Remedial Development." In *The Nile: Sharing a Scarce Resource: A Historical and Technical Review of Water Management and of Economic and Legal Issues*, edited by P. P. Howell and J. A. Allan, 243–280. Cambridge: Cambridge University Press, 1994.

Hukill, Traci. "The World's Forgotten Emergencies." *National Journal* 22 (14 January 2004).

Hulme, Michael. "Global Climate Change and the Nile Basin." In *The Nile: Sharing a Scarce Resource: A Historical and Technical Review of Water Management and of Economic and Legal Issues*, edited by P. P. Howell and J. A. Allan, 139–162. Cambridge: Cambridge University Press, 1994.

———. "The Changing Rainfall Resources of Sudan." *Transaction for the Institute of British Geographers* 15, 1 (1990): 21–34.

Hvidt, Martin. "Water Resource Planning in Egypt." In *The Middle Eastern Environment*, Selected Papers of the 1995 Conference of the British Society of Middle Eastern Studies, edited by Eric Watkins, 90–100. Cambridge, MA: St. Malo Press, 1995.

Independent Evaluation Group. *Natural Disasters Evaluation.* Washington D.C.: World Bank, April 2006.

Innocenti, Nicol Degli. "Farming Could Be a Growth Engine in a Land of Rich Soil Agriculture." *Financial Times* [London] (6 April 2004).

International Food Policy Research Institute. "Looking Ahead: Long-term Prospects for Africa's Agricultural Development and Food Security" (August 2005). Available at http://www.ifpri.org/2020/dp/vp41.asp.

International Law Association. "Helsinki Rules on the Uses of Waters of International Rivers." 52I.L. 484. The Hague: International Law Association, 1966.

International Rivers Network. "Environmental Problems of the Merowe Dam" (22 March 2006). Available at http://www.irn.org//programs/merowe/.

———. "Escalating Conflict over the Merowe Dam" (30 November 2005). Available at http://www.irn.org/programs/merowe/.

IRIN. "Food Stituation Getting Worse, Warns FEWS Net." 28 March 2006.

Johnson, T. C. et al. "Climatic and Tectonic Effects on Sedimentation in a Rift Valley Lake." *Geological Society of American Bulletin* (April 1987): 439–447.

Jones, Walter S. *The Logic of International Relations.* New York: HarperCollins, 1991.

Kaikati, Jack G. "The Economy of Sudan: A Potential Bread Basket of the Arab World?" *International Journal of Middle East Studies* 11, 1 (February 1980): 99–123.

Kashimbiri, Nimihirwa et al. "Assessment of Effects of Human Development on the Environment by Using System Dynamic Modeling Technique: A Case Study of the Mkomazi Watershed Basin in Northeastern Tanzania." *Human and Ecological Risk Assessment* 11, 2 (April 2005): 451–467.

Kaufman, L. "Asychronous Taxon Cycles in Haplochromine Fishes of the Greater Lake Victoria Region." *Southern African Journal of Science* 93, 11–12 (November–December 1997): 601–666.

———. "Catastrophic Change in Species-Reach Fresh Water Ecosystems." *Bioscience* 42, 11 (December 1992): 846–858.

Keller, Edmond J. *Revolutionary Ethiopia: From Empire to People's Republic*. Bloomington: Indiana University Press, 1989.

Kellett, Francisca. "Kenya's Castaways." *New African* (June 2003).

"Kenya: After Famine Comes the Storm." *The Nation* [Nairobi] (10 January 2006). Available at http://www.lexis-nexis.com/universe.

"Kenya: Degradation Finally Takes its Toll on Lake Jipe." *Africa News* (11 April 2005).

"Kenya Economy: East African Budgets Diverge." EIU News Wire (10 June 2005).

"Kenya: New Scramble for Lake Victoria Fish." *The East African Standard* [Nairobi] (23 January 2005).

"Kenya: One Million Still in Need of Food Aid." IRIN (5 September 2005). Available at http://iys.cidi.org/humanitarian/irin/ceafrica/05b/ixl8.html.

"Kenya: Millions Facing Starvation." *The Nation* [Nairobi] (13 January 2006). Available at http://www.lexisnexis.com/academic/.

"Kenya Spends More on Rice Imports." Pan-African News (23 July 2005). Available at http://www.lexisnexis.com/academic/.

"Kenyan Assistant Minister Dismisses Nile Treaty as Unrealistic." BBC Monitoring International Reports (16 March 2005).

"Kenyans' Fear Further Killer Raids." BBC News Online (14 July 2005). Available at http://www.news.bbc.co.uk/.

Khalil, Essam. "Water Strategies and Technological Development in Egyptian Coastal Areas." *Desalination* 165, 1–3 (May 2004): 23–30.

Khor, Martin. "Northern Domination of the Global Economy and Its Consequences for the Human Rights of Humanity" (2002). Available at http://www.arrc/hre.com/publications/hrepsek1page50.html.

Kilbride, Philip et al. *Street Children in Kenya: Voices of Children in Search of a Childhood*. Westport, CT: Bergin & Garvey, 2000.

Kitissou, Marcel. "Resolving Conflicts and Reshaping Cooperation: The Role of River Basins in Africa." *Africa Analysis* (30 April 2004). Available at http://www.lexisnexis.com/academic/.

Kjekshus, Helge. *Ecology Control and Economic Development in East Africa: The Case of Tanganika, 1850–1950*. Berkeley: University of California Press, 1977.

Korten, David C. *When Corporations Rule the World*, 2nd ed. Bloomfield, CT: Kumarian Press, 2001.

Kuehls, Thom. "Between Sovereignty and the Environment: The Exploration of the Discourse of Government." In *The Greening of Sovereignty in World Politics*, edited by Karen T. Litfin, 79–108. Cambridge: MIT Press, 1988.

Lange, Karen E. "The Nuba." *National Geographic* 203, 2 (February 2003): 60–67.

Lele, Sharandra M. "Sustainable Development: A Critical Review." *World Development* 19, 6 (1991): 607–621.

Leslie, Jacques. *Deep Water: The Epic Struggle over Dams, Displaced People, and the Environment.* New York: Farrar, Straus, and Giroux, 2005.

Levinas, Emmanuel. *Humanism of the Other.* Translated by Nidra Poller. Urbana-Champagne: University of Illinois Press, 2003.

Library of Congress. "Sudan: Irrigated Agriculture" (June 1991). Available at http://www.photius.com/countries/sudan/economic/.

"Lions Eat Twenty People, Wound Ten Others in a Week in Ethiopia." Associated Press (20 September 2005).

Linklater, Andrew. *Men and Citizens in the Theory of International Relations.* London: Macmillan, 1990.

Lipschutz, Ronnie. "The Nature of Sovereignty and the Sovereignty of Nature: Problematizing the Boundaries between Society, State and System." In *The Greening of Sovereignty in World Politics,* edited by Karen T. Litfin, 109–136. Cambridge: MIT Press, 1988.

Lobe, Jim. "Asia, the World's Top Arms Importer." *Z Magazine* (7 September, 2005.) Available at http://leftnews.org/archives/2005/09/08/2418/.

Lore, David. "Glaciers, Source of Water for Many, Are Vanishing." *Columbus Dispatch* (25 February 2001).

Lowe-McConnell, Rosemary. "EAFRO and After: A Guide to Key Events Affecting Fish Communities in Lake Victoria." *Southern African Journal of Science* 93, 11–12 (November–December 1997): 570–574.

Lwanga, J. S. et al. "Tree Population Dynamics in Kibale National Park, Uganda 1975–1999." *African Journal of Ecology* 499, 1–3 (September 2000): 85–92.

Lynch, Karen. "The Nuba." *National Geographic* (February 2003): 60–67.

M.J. "Funding for Water Sharing." *Environmental Policy and Law* 3, 4–5 (2001): 34–40.

Madsen, H. et al. "Distribution of Fresh Water Snails in Irrigation Schemes in the Sudan." *Journal of Applied Ecology* 25 (1988): 853–866.

Maganga, Faustin P. "Domestic Water Supply, Competition for Water Resources and IWRM in Tanzania" (August 2001). Available at http://www.iwsd.co.zw/symposium2001/papers2/maganga.pdf.

Magbadelo, Olushola John. "Westernism, Americanism, Unipolarism, Globalism and Africa's Marginality." *Journal of Third World Studies* 22, 2 (Fall 2005): 89–101.

Mageria, David. "Kenya Seeks End to Egyptian Veto Over Nile Waters." *The Scottsman* (19 February 2002): 11.

Magor, Larry. "Tanzania Economy: Contract Spat Puts Focus on Aid Dilemma." EIU Newswire (29 June 2005).

Majtenyi, Cathy. "Even the Forests Are Being Privatized." *New African* (December 2001).

Marx, William. *The Holy-Order of Water: Healing Earth's Waters and Ourselves*. Great Barrington: Bellpoot Books, 2001.

Matheson, Ishbel. "Kenya's Fight for a Constitution." BBC News Online (22 July 2005).

May, Elizabeth. "The Environment: A Place to Visit." *Women and Environments* (Fall 2003): 8.

McFarlane, J. "The Production of Cotton in Egypt." *Journal of the Royan African Society* 8, 32 (1909): 372–382.

McGowan, Patrick J., and Phillip Nel. *Power, Wealth and Global Equity: International Relations Text for Africa*. Capetown, SA: Juta Academic, 2004.

McGrath, Cam, and Sonny Inbaraj. "East Africans Consider Pulling Out of Nile Water Treaty." *Global Information Network* (15 January 2004).

McLymont, Rosalind. "Beauty of the Beast: When Tourism and World Trade Meet." *Network Journal* (May 2005): 23–24.

Melvin, Don. "Kenyan Farmers Aim at Markets in Europe." *Atlanta Journal Constitution* (17 March 2004):1F.

Miller, F. DeWolfe et al. *Human Intestinal Parasitic Infections and Environmental Health Factors in Rural Egyptian Communities: A Report to the U.S.-Egyptian River Nile and Lake Nasser Research Project*. Athens, GA: Environmental Research Laboratory, Office of Research and Development,1980.

Millennium Ecosystem Assessment. *Living Beyond Our Means: Natural Assets and Human Well-Being* (2005). Available at www.millenniumassessment.org/.

Mitchell, Tara. "International Conflict and the Environment: Rwanda Case" (Spring 1997). Available at http://www.american.edu/ted/ice/rwanda.htm.

Moghalu, Kingsley C. *Rwanda's Genocide: The Politics of Global Justice*. New York: Palgrave, 2005.

Moncrief, Colin, and C. Scott. "Egyptian Irrigation." *The Geographical Journal* 35, 4 (April 1910): 425–428.

Mostafa, Hadia. "Water Shortage Looms in Egypt as Population Soars." *Mathaba Network* (August 2003).

MTTI Library Team. "January Press Review: Uganda Reaps Big in World Food Support" (11 January 2006): 56. Available at http://www.mtti.go.ug/docs/Press%20Review%20January%202006.pdf.

Mulama, Joyce. "Kenya Unveils an Investor-Friendly Budget." *Global Information Network* (13 June 2005).

———. "Kenya Trying to End Its Unending Cycle of Famine." *New York Amsterdam News* (9 September 2004).

———. "Nile Treaty Partners to Share Rich Resource." *Global Information Network* (22 March 2004).

Mulinge, Munyae M., and Gwen N. Lesetedi. "Corruption in Sub-Saharan Africa: Towards a More Holistic Approach." *African Journal of Political Science* 4, 1 (June 2001): 51–67.

Murakami, Masahiro. *Managing Water and Peace in the Middle East.* Tokyo and New York: United Nations University Press, 1995.

Murphy, Dan. "Discontent Flaring in Rural Egypt." *Christian Science Monitor* (6 May 2005): 1.

Myangito, Hezron O. et al. "Realizing Agricultural Productivity in Kenya." In *Restarting and Sustaining Economic Growth and Development in Africa: The Case of Kenya,* edited by Mwangi S. Kimenyi et al., 191–218. Burlinton, VT: Ash Gate, 2003.

Myers, Norman. "The World's Forests and Their Ecosystem Services." In *Nature's Services: Societal Dependence on Natural Ecosystems,* edited by Gretchen C Daily, 215–235. Washington, D.C.: Island Press, 1997.

Nathanson, Jerry A. *Basic Environmental Technology: Water Supply, Waste Management, and Pollution Control,* 2nd ed. Upper Saddle River, NJ: Prentice-Hall, 1997.

National Research Council. *Irrigation-Induced Water Quality Problems: What Can Be Learned from the San Joaquin Valley Experience.* Washington, D.C.: National Academic Press, 1989.

"New Report Warns of Water Catastrophe." *Africa News* (31 January 2006). Available at http://www.lexinexis.com/academic/.

Newbury, Catharine. *The Cohesion of Oppression: Clientship and Ethnicity, 1860–1960.* New York: Columbia University Press, 1988.

Newbury, David. "Precolonial Burundi and Rwanda: Local Loyalties, Regional Royalties." *International Journal of African Historical Studies* 34, 2 (2001): 255–314.

Newmark, W.D. *Conserving Bio-Diversity in East African Forests: A Study of the Eastern Arc Mountains.* New York: Springer, 2002.

Ngotho, Kamau. "Eyeing Forests." *The Standard Online* (16 July 2005). Available at http://www.eastandard.net/archives/cl/hm_news/news.php?articleid=25358.

Niblock, Tim. "Sudan's Economic Nightmare." *Middle East Research and Information Project* 135 (September 1985): 15–18.

Njuriri, B. "Nile Waters for Sale?" *New African* (August–September 2003): 27.

Nkrumah, Gamal. "Fresh Water Talks: Nile Basin Countries Redouble Efforts to Work Out a Way of Sharing and Managing the Region's Water Resources." *Al-Ahram Weekly* (11 June 2004).

Ntiba, M. J. "Management Issues in Lake Victoria Water Shed." *Lakes and Reservoirs* 6, 1 (September 2001): 211–216.

O'Brien, Jay. "Sudan: An Arab Bread Basket?" *Middle East Research and Information Project* 99 (September 1981): 20–26.

Odek, Otieno et al. *The Challenges and the Way Forward for the Sugar Sub-Sector in Kenya.* Nairobi: Friedrich Ebert Stiftung, 2003.

Odum, Eugene P. *Basic Ecology.* Philadelphia: Saunders, 1983.

Ohito, David. "Dominion to Raise Rice Production by 100,000 Tonnes" (2006). Available at http://www.eastandard.net/hm_news/news.php?articleid=1143952215.

Ojany, Francis F., and Rueben Ogendo. *Kenya: A Study in Physical and Human Geography.* Nairobi: Longman, 1973.

Oki, Taikan. "Global Water Issues Today and Future Perspectives." *Asia-Pacific Review* 10, 2 (November 2003): 60–77.

Okidi, C. O. "History of the Nile Basin and Lake Victoria Basins through Treaties." In *The Nile: Sharing a Scarce Resource: A Historical and Technical Review of Water Management and of Economic and Legal Issues,* edited by P. P. Howell and J. A. Allan, 321–350. Cambridge: Cambridge University Press, 1994.

Olmstead, Sheila M. "What's Surprise Got to Do with It?" *Environment* 45, 10 (December 2003): 22–34.

Ololdapash, Meitamei. "Kenya: Mau Forrest Destruction: Human and Ecological Disaster in the Making." *Cultural Survival Voices* (31 July 2005): 1–4.

Oluoch, Fred. "The Growing Land Issue." *New African* (June 2002): 22.

Opio, Dave. "Nile Perch Stocks Fallings Rapidly." *East African* [Kenya] (9 January 2007). Available at http://www.lexis-nexis.com/academic/.

O'Reilly, Catherine et al. "Climate Change Decreases Aquatic Ecosystem Productivity of Lake Tanginika, Africa." *Nature* 424, 950 (14 August 2003): 766–768.

"Ornamental Plant Threatens Lake Victoria." *Water and Environment International* 8, 61 (September 1999): 9–14.

Otieno, Derek. "Kenya: Tourism Bounces Back." *African Business* (March 2005): 55.

Owen, Roger. *State, Power and Politics in the Making of the Modern Middle East.* New York: Routledge, 2004.

Pepper, David. *Eco-Socialism: From Deep Ecology to Social Justice.* New York: Routledge,1993.

Pflanz, Mike. "Kenya Losing Battle Against Corruption." *The Daily Telegraph* [London]. (11 August 2005).

Phombeah, Gray. "Corruption Haunts Kenya's Leader." BBC News Online (23 February 2005).

Pine, Shawn. "Egypt's True Defense Expenditures: $2.7 or $14 Billion?" *Native Online, A Journal of Politics and Arts, Policy Paper* 6 (2003).

Place, Frank, and K. Otsuka. "Land Tenure Systems and Their Impacts on Agriculture Investments and Productivity in Uganda." *Journal of Development Studies* 38, 6 (August 2002): 105–128.

Poincelot, Raymond P. *Toward a More Sustainable Agriculture.* Westport, CT: Avi, 1986.

Postel, Sandra. "Fresh Water Supplies and Competing Uses." In *Perspectives on Water Uses and Abuses*, edited by David H. Speidel et al., 103–108. New York: Oxford University Press, 1988.

———. *Pillar of Sands: Can the Irrigation Miracle Last?* New York: W. W. Norton, 1999.

Postel, Sandra, and Aaron T. Wolf. "Dehydrating Conflict." *Foreign Affairs* (September–October 2001): 60–67.

Power, Samantha. *"A Problem from Hell": America and the Age of Genocide*. New York: Basic Books, 2002.

Princen, Thomas. *The Logic of Sufficiency*. Cambridge: MIT Press, 2005.

Prugh, Thomas et al. *The Local Politics of Global Sustainability*. Washington, D.C.: Island Press, 2000.

Prunier, Gerard. *The Rwanda Crisis: History of a Genocide*. New York: Columbia University Press, 1995.

Purcell, R. "Potential for Small-Scale Irrigation in Sub-Saharan Africa: The Kenyan Example." Paper presented at the FAO subregional workshop, Harare Zimbabwe (14–17 April 1997). Available at http://www.fao.org.

Radford, Tim. "Species Struggle as Humans Grab Resources." *The Guardian* [London]. (2 August 2002): 7.

Rahaman, Muhammad Mizanur et al. "EU Water Framework Directive vs. Integrated Water Resources Management: The Seven Mismatches." *International Journal of Water Resources Development* 20, 4 (December 2004): 565–575.

Rainforest Foundation. "World Bank Oversees Carve-up of Congo Rainforests" (February 2004). Available at http://www.rainforestfoundationuk.org.

Rajan, A. Meenkshi Sundara et al. " Impact of Economic Reforms on Economic Issues: A Study of Ethiopia." *African Development Review* 17, 1 (April 2005): 138–150.

Reeves, Eric. "Genocide by Attrition." *Dissent* 52, 1 (Winter 2005): 21–25.

Reina, Peter. "Huge Projects Under Way to Bring Water to Egyptian Deserts." *Engineering News-Record* (7 May 2001): 20.

———. "Chinese Contractors Flex Lean Muscles in Sudan." *Engineering News-Record* (12 April 2004).

"Relief in Sight." *Canada and the World Backgrounder* (March 2005).

Renner, Michael et al. *State of the World*. New York: W. W. Norton, 2005.

"Report Details Kick Backs for Iraq." *USA Today* (25 October 2005): A1.

Rickleff, Robert E. *The Economy of Nature: A Textbook in Basic Ecology*, 4th ed. New York: W. H. Freeman, 1997.

Roden, David. "Regional Inequality and Rebellion in the Sudan." *Geographical Review* 64, 8 (October 1974): 498–516.

Rosenblum, Mort. "Who Owns the Water?" Associated Press (20 August 2002).

Roudi, Farzaneh (Nazy). "Population Trends and Challenges in the Middle East." *United Nations Population Division, World Urbanization Prospects, the 1999 Revision: Key Findings.* New York: UN Population Division, 1999. Available at http://www4.gvsu.edu/coler/GPY355/Readings/Population%20ME.htm.

"Rows Drying Up Irrigation Scheme." *Africa News* (11 August 2005).

Russett, Bruce M. et al. *World Politics: The Menu for Choice,* 8th ed. New York: Thompson-Wadsworth, 2006.

"Rwanda Faces Serious Deforestation Problems." Pan-African News Agency (16 October 2000). Available at http://www.lexisnexis.com/academic/.

Sachs, Jeffrey D. *The End of Poverty: Economic Possibilities for Our Time.* New York: Penguin Press, 2005.

Salopek, Paul. "Who Rules the Ituri Forests?" *National Geographic* (September 2005): 81–100.

Sarnowiski, Andrea Von. "The Artisnal Fisheries of Lake Albert and the Problem of Over-Fishing." Available at http://www.tropentag.de/2004/abstracts/full/9.pdf.

The Saudi Arabian Information Resource. "Desalination." Available at http://www.saudinf.com/main/a541. 2005.

Schindler, Daniel E. et al. "Ecological Consequences of Gill Net Fishers for Nile Perch in Lake Victoria." *Conservation Biology* 12, 1 (February 1998): 56–64.

Scott, Christopher. "Conference Report: Water Management in the Future." *Water Resources Development* 19, 3 (September 2003): 513–515.

Seckler, David. "Tapping Technology." *UN Chronicle* (1999): 45–46.

Shikwati, James. "Will the Destruction of Coffee Stocks Save Kenyan Farmers?" (17 September 2002). Available at http://www.policynetwork.net/main/news_archives.php+Will+the+Destruction+of+Coffee+Stocks+Save+Kenyan+Farmers+ IREN&hl=en &gl=us& ct=clnk&cd=1&client=firefox-a.

"Shrinking Lake Leaves Transporters Very Worried." *The Nation* [Nairobi] (19 January 2006). Available at http://www.lexis-nexis.com/academic/.

Skarstein, Rune. "Economic Liberalization and Small Holder Productivity in Tanzania: From Promised Success to Real Failure, 1985–1998." *Journal of Agrarian Change* 5, 2 (June 2005): 334–362.

Skjekshus, Helge. *Ecology Control and Economic Development in East Africa: The Case of Tanganika, 1850–1950.* Berkeley: University of California Press, 1977.

Smith, Gerald Alonzo. "Humanist Economics: From Homo Economicus to Homo Sapiens." In *Beyond Neoclassical Economics: Heterodox Approaches to Economic Theory,* edited by Fred E. Foldvary, 115–133. Brookfield, VT: Edward Elgar Publishers, 1996.

"Sold Down the River." *Forests Monitor* (March 2001). Available at
     http://www.forestsmonitor.org/reports/solddown/river/drc.htm.
Springle, Robert M. "The Nile Perch in Lake Victoria: Local Responses
     and Adaptation." *Africa* 75, 4 (2005): 510–528.
Stanhill, G. "Irrigation in Arid Lands." *Philosophical Transactions of the
     Royal Society of London* 316, 1537 (February 1986): 261–269.
Starr, J. R. "Of Water Wars." *Foreign Policy* 82 (Spring 1991): 17–36.
Stein, Arthur S. "Coordination and Collaboration: Regimes in an Anar-
     chic World." In *International Regimes*, edited by Stephen D. Kras-
     ner, 116–140. Ithaca, NY: Cornell University Press, 1983.
Sternberg, J.M. "Human African Trypanosomiasis." *Parasite Immunol-
     ogy*, 26, 11–12 (November 2004): 469–476.
Stevenson, Mark. "Critics Rail against 'Stealth' Privatization as World
     Water Forum Opens." The Associated Press (20 March 2006).
Stewart, Dona J. "Cities in the Desert: The Egyptian New Town Program."
     Annals of the Association of American Geographers (1996):
     459–480.
Stiassony, Melany L., and Axel Meyer. "Cichlids of the Rift Lakes."
     Scientific American (February 1999): 64–69.
"Sudan: Alsunut Launches Almogran Real Estate Development."
     Al Bawaba [London]. (19 September 2005).
"Sustainable Jobs Growth Is Key to Poverty Reduction in Africa."
     UN News Service (December 2005).
Sutcliffe, John V., and F. P. Parks. *Hydrology of the Nile*. Wallingford, En-
     gland: International Association of Hydrological Sciences, 1999.
Swain, Ashok. "Ethiopia, the Sudan and Egypt: The Nile River Dispute."
     Journal of Modern African Studies 35, 4 (December 1997): 675–693.
Tafesse, Tesfaye. *The Nile Question: Hydropolitics, Legal Wrangling,
     Modus Vivendi and Perspectives*. Munster: Lit Verlag, 2001.
Tangley, Laura. "How Much Is a Forest Worth?" *U.S. News and World
     Report* (26 May 1997): 60–61.
"Tanzania: FAO/WFP Special Report on Crop and Food Supply." *IRIN*
     (16 February 1999).
"Tanzania: Hundreds of Thousands in Need of Food Aid." *IRIN* (3 May
     2005).
"Tanzania: Move to Save Forests Angers Loggers." *Africa News* (7 Feb-
     ruary 2006). Available at http://www.lexisnexis.com/academic/.
"Tanzania Ranks as One of Africa's Better Performers." EIU ViewsWire
     (12 April 2005). Available at http://www.proquest.umi.com.
Taylor, Jeffrey. "Foreign Affairs: Worse than Iraq? Nigeria's President
     and One Time Hope for a Stable Future Is Leading His Country
     toward Implosion and Possible U.S. Military Intervention." *The
     Atlantic Monthly* (April 2006): 33–35.
"Threats to Zaire's Virunga Park." *Unesco Courier* 41 (April 1995).

Thurow, Lester C. *The Future of Capitalism: How Today's Economic Forces Shape Tomorrow's World*. New York: William Morrow, 1996.

Thurow, Roger. "Changing Course: Ravaged by Famine, Ethiopia Finally Gets Help from the Nile." *Wall Street Journal* (26 November 2003): A1.

Tilman, David. "Biodiversity and Ecosystem Functioning." In *Nature's Services: Societal Dependence on Natural Ecosystems*, edited by Gretchen C Daily, 93–112. Washington, D.C.: Island Press, 1997.

Tully, Shawn. "Water, Water Everywhere." *Fortune* (15 May 2000): 342–349.

"Uganda: Egypt Gives $5 Million for Water Hyacinth." *Africa News* (20 November 2006). Available at http://www.lexis-nexis.com/academic/.

"Uganda: Forests, A Dream of the Past." *Africa News* (23 August 2005). Available at http://www.lexisnexis.com/academic/.

"Uganda's Habitats for Endangered Species under Threat from Encroachers." Xinhua News Agency (18 January 2005). Available at http://www.lexisnexis.com/academic/.

"Uganda's Water Corporation To Pump More Water for Capital City." Xinhua General News Service (20 January 2006). Available at http://www.lexisnexis.com/academic.

"UN Warns of Food Crisis in Eastern Africa." Agence France Presse (17 January 2006). Available at http://www.lexisnexis.com/academic/.

United Nations. "Stockholm Declaration of the United Nations Conference of the Human Environment." U.N.DOC.A/Conf48/Rev.1 (1973). *UNEP*. Available at http://www.unep.org/Documents.multilingual/Default.asp?DocumentID=97&ArticleID=1503.

United Nations Conference on Trade and Development. "Economic Development inAfrica: Trade Performance and Commodity Dependence" (2004). Available at http://www.unctad.org/ANCTAD/press/Pr/2004/2003.

United Nations Convention to Combat Desertification. "Desertification: A Global Problem of Transnational Magnitude" (5 June 2006). Available at http://www.unccd.int/main.php.

United Nations Development Program. "United Nations Human Development Indicators" (2002). Available at http://www.undp.org.

United Nations Development Program. "Lake Jipe Surrounded by Typha Weed" (2004). Available at http://www.ke.undp.org/GEF/SGP/Lake20Jipe.

United Nations Environmental Protection. "Water Demand." In *Perspectives on Water Uses and Abuses*, edited by David H. Speidel et al., 97–102. New York: Oxford University Press, 1988.

United Nations Food and Agricultural Organization. "Special Report: FAO/WFP Crop and Food Supply Assessment Mission to Ethiopia" (January 2001). Available at http://www.FAO.org.

United Nations Population Fund. "The State of World Population 2005: The Promise of Equality" (24 October 2005). Available at http://www.web.lexis-nexis.com/universe.

United Republic of Tanzania. "Lake Jipe Awareness Raising Strategy, 2005–2007." Dar Es Salam, Yanzania: Ministry of Natural Resources and Tourism, 2004.

United States Department of the Interior, Bureau of Reclamation. *Land and Water Resources of the Blue Nile Basin, Ethiopia.* Washington, D.C.: U.S. Government Printing Office, 1964.

USAID. "Eritrea: Complex Food Security Crisis" (7 July 2005). Available at http://www.usaid.gov.

US Department of State. "Ethiopia: Background Notes" (May 2003). Available at http://www.state.gov.

US Department of State, Bureau of Verification and Compliance. "Fact Sheet: World Military Expenditures and Arms Transfers 1998, 27th Series Report" (21 August 2000). Available at http://www.fas.org/man/docs/wmeat98/wmeat98fs.html.

US Fed News. "Environmentalists Blast Uganda President for Plans to Clear-cut Forests" (14 December 2006).

US Geological Survey. "Pesticides in the Nation's Streams and Ground Water, 1992–2001" (3 March 2006). Available at http://pubs/.usgs.gov/circ/2005/1291/.

Vesley, Milan. "Africa Goes Credit Card Crazy." *African Business* (April 2005): 60–61.

Villiers, Marq D. *Water: The Fate of Our Most Precious Resource.* Boston: Houghton Mifflin, 2000.

Wahby, Wafeek. "Technologies Applied in the Toshka Project of Egypt." *Journal of Technology Studies* 30, 4 (Fall, 2004): 86–91.

Wainaina, Binyavanga. "Inventing Nairobi." *National Geographic* (September 2005) 37–50.

Waithaka, J. K. et al. "Aging and Poverty in Kenya, Country Report for the Original Workshop on Aging and Poverty in Sub-Saharan Africa." October 2003. Available at http://www.un.org/esa/socdev/ageing/.orkshops/tz/kena.pdf.

Wallach, Brett. "Irrigation in Sudan since Independence." *Geographical Review* 78, 4 (October 1998): 417–434.

Walsh, Declan. "Kenyans Fear Harvest of Tree-Cutting from Tea to Water." *Boston Globe* (10 February 2002): A4.

Walsh, P. D. et al. "Recent Rainfall Changes and Their Impact on Hydrology and Water Supply in the Semi-Arid Zone of the Sudan." *Geographical Journal* 154, 2 (July 1988): 181–197.

Ward, Veronica. "Marxism, Sovereignty and Ecosystem Management: Clash of Concepts and Boundaries." In *The Greening of Sovereignty in World Politics*, edited by Karen T. Litfin, 79–108. Cambridge: MIT Press, 1998.

"The Water Hyacinth Is Back." *Africa News* (31 December 2006). Available at www.lexis-nexis.com/academic/.

"Water Hyacinth Rolls Back on Lake Victoria." Xinhua General News Service (4 February 2007). Available at http://www.lexis-nexis.com/academic/.

Waterbury, John. *Hydropolitics of the Nile Valley*. Syracuse: Syracuse University Press, 1979.

———. *The Nile Basin: National Determinants of Collective Action*. New Haven: Yale University Press, 2002.

Watson, Catherine. "The Death of Democracy." *Africa Report* 39, 1 (January–February 2004): 26–31.

Webster, Normon. "Corruption Is Crushing Kenya." *The Gazette* [Montreal] (11 June 2005).

Weinbaum, Marvin G. "Dependent Development and U.S. Economic Aid to Egypt." *International Journal of Middle East Studies* 18, 2 (May 1986): 119–126.

"WFP Estimates 3.5 Million Now Need Food in Darfur." *The Nation* [Nairobi] (5 June 2005). Available at http://web.lexis-nexis.com/universe.

Whibb, Krist. "The Nile River: Potential for Conflict or Cooperation in the Face of Water Degradation." *Natural Resources Journal* 41, 3 (Summer 2001): 731–754.

White, David. "The Private Sector: Private Capital Is a Pillar of the Plan for Economic Revival." *Financial Times* [London] (21 November 2006): 2.

Whittington, Dale, and Elizabeth McClelland. "Opportunities in Regional and International Cooperation in the Nile Basin." *Water International*. 17 (1992): 144–154.

"Why Fishermen Are Not Rejoicing." ReadNews (1 January 2005). Available at en.cppma.com/news/readnews.asp?newsd_12190.

Withgott, Jay. "Bees from the Rainforest Add Up to a $62,000 Coffee Buzz." *Science* (20 August 2004): 1100–1101.

World Bank. "Where Is the Wealth of Nations? Measuring Capital for the 21st Century." Washington, D.C.: World Bank, 2006.

——. "Questions and Answers: World Bank Support to Sustainable Management of Forests in the Democratic Republic of Congo" (11 January 2006). Available at http://www.worldbank.org.

———. "Kenya: Natural Resources Management Project" (October 2005). Available at http://www.wds-worldbank.org.

———. "Country Briefing" (September 2005). Available at http://www. worldbank.org/ethiopia.htm.

———. "Anti-Corruption Initiatives in Sub-Saharan Africa, No. 38" (March 1999). Available at http://www.worldbank.org.

———. "Lake Victoria: A Case in International Cooperation; World Bank Staff Appraisal Report for the Lake Victoria Environmental Management Project, Report No. 15429-AFR." Washington, D.C.: World Bank, 1996.

"World Bank Pledges Support for Water Reform in Kenya." Xinhua General News Service. (31 October 2005).

World Commission on Dams. *Dams and Development: A Framework for New Decision Making*. London: Earthscan, 2000.

World Health Organization. "Health Hazards of Water Pollution." In *Perspectives on Water Uses and Abuses*, edited by David H. Speidel et al., 231–235. New York: Oxford University Press, 1988.

World Resources Institute. "Earth Trends: Agriculture and Food—Ethiopia" (2003). Available at http://www.earthtrends.wri.org.

"Yangtze River Cancerous with Pollution." Xinhua General News Service (30 May 2006).

Yohannes, Okbazghi. *The Political Economy of an Authoritarian Modern State and Religious Nationalism in Egypt*. New York: Edwin Mellen Press, 2001.

———. *The United States and the African Horn: Pattern and Process*. Boulder: Westview Press, 1997.

Zimmerman, Tim. "The Mystery of Lake Nikuru." *US News and World Report* (5 August 1996).

Index